India's Open-Economy Policy

This book is the first major exploration of Indian political economy using a constructivist approach. Arguing that India's open-economy policy was made, justified, and continued on the basis of the idea of openness more than its tangible effect, the book explains what sustained the idea of openness, what philosophy, interpretations of history, and international context gave it support, justification, and persuasive force.

Drawing on a wide range of contemporary and historical sources, and going as far back as the nineteenth century, the author reconstructs the way in which Indian policymakers have interpreted economic priorities, perceived success and failure, and evaluated the destiny of their nation. By the 1990s, their imperatives increasingly highlighted a sense of rivalry, especially with China, and globalism, a desire to play a strong role in world affairs. The book shows how a sense of nationalist urgency was created through globalism and rivalry, allowing policymakers to privilege international needs over domestic political demands, replace economic independence with interdependence as a priority, and ensure that the broad basis of India's openness could not be challenged effectively even though certain policies faced severe opposition.

This book will be of interest to those working on International Political Economy, Globalization, Economic History, Public Policy, and South Asian politics.

Jalal Alamgir is Assistant Professor of Political Science at the University of Massachusetts, Boston, specializing in the relationships between globalization and representational politics.

Routledge contemporary South Asia series

1 **Pakistan**
Social and cultural transformations in a Muslim nation
Mohammad A. Qadeer

2 **Labor, Democratization and Development in India and Pakistan**
Christopher Candland

3 **China–India Relations**
Contemporary dynamics
Amardeep Athwal

4 **Madrasas in South Asia**
Teaching terror?
Jamal Malik

5 **Labor, Globalization and the State**
Workers, women and migrants confront neoliberalism
Edited by Debdas Banerjee and Michael Goldfield

6 **Indian Literature and Popular Cinema**
Recasting classics
Edited by Heidi R.M. Pauwels

7 **Islamist Militancy in Bangladesh**
A complex web
Ali Riaz

8 **Regionalism in South Asia**
Negotiating cooperation, institutional structures
Kishore C. Dash

9 **Federalism, Nationalism and Development**
India and the Punjab economy
Pritam Singh

10 **Human Development and Social Power**
Perspectives from South Asia
Ananya Mukherjee Reed

11 **The South Asian Diaspora**
Transnational networks and changing identities
Edited by Rajesh Rai and Peter Reeves

12 **Pakistan–Japan Relations**
Continuity and change in economic relations and security interests
Ahmad Rashid Malik

13 **Himalayan Frontiers of India**
Historical, geo-political and strategic perspectives
K. Warikoo

14 **India's Open-Economy Policy**
Globalism, rivalry, continuity
Jalal Alamgir

India's Open-Economy Policy

Globalism, rivalry, continuity

Jalal Alamgir

Routledge
Taylor & Francis Group
LONDON AND NEW YORK

First published 2009
by Routledge
2 Park Square, Milton Park, Abingdon, Oxon OX14 4RN

Simultaneously published in the USA and Canada
by Routledge
711 Third Avenue, New York, NY 10017

Routledge is an imprint of the Taylor & Francis Group, an informa business

Typeset in Times by Wearset Ltd, Boldon, Tyne and Wear

British Library Cataloguing in Publication Data
A catalogue record for this book is available from the British Library

Library of Congress Cataloging in Publication Data
Alamgir, Jalal, 1971–
India's open-economy policy: globalism, rivalry, continuity/Jalal Alamgir.
p. cm. – (Routledge contemporary South Asia series; 14)
Includes bibliographical references and index.
1. India–Economic policy–1991– 2. Globalization–India. 3.
Competition–India. I. Title.
HC435.3.A43 2008
338.954–dc22 2008022604

ISBN13: 978-0-415-77684-4 (hbk)
ISBN13: 978-0-203-88697-7 (ebk)

For Amma and Abba

Contents

Figures

Tables

Preface

This book uses a constructivist approach to explain why India's open-economy policy has continued apace and become established despite political turmoil. When I began the initial research a decade ago, India was teeming with "a million mutinies," as V. S. Naipaul put it. Everything about the country, especially its economic policy, was shaped inexorably by material immediacies. Or so it seemed. As I dug deeper, I began to find that explanations based on material factors, whether political or economic, were weaker than they initially appeared: they could not account for the tenacity of India's open-economy policy. Nor could they adequately explain how a policy, especially one considered a radical departure, is marketed such that its political risks are reduced and that the policy becomes embedded enough to survive changes in government. To entrench policy is not an easy task – and particularly so in a society that is incredibly diverse, spectacularly complex, and typically "argumentative." Yet this is exactly what has happened in India since 1991: economic openness has come to be accepted in society as a core national value, on a par with other fundamental values that the state is committed to protect. I explore the ideational basis of this acceptance.

My research and writing proceeded in three phases. I did initial fieldwork and interviews in South Asia in 1997–98, which, in hindsight, turned out to be an opportune point between the initiation and consolidation of India's open-economy policy. The Centre for Policy Research in New Delhi, the Centre for Policy Research and Analysis at the University of Colombo, and the Centre for Social Studies at the University of Dhaka hosted my fieldwork in the subcontinent. I am especially indebted to Isher Judge Ahluwalia, Jayedeva Uyangoda, and Borhanuddin Khan Jahangir for their strong leadership and advocacy in facilitating the research. During this time I also received suggestions from Balveer Arora, Sanjaya Baru, Amit Bhaduri, C. P. Bhambri, B. Bhattacharya, Bishwajit Dhar, Ayesha Jalal, Atul Kohli, Deepak Nayyar, V. A. Pai Panandiker, and Eswaran Sridharan. I should add the disclaimer that not everyone here shared my views. I am indebted to Mr. and Mrs. Fazlul Ahad, who insisted on having me stay for four months in their house in New Delhi, and quickly became a second family to me, and to Anne Ranasinghe, who hosted me in her lovely bungalow in Cinnamon Gardens in Colombo, and shared with me her politics and poetry, not to mention the post-dinner Scrabble games, which she insisted were essential "to keep our faculties running."

I conducted additional research at the Southern Asian Institute at Columbia University and the Watson Institute for International Studies at Brown University between 1999 and 2003. I received encouragement and feedback from many, including Richard Francis, Rodney Bruce Hall, Rounaq Jahan, Deepa Kumar, Andrew Marble, Craig Murphy, Baldev Raj Nayar, Nagesh Rao, Grahame Thompson, and Linda Weiss. Four mentors were critical to the success of this project. For their guidance, feedback, and benign neglect of my occasional foibles, I thank: Thomas Biersteker, who influenced my thoughts on globalization and constructivism; Robert Wade, who helped me understand better the political economy of development; Dietrich Rueschemeyer, who emphasized the socio-historical importance of the state; and Linda Miller, who not only prodded me with affection to write clearly, but also, as editor of *International Studies Review*, where I worked, allowed flexibility in my schedule to accommodate the composing of initial drafts.

The third phase of the work, including additional research, presentations, and substantial writing, took place at the University of Massachusetts, Boston. I received support and strength from many faculty: Elizabeth Bussiere, Elora Chowdhury, Leila Farsakh, Thomas Ferguson, Arjun Jayadev, Ruth Miller, Pratima Prasad, Heike Schotten, Rajini Srikanth, Primo Vannicelli, Ananya Vajpeyi, and Paul Watanabe, among others. I am thankful to my consulting colleagues, Cindy Carpenter and Matthew Sullivan, for allowing me, wholeheartedly, time off project work so I could concentrate on the book. A bow of thanks also goes to 1369 Coffee House in Cambridge, Massachusetts, where I spent many a morning caffeinated, writing and editing. The College of Liberal Arts at UMB provided financial assistance for part of the work, including indexing. Earlier parts of the research were funded by fellowships from the Center for the Comparative Study of Development, Brown University Graduate School, and the Watson Institute for International Studies.

Certain aspects of the research have been published elsewhere. I thank Cambridge University Press for granting permission to include extracts from Jalal Alamgir, "Managing Openness in India: The Social Construction of a Globalist Narrative," in Linda Weiss ed., *States in the Global Economy*, 2003, and the Taylor and Francis Group for permission to use extracts from Jalal Alamgir, "Narratives of Open-Economy Policies in India, 1991–2000," *Asian Studies Review* 31 (2), 2007.

Although the research and writing of this book, from start to finish, have taken many years, I believe that the book as a result has enjoyed the spirit and benefits of a longitudinal study. It has allowed me time to confirm the gradual political embedding of economic openness in India. But the lengthy gestation also means that my list of friends and family to thank has grown too long to name individually. I appeal for their forgiveness. I have come to realize that the pursuit of a book project involves inadvertently many more beyond the person who pens it. Among those who have been forced to share hard times and yet been patient and generous, I am particularly grateful to my wonderful fiancée Fazeela, my diligent brother Joy, my loving aunt Ruby and uncle Mansur, and my parents, who are fighters, victims, and an inspiration for the cause of decent democratic politics.

Abbreviations

Assocham	Associated Chambers of Commerce and Industry of India
BJP	Bharatiya Janata Party
CII	Confederation of Indian Industry
CNPC	China National Petroleum Corporation
CTBT	Comprehensive Test Ban Treaty
EPZ	Export Processing Zone
FDI	Foreign Direct Investment
FPI	Foreign Portfolio Investment
FICCI	Federation of Indian Chambers of Commerce and Industry
G77	Group of 77
GATT	General Agreement on Tariffs and Trade
GDP	Gross Domestic Product
HDI	Human Development Index
IFI	International Financial Institution
IMF	International Monetary Fund
INC	Indian National Congress
ISRO	Indian Space Research Organisation
NAM	Non-Aligned Movement
NPT	Nuclear Non-proliferation Treaty
NRI	Non-Resident Indian
OECD	Organisation for Economic Cooperation and Development
ONGC	Oil and Natural Gas Corporation (India)
PIO	People of Indian Origin
PPP	Purchasing Power Parity
PSU	Public Sector Unit
R&D	Research and Development
SEZ	Special Economic Zone
SOE	State Owned Enterprise
UN	United Nations
UNCTAD	United Nations Conference on Trade and Development
UNDP	United Nations Development Programme
WTO	World Trade Organization

1 Explaining the continuity of openness

> Given the democratic nature of our political system, it's a miracle we have got this far.
>
> Manmohan Singh, Indian Finance Minister (Congress Party), 30 September 1993

> Reversing economic liberalization is ruled out.
>
> Deve Gowda, Indian Prime Minister (United Front), 16 December 1996

> We in India are committed to globalization.
>
> Yashwant Sinha, Indian Finance Minister (BJP), 1 February 1999

The world's largest democracy, India, is instructive for those interested in counter-intuitive politics. In the last decade and a half, Indian leaders, regardless of party, endured considerable political turmoil to implement a set of policies to move India from a relatively closed economy focused on domestic planning to one that espouses free markets and international trade. To be sure, elements of freedom were present in India's economy before, and conversely, trace elements of centralized planning remain today. But the organization of the economy – how income is earned and spent, how capital is raised, how business is run, how labor is employed and work done, how goods and services are traded across borders, how profits are shared, re-invested, and taxed, and how the state treats private enterprise – became by the mid-2000s fundamentally different from how it was in 1990. The change is visible not only statistically; everyday economic and social life was also noticeably different for many Indians, as observed by residents and travelers alike. Today, the difference has been internalized and accepted as normal: an increasingly larger part of society has settled down into the newer ways of conducting life, and of defining success in life. All told, it is not an exaggeration to claim that what the Indian political economy has gone through is one of the great transformations of the last century.

Paradoxically, this *change* could not have been possible without *continuity*. It was by continuing with open-economy policies, thereby building momentum incrementally and relentlessly, that policymakers could shift the direction of the economy. The move was risky. India's political and economic circumstances were fragile in the early 1990s. Two years into the process the Finance Minister still reckoned that it would take a "miracle" to sustain economic openness in a country as diverse and politicized as India. In the seventeen years since reforms began, policymakers have endured a wave of protests, strikes, lockouts, violence, even mass suicide – from social groups, organized labor, trade associations, farmers, nationalist parties, environmentalists, and intellectuals. The period saw seven changes in government, but only one notable policy retraction from economic openness.[1] Even that happened prior to the passing of the policy; once enacted, no major pro-openness policy has been curtailed or withdrawn since 1991. Successive Indian governments, regardless of party, have "ruled out" any reversal in India's new economic orientation.

What is remarkable about India's story is not why policies were changed, but why they have been sustained. One would expect that during lengthy periods of turbulence elected politicians would be doubly sensitive to the demands of their constituencies. It may make sense for them to bear short spurts of unrest. But in India political upheaval against open-economy policies continued for a decade and a half. Even the most recent general elections, in 2004, were won and lost mainly on the question of globalization.[2] Though contested on many issues, the election results underscored the ongoing problem of managing the unequal benefits of economic openness. The pro-openness policy trajectory of BJP, the party that was in power, had raised the visibility of the trading and financial elite as the primary policy beneficiaries, which alienated many Indian voters who perceived themselves still steps and years removed from the trickling down of wealth. Yet India's open-economy policy continues, and indeed for the past seventeen years, politicians in power have been trying to build bridges across political interests in support of increasing, not limiting, the scope of openness in Indian economy. What explains this continuity?

This book offers an answer by highlighting the fundamental role played by ideas and beliefs. Policy continuity is essentially a consistent progression of decisions and actions taken by policymakers. To investigate continuity, we need to discount the significance of an individual policy or event, and try to identify patterns instead. A triggering event or an individual policy can be arbitrary: other events could have substituted for it. The event that triggered India's open-economy policy was a devaluation of its currency in 1991, undertaken to address a severe shortage of foreign exchange needed for external payments. In another case the trigger could well have been an energy crisis, a treaty deadline, lobbying by exporters, or a palace coup. In other words, I am less interested in asking why a certain decision was made, but more in understanding the basis on which a series of policies was sustained. It is in understanding this basis that the role of ideas becomes significant. How can certain ideas be powerful enough to override a torrent of political disincentives? What makes them useful enough to be marketed to the broad populace, such that policies eventually come to be established and accepted, thus lowering the risk of changes and uncertainties?

The central role of ideas becomes clearer if one considers, conceptually, how economic openness or any such value orientation can become established, starting from being set up as a tentative policy championed by a small group of policymakers, to being accepted eventually as a standard by society at large. The process, with all its attendant arguments, persuasions, narratives, manipulations, selling and marketing, takes place predominantly in the realm of ideas. To the extent that one considers statistics "real," economic openness can be measured statistically, using the ratio of a country's trade to gross domestic product (GDP), for instance. But until those ratios can be calculated, shown to be different a few years later, and confirmed to be sustainable still a few more years later, openness remains *ideational*. In other words, until beneficial shifts are evident in life, which can take many years, open-economy policy has to be made, justified, and continued on the basis of the *idea* of openness rather than its tangible effect. Indian policymakers needed to persist with their unpopular policy, and at the same time, win a series of ideational battles over free trade, foreign investment, withdrawal of subsidies, welfare programs, and indeed, the very definition of nation. The victory of pro-openness policymakers was far from assured, but is evident in the fact that even Indian states governed by communist parties, such as the states of West Bengal and Kerala, began to pursue their own open-economy policies by the second half of the 1990s. My aim is to discuss what sustained the idea of openness in India and what ensured that it had the persuasive political force needed to withstand its discontents.

An exploration of ideas will necessarily involve navigating "perception" and "construction." The terms can add enormous complexity, and also baggage, covering a wide range of approaches from social psychology and cognitive science to post-positivism and postmodernism; for the purpose of this study the only differentiation I draw is that perception is passive while construction is proactive. One can perceive reality in a descriptive fashion ("this has happened"), but one constructs reality in the active effort of trying to make sense of it ("this has happened because..."; "this will happen if..."). Notions of collective identity, theory, historiography, policy statements, textbooks, political speeches, publications, debate, academic and professional training, government sponsorship of arts or cultural rituals – the production and practice of all of these can cumulate into systematic social construction that privileges certain ways of interpreting complex political and economic realities, and eventually informs and governs policy behavior.[3]

In much of this book, we will attempt to put ourselves in the mindset of the perceptive and constructive policymaker, recognizing the role of both introspection and extroversion inherent in sustaining macro policies aimed at accomplishing political and economic change. In more straightforward terms, we will look at how pro-openness policymakers perceived India and its ambitions internally as well as externally in relation to a broader society of states. The assumption is that societal change involves introspective national and nationalist imaginings, and nationalist perceptions become sharper and urgent only in relation to the *inter*national, the outside, or the foreign. Policymakers had to place their initiatives to open up India's economy into a vision more encompassing than merely "free trade" or "capitalism"; they had to perceive for themselves and construct for others a larger milieu that could provide justification for controversial policies, such that India's economy could be integrated with the world outside without losing national imaginings of what "India" means. For example, India's primary economic objective, for most of its history, has been poverty alleviation. The primary goal noted in key policy documents nowadays is quite different, as Chapter 4 of this book will point out. Does that mean that a core national value has been compromised? Can fundamental changes such as these be reconciled in the context of broader ideas? The continuity of open-economy policy involved the rationalization, marketing, and acceptance of ideological changes that were politically very sensitive; orchestrating it required perceiving and constructing "reality" in a way that could convey consistency with cherished national aspirations despite change.

Whether structural conditions or "hard economic reality" become relevant to policy depends significantly on perception and construction, especially of self and other. It is now commonplace to perceive India and China as competitors. A growth industry has boomed in international business and international relations literature seeking to compare India and China, producing every year a torrent of catchy titles that together could describe a veritable zoo, complete with dragons, giants, tigers, elephants, lions, and mongooses.[4] Most of these works feed off an automatic assumption of rivalry. But how did these two countries become rivals? And what does rivalry mean from the perspective of a policymaker? Business literature frequently compares the foreign direct investment (FDI) coming into India and China. But does FDI into China crowd out FDI into India, as presumed whenever analysts urge for policy reform? It generally does not, since most investors spread assets across both India and China to diversify risk and to access both markets – which is partly why FDI into both countries has been rising simultaneously. Moreover, just because China has a greater inflow of FDI does not necessarily mean India needs to attain that level. The appropriate level of FDI would be determined by a variety of factors, including domestic savings-investment gap and absorbability. But because rivalry is imagined and constructed, any difference between the two countries, whether relevant or not, becomes a matter of gain/loss: a greater level of FDI into China is conveyed and interpreted automatically as a relative loss for India, and accompanied with urgent policy prescriptions and allusions. Later chapters will show that China was imagined to be India's rival long before they competed materially in any significant way. It was the imagining, the perception, not the "material" competition, that became policy-relevant.

Ideational motivations centered on these two dimensions – one about national ambition ("what do we want to achieve as a nation") and the other about national placement ("where are we placed relative to other nations") – had begun to intertwine powerfully in Indian policy-thinking long before a crisis hit the economy in 1991. As a result of the specific ways that these motives combined, the mindset of Indian policymakers was already attuned sharply to the *external* world; their imaginings of India had already become globalized. We will, in the course of this book, explore how this happened, how it encouraged policy continuity, and how it induced an increasingly greater part of policymakers as well as the public, over time, to associate India's open-economy policy with aspirations of the nation-state rather than with the platform of a specific party. We must also consider seriously the influence of social construction and ideas on economic policymaking because the guidance offered by existing approaches to openness, outlined briefly below, does not fully account for continuity. Much scholarship on national economic policy since the end of the Cold War has cast disproportionate attention on "material" change. Continuity has either remained obscure or taken for granted.

Approaches to continuity

Conventional discussions on Indian economy attributed the shift toward openness to a balance of payments crisis in 1991, in the wake of the Persian Gulf War. This view is consistent with mainstream economic studies that have identified a similar pattern of crisis-led policy change elsewhere in the developing world.[5] Leftist perspectives also acknowledge the role of the crisis, and indicate, in addition, the influence of Indian businesses, restating the classic argument that the move toward a market economy has been orchestrated and sustained collectively by the interests of capital, that is, "the bourgeoisie."[6] But questions remain. The bourgeoisie was not a unified whole in support of open-economy policies; it was in fact deeply divided over policy continuity.[7] Moreover, if economic crisis prompted a policy response, we should expect that constant political crises and turbulence would also prompt appropriate policy responses. It is not rational for weak coalition governments to continue openness at substantial political cost – costs that became evident in Indian voter behavior nationally and regionally. Earlier efforts at liberalization were piecemeal and extinguished prematurely mostly because of domestic political difficulties.[8] One possible explanation of how the post-1991 economic reforms were politically sustained in India is offered in Rob Jenkins's study. Jenkins argues that given the resistance and hurdles, reformist policymakers often resorted to underhanded techniques of manipulation, while using India's layers of democracy and politics, from local to state to federal, as protection in order to carry on with their reform program. It was essentially reform by "obfuscation and stealth" (Jenkins uses these terms not pejoratively, but descriptively). This approach illuminates the political mechanism involved, but it does not satisfactorily answer why reformist policymakers would be so determined to continue open-economy policy in the first place, when the easier option, from the perspective of both political costs and political incentives, is to desist and fall back toward the pre-reform status quo.[9]

Another perspective underscores the influence of international financial institutions (IFIs), such as the World Bank and the International Monetary Fund (IMF). Since the Third World Debt Crisis in the early 1980s, much lending from IFIs to troubled economies has been conditional on policy adjustment toward openness, especially in countries with payment problems.[10] Opening up the economy, however, is not the only way that countries have responded to crises.

They have turned inward at times, and many borrowers adopted a "heterodox" mix of policies, including incomes policies, subsidies, price controls, or capital controls that were not part of conditionalities.[11] The impact of IFIs has been limited because of "powerful sources of conflict between the policy strictures of the external actors and the political interests of many developing country governments."[12] An in-depth analysis by Mosley, Harrigan, and Toye on the influence of World Bank policies found that only two countries (Turkey and Thailand) among the nine cases studied met more than 65 percent of the loan conditions. Even small (read: weak) countries such as Kenya, Guyana, and Ecuador implemented only about a third of the stipulations.[13] During the ravages of the Asian Financial Crisis in the late 1990s, Malaysia contravened IMF's prescription and imposed capital controls. Poland set the scope and pace of economic transition from communism to capitalism mostly on its own terms, rejecting the shock therapy advised by the IMF and the US Treasury.[14] India is a large and resourceful country, with a strong prior record of independence from pressures by international organizations. Moreover, as this study will show, most of India's policy struggles with IFIs have been about fiscal deficit, and domestic, not external, liberalization. Indian policymakers seem to have implemented pro-openness policies pre-emptively and out of their own volition.[15] What explains their commitment to openness?

"Social learning" may have provided the basis, as contended by some analysts. The idea is that policymakers in developing countries "may have finally 'seen the light' and accepted the superiority of the liberal economic ideas."[16] National policymakers, many of whom had stints as staff members of IFIs or regional and international development banks, learned about successful techniques of economic transformation through previous experience with failed models, or from observing other countries, or from continual policy dialogue with IFIs. Devesh Kapur's research shows the extent and some of the effects of the overseas exposure of India's policy elite – through international migration, education, and return – since India's colonial days.[17] Social learning eventually becomes institutionalized, providing ideational continuity despite political change. However, this line of research has usually put the source of the ideas in the West; the implication is that Indian policy would change as the West changes. As Achin Vanaik wrote, explaining the source of the 1991 reforms, "the apex of the state bureaucracy in India … [was] increasingly drawn into the mental orbit of their counterparts in the West."[18] But social learning can also *threaten* continuity, especially if elements of the initial policy package are controversial, as they were in India, and fail to deliver the anticipated results. In addition, as Haggard and Kaufman note, "it is difficult to pin down precisely processes of learning and socialization that determine the way such ideas are adopted by particular sets of national leaders or incorporated into specific policy contexts."[19] Why were post-1991 reforms different from previous episodes with regard to policy continuity? This book contributes evidence of social learning, but also identifies nation-centric interpretations that give such learning significance toward policy continuity instead of policy reversal.

Bureaucratic competence or insulation of technocrats from political demands provides support for risky policies, according to another influential strand of scholarship. But major studies of India's bureaucracy, especially those up to the 1990s, report downbeat results, contending that inefficiency, corruption, patronage, and a lack of professionalism, coupled with "giantism" and democratic restraints, had turned India into a "failed developmental state," particularly compared to East Asian bureaucracies that successfully harmonized the costs of openness with domestic political interests.[20] Although technocrats played a crucial role in devising economic policies, India's bureaucracy alone seemed hardly capable of mustering the level of political wherewithal needed to continue policies toward openness through thick and thin. Could it have become agile suddenly in the 1990s? This is unlikely – even as recently as 2008, *The Economist* identified India's "bloated civil service" as the main threat to sustaining economic growth and extending the political will toward further liberalization.[21] Insulation of technocrats and bureaucrats, furthermore, can make the government unresponsive and inefficient in identifying problems, which, by stifling "effective channels for communicating with affected political interests," can threaten long-term policy stability.[22] Insulation helps, concludes John Waterbury, but insulated "change teams" have been instrumental mostly during policy initiation, not consolidation.[23] Going further, Dani Rodrik's analysis shows that it is not insulation but participation, that is, access to political institutions by non-elites, that historically resulted in better performance in adjusting to macroeconomic shocks.[24] The World Bank has also begun to view the promotion of "inclusiveness" as one of the keys to ensure sustainable development with a market economy.[25]

Some scholars point out the role of performance and material interests: if policies are successful in raising the external balance, investment, and growth rate, they create new constituencies and interests to support the continuity of those policies.[26] Continuity, hence, rests on support from its material beneficiaries.[27] This argument makes intuitive sense, especially if one considers the pressures toward sustaining open-economy policies created by some parts of India's private sector and almost all parts of the overseas investment community. But it cannot fully explain why policies are continued. In some cases policies have been withdrawn in response to demands from material interests, and in other cases they have continued despite strong opposition. As Robert Bates and Anne Krueger conclude from their study of policy reform in eight countries: "variations in the pattern of interest group representation failed to account for variation in the success of different governments to implement economic policy reforms."[28] Social groups have complex interests. Especially in a country as diverse as India, other cleavages often cut across material interests, making it difficult – except for some clear-cut groups like overseas investment banks or venture capital funds – to translate in any straightforward way a group's imputed material position into consistent policy preference. What further complicates the argument based on interest and performance is that the benefits and costs of reform are often diffuse and uncertain, and difficult for many to grasp. Openness in India, as in many other countries, has been accompanied by worsening inequality. In a 2002 survey, Angus Deaton and Jean Drèze find in India "strong indications of a pervasive increase in economic inequality in the nineties," which, the authors conclude, is a new phenomenon compared to historical trends.[29] Indian constituencies have not hesitated to act against this increase, both with the ballot and on the streets. Therefore it needs to be specified how pro-openness political forces would strengthen without marked improvement in disparity, especially under India's democratic and federal system with frequent coalition governments and a long history of apprehension about free markets. This is why, after BJP's electoral defeat, the post-2004 Congress Party government became more serious about "inclusive growth," though foreign investors tried to deride it as unnecessary populism. Eyeing the 2009 elections, the government announced a massive $15 billion debt-relief program for the country's small farmers. While it is easy for Wall Street to take India's economic openness for granted because of an exponential growth in India's urban-based private sector, openness still needs to be sustained politically by extending direct material interventions for the majority of voters, who happen to be in rural India. The problem was even more acute in the early days of reform. Policymakers made it amply clear that economic performance would come only through prolonged austerity. These economic warnings indicated political worry, and yet the choice to weather austerity and accept the penalties associated with it indicated, more importantly, some kind of ideational determination across different parties that have held the helm of governance in India.

As a final turn in searching for explanations, we may refer to a broader literature that looks at the global system. Critical perspectives on the world system assume that there is no *dis*continuity in the first place, that the wave of economic openness is merely a stage in the same chronology of globalization that dates back to the seventeenth century or earlier. The continuity of openness does not require a separate explanation: it is subsumed within the logic of capitalism; hence, it is relentless, systemic, and to an extent inevitable. Consider Robert Cox's claim:

> [C]apitalism has always been global, whether its origins are traced to the seventeenth-century Eurocentric world or to more ancient civilizations – global in vocation if not in geographic extent. In this perspective, there is nothing different about the last three decades of the twentieth century.[30]

Focusing precisely on those last three decades with titles like "The Twilight of Sovereignty," "The Retreat of the State," and "Surrendering to Markets," more mainstream approaches assume that the same factors (usually transnational corporations, technology, and financial markets) propelling globalization also result in policy continuity by circumscribing the state's power and authority.[31] From this perspective, policy continuity is really an unspoken by-product of policy paralysis.

Structuring ideas

This book is about ideas. In explaining policy continuity, I use an approach influenced by constructivism to address some of the limitations reviewed above. I highlight two sets of ideas that serve as *ideational frameworks*: they act as frames or structures within which Indian nationalist policymakers defined the international political and economic environment that they inhabit, understood core aspects of national identity, interpreted the role of power, and constructed and prioritized long-term objectives of national policy. The first, and the broadest, ideational framework that I will examine is *globalism*, by which I mean the desire to play a strong role in world affairs. The second is *rivalry*, which denotes an interpretation of the state's external context of economic and political decision-making in relation to certain other states or referents. The former is often normative, pointing to "what should be": "What should be the role of our country in world affairs? What should be its power position?" The latter focuses attention on what are usually understood to be material dimensions. It describes "what is." The former serves as a wide-angle lens, so to speak, through which a nation can be seen in the context of the world, and also in the context of its distant past and long-term future. The latter narrows the focus to help interpret the immediate external environment, spatially, and policy urgencies, temporally.

I will endeavor to show how globalism and rivalry have aligned and complemented each other to provide impetus for the continuity of open-economy policies in India. Much of this alignment happens in the realm of logic and perception. Globalism and rivalry are not necessarily the language used by Indian policymakers; these are frameworks that I use to analyze perceived and constructed realities and possibilities in the mindset of political actors. Policymakers with a strong sense of globalism and rivalry will tend to evaluate the state's interest, eliminate options, and make a series of strategic decisions in ways different from those with a weaker disposition or attachment toward these two ideational frameworks. Both of these constructs are informed by the same underlying inquiry: what are the sources that convey meaning and provide momentum toward continuing with economic openness through material and political hardship?

Globalism

Globalism is the desire to play a significant role in world affairs. Though it is focused outwards, globalism is fundamentally about self-identity. It is based on a strong awareness of where the state should be in the international distribution of power and status, and a perceived *value* in being oriented globally or connected globally.[32] A globalist policymaker deems it good for the state to live in an interconnected world in which the aspirant state's objectives can disseminate easily and globally. Globalism aims to project into the world what are considered indigenous values, on the conviction that such projection externally of what is considered valuable internally should be one of the goals of the state in a world inhabited by competing states and competing values. For states at the top of the hierarchy of global power, globalism is likely to be conservative, an ideological instrument to justify and retain their dominant position. For rising states, that is, states that have the desire of a world role but yet to prove their global capabilities, globalism is likely to be revisionist or reformist, in which a change in world order is deemed necessary so that it comes to reflect a value system different from the dominant one. The globalist aims of socialism or Islamism are examples.

A state's political events as well as constructed and reconstructed history, resource base as well as nationalist imaginations – all come together to give policymakers a sense of where the state should belong in the amalgam of states in the world. Some states, because of their size, resources, sense of history, or ideological goals, may aspire to play a world role more readily than others. In the case of Britain and the US, a world role has been largely a function of rising capabilities, especially the domination and industrial application of new technologies.[33] But their rise to power captured the fancies of the nation to the extent that both British and US policymakers, during their respective turns, came to believe that playing a world role was part of their identity, responsibility, or destiny. Walter LaFeber, for instance, shows that US expansion in the late nineteenth century was fueled strongly by imaginative thinking (in contrast to material costs and benefits) about what the US role should be in world affairs.[34] Similarly, in his sketch of US foreign policy, Stephen Ambrose uses "globalism" (as opposed to isolationism) as the term that best captures the motivation and foreign policies of US since its involvement in World War II.[35] For Ambrose the term conveys the US's sense of destiny as a world power, the values that shaped its ambitions, as well as the policies to increase and project power globally. Similarly, Paul Kennedy remarked in his review of British hegemony: "Like all other civilizations at the top of the wheel of fortune … the British could believe that their position was both 'natural' and destined to continue."[36] This is what I want to convey by using the term globalism: ideological and normative imaginings of a world role, pertaining to identity, awareness, commitment, and a sense of destiny.

Once constructed, globalism informs policymakers where the state *should be*, or deserves to be, in the future, especially in relation to other states in the world. Globalism in that sense may give an "end" to policymakers' view of progress, allowing them to be unfazed by short-term domestic political fluctuations that can challenge policy continuity. In that, crucially, globalism is the international manifestation of successful nationalism. This does not mean that all nationalist movements are simultaneously globalist. The reverse is more likely: globalist ideology has been simultaneously nationalist. A strongly globalist state is likely to consider the desire to play a prominent role in world affairs as a part of its nationalist project. It becomes part of the national ambition, of popular imagination, as it became in Britain and the US, and it asserts the judgment that being oriented or influential globally is good for the nation as well as for the world. International pretensions and policy successes shore up nationalism in support of either the regime in power or the continuity of its policies. The nationalist wave in India after its nuclear testing in May 1998 is an example. For a non-globalist state, nationalism, relatively speaking, might be reinforced more by images and projects that look inward into indigenous history or culture to enhance the perception of national unity. By wedding outward orientation with nationalism, globalism can heighten domestic support for the idea of external openness.

Another effect of globalism, less explicit but still significant, is to incline policymakers to opt for outward-oriented policies when cost-benefit analyses or jockeying among various interests yield ambiguous results. Globalism encourages policymakers to make choices normatively, if not empirically. For example, consider two hypothetical states that are undergoing the same economic phenomenon experienced by many developing countries in the last decade: rising trade but worsening inequality. All else equal, a state with globalist aspirations is more likely to draw positive conclusions from the phenomenon. In the eyes of globalist policymakers the benefits of trade will outweigh the costs of inequality, providing incentives to continue openness despite social discontent or turmoil. The non-globalist state might draw the opposite conclusions. Comparing trade with inequality is somewhat like the proverbial comparing of apples and oranges: since there is no objective way of determining which one is inherently more desirable, subjective values will shape the decision.

Finally, by promoting continuous awareness of the state's position in the world order, globalism *relativizes* the nation and begins to frame or enhance the perception of rivalry.[37] Globalism, in other words, entails a heightened importance of the Foreign, a vigilance on what is happening elsewhere in the world, and a constant comparing of one's own society to others. A globalist state, thus, becomes sensitive to the construction and perception of relative identity, such as poor or rich, open or closed, free or restricted, fast-growing or stagnant, modern or traditional, industrialized or agricultural, and most importantly, powerful or weak. The significance of each of these adjectives in the construction of a national identity, an awareness of self, is more poignant in a globalist state than it is in a non-globalist state.

Like all constructs, globalism evolves, and consideration of the effect of its evolution will be important for this study. As globalism develops from an idea to an ideology, its role expands from exerting a predisposition for certain policies during cost-benefit analysis (as mentioned before) to excluding some policy options or questions from deliberation altogether. In some cases, such exclusion may be interpreted as passive, as paralysis or unwillingness, and in other cases, as an active commitment. One example is the French government's failure to use economic policies to reduce unemployment in the 1990s. This was explained conventionally as policy paralysis induced by strictures of the European Union. But Paul Krugman argues that there may have been a more important reason: "French policy is indeed paralyzed – not, however, by impersonal market forces but by the determination of its prestige-conscious politicians not to let the franc decline against the German mark."[38] Similarly, a number of economists have argued that globalization does not automatically constrain the state's capacity to maintain egalitarian income distribution policies. Much of the policy incapacitation, in their view, lies in a lack of will, manifest not in material cost-benefit calculations but in an unquestioned or passive acceptance of neoclassical economic orthodoxy.[39]

In India, as the next chapter describes in detail, numerous analysts interpreted the continuity of pro-openness policies, and indeed aspects of globalism, as a similar type of paralysis or weakness, as a reluctant and passive acceptance of the Washington Consensus or IMF conditionalities. By tracing the evolution of globalism in India, this book makes the case that the ideology indeed excluded policy options from consideration, but not because of powerlessness. Rather, it was out of a sense of empowering India globally; and as such, it was proactive commitment, not passivity or paralysis. Drawing the distinction is important. Commitment can politically support continuity to an extent that passive acceptance may not. On the other hand, depending on circumstances, being committed to a policy path can also be politically more dangerous than keeping options open, especially if politicians fail to extend the commitment into the broader society.

A clear consequence of commitment is that it limits some policy options primarily on an ideational or ideological basis. Consider a state's commitment to protect territorial integrity. This commitment is so deep-rooted in the modern state that it does not waver with changes in government. Indeed, it is treated as non-negotiable, and inculcated through nationalist ideology from an early age. Thus secessionist sentiments, including those in India, are usually treated with coercive measures regardless of costs or implications, and the commitment to preserve territorial integrity supercedes the commitment to tolerate dissent or to uphold human rights. A position that reflects a short-term financial problem, such as the prescription that India needs to devalue its currency and increase exports to meet a deficit in its balance of payments, reflects a material cost-benefit calculation, and does not reveal any obligation beyond simply maintaining a modicum of economic health. But a position that emphasizes openness to the outside world as a timeless value characteristic of Indian civilization shifts the discourse fundamentally. Believers of openness can justify greater costs internally, and adversaries of openness are confronted with the risk of questioning a national-historical continuity.

Rivalry

The international political system, composed of states that claim to be sovereign, and extended hand-in-hand with the spread of capitalism worldwide over the last 400 years, reflects and edifies the primacy of ownership and competition. Regardless of its moral and ideological implications, the current state-centric international system is such that competition is endemic, competitiveness is considered a virtue, and policies that clearly enhance a state's competitive position against its rivals are rarely questioned. The context of rivalry, that is, the context in which a state makes competitive decisions, is shaped historically, influenced by both events and the evolution of dominant ideas. Eventually it can take a life of its own. As William Thompson explains it:

> Rivalries persist ... because states have conflicting interests that go unresolved. They wish to occupy the same territory, control the same markets, or monopolize overlapping positions of influence. In the process they become competitors for these objectives. Given sufficient time, it may not matter much that some of the contested objectives are no longer in conflict. Intense rivals will find new sources of conflict as time goes by.[40]

Thompson's lucid description alludes to the notion that rivalry is at its heart a matter of perception and construction. State leaders can take intense rivalry as a given, regardless of material circumstances. Rivalries can simply be inherited, having little to do with present circumstances, policies, or leaders. Non-material perceptions, such as ego or pride or sense of destiny, can become, in the context of constructed rivalries, cause for not just a mere disregard of domestic politics but also major war. Conversely, significant shifts in material circumstances or changes in their interpretation can lead to an escalation of hostility just as swiftly as they can spawn friendship, even formal alliances. A new generation brought up in peace will likely perceive rivalry differently from an older one scarred by war. The meaning of an "enemy" can be reconstructed sometimes simply by a change in political leadership. Rivalry in international politics is a human construct, and subject to the same tendency to be volatile and to err.

However, when strategic rivalries are perceived to exist, the decision-making context can be particularly intense if state leaders see the same outstanding rival in multiple "arenas," from economic to political to military – a situation that we can call dense rivalry. In the early years of the modern state, rivalry between England and the Netherlands began from a commercial rivalry and expanded into a military-strategic rivalry culminating in three naval wars in 1652–54, 1665–67, and 1672–74. Such expansion from one-dimensional rivalry to multi-dimensional rivalry was "a frequent source of war" during that time.[41] The United States and Japan shared a "dense" multi-dimensional strategic context in the interwar years, but they are no longer military rivals now.[42] Similarly, India's strategic context with China in the 1960s used to be primarily military. The context has become more dense, and therefore more intense, as India perceives itself to compete against China increasingly in economic, diplomatic, and technological arenas. From the perspective of Indian policymakers, Pakistan, in contrast, remains mainly a military and political rival (leaving aside for the moment their legendary rivalry in cricket).

Dense or intense rivalry supports policy continuity by serving three functions. First, relative to domestic political needs, it elevates the importance of an external rival in the decision-making calculus of national policymakers. This can manifest itself in various ways. Policies that solve domestic problems will be considered more attractive if they also enhance a state's competitive position against its perceived rival. Dense rivalry also can make the rival visible, as a constant presence, in the shadow of which policies need to be made. For example, at an operational level in India, China features increasingly in research, deliberations, speeches, and planning in multiple ministries: Finance, Defense, External Affairs, Commerce and Industry, Communications and Information Technology, and Science and Technology, as well as the Department of Atomic Energy and the Department of Space. References to China come up in cabinet meetings and in parliament, becoming more frequent and covering more diverse topics. Books and articles come out every year comparing different aspects of these two "Asian Giants," as though such comparison is only natural. Eventually the construction, appearance, and re-appearance of the same rival in multiple arenas prompts coordination, and it raises the possibility of reaching high-level consensus across different policymaking bodies. Even though inter-departmental coordination on issues relating to China remains ad hoc in India, evidence indicates that it has become relatively more regular for policymakers and more pressing in the perception of analysts. A sense of dense or multi-dimensional rivalry can elevate issues about international position and competitiveness to state-level priorities, transcending the partisan agenda of any one particular party. Rivalry, whether tangible or not, can then become an uncontested belief.

Dense rivalry promotes the adoption of a strategic and longer-term approach to envisioning and prioritizing the state's goals. As rivalry spreads to cover additional spheres, from military to economic, as in the case of India–China, we can expect the cost of policy failure to increase. Under a dense context, a policy failure in one arena, say, economic arena, can translate into not only economic, but also political or military advantages for a state's rival.[43] The possibility of spillover can provide incentives for *strategic* decision-making: forecasting and making policy "moves" based on a rival's prior and expected future moves. The significance of an individual policy move at a random point in time is eclipsed by the importance of a series of moves over time.[44] In other words, a strategic policymaker operating under a dense context of rivalry would be willing to bear short-term domestic costs in view of longer-term benefits to the state's international power and status. This stance privileges strategic continuity over the kind of discontinuity that is created by ad hoc policymaking. To tease this out without getting distracted by the importance of a single policy event, the study takes a close look at the overall effects of the historic evolution of India's perception of rivalry with China.

Third, the more dense or concentrated the context of rivalry, the greater the incentive to match or excel a rival's policies. This mode of competitive behavior is described and explained persuasively by strategic trade theory in economics.[45] What is important to note is that this matching or mirroring is reflected in the intent more than the content of the policymaking process. For example, imagine that China and India are competitors in the international tea market. If China intervenes in its domestic tea market to raise the international competitiveness of its tea, Indian policymakers might feel compelled to respond. But they can choose from a variety of avenues to maintain or enhance its competitive position. They may offer subsidies for inputs, or defray transaction costs by organizing tea auctions, or offer direct tax benefits or better credit terms for producers, or deregulate to promote additional private investment in the tea sector – to name a few. Any or all of these interventions can change the price of Indian tea relative to China's.[46] The policy intent is achieved even though the policy content is different. Strategic policymaking does not guarantee identical or convergent policies. But, as later chapters will argue, the more that Indian policymakers and analysts began to interpret success and failure through the prism of external rivalry and competitiveness, the more they displayed an intent to match Chinese economic policies in a variety of sectors.

Combined, these three features – the presence of singular rival in multiple arenas, a longer-term horizon for cost-benefit calculations, and strategic policy matching – induced a kind of policy-thinking in India that was driven less by domestic politics and more by the outcome of policies pursued outside, especially by China. China's economic success in the 1980s began to spill over to multiple spheres in the 1990s, from the modernization of its military, to its underwriting of the US deficit, to even a successful bid to host the Olympic Games – all of which were observed and analyzed in Indian policy circles, heightening a sense of relative loss for India and a potential dent in India's globalism. By 2007, Chinese products were competing strongly against Indian goods within India, which persuaded Indian policymakers to promote more flexibility in its domestic labor market, even though it would be a dangerous venture politically. In fact, labor market intervention was partly responsible for BJP's electoral failure in 2004. Had India's strategic context remained dispersed, the immediacy of international competition would have been less significant relative to domestic needs and political calculations. In that case, interest-based domestic politics may have had a greater influence on whether policies were continued or abandoned.

Globalism, rivalry, and open-economy policy

This book proposes that the continuity of India's open-economy policy has been the result of a strong sense of unfulfilled ideological mission, the power of which was situated in interpretations of India's role aspirations in world affairs and its strategic behavior relative to its rivals. The relationship is dialectic: globalism and rivalry have evolved and combined in different ways in different historical and political settings to provide complementary or contradictory incentives toward policy continuity. In the chapters to come, I intend to show that the dominant ideational influence on Indian policymaking shifted between the 1890s and 1990s from being non-globalist with a perception of dispersed rivalries toward strong globalism with a sense of dense international rivalry. This evolution of globalism and rivalry eventually privileged India's international goals over domestic political demands, and helped justify outward orientation to domestic constituencies, providing stronger incentives for policy continuity toward openness. There was a time when the historic mission of the Indian state was focused internally, dwelling on development, *swadeshi*, self-reliance, or poverty alleviation. Globalism was important as an uncontested background theme, but the determinants of policy continuity were primarily internal. The main influences on economic policy were incentives and disincentives arising from domestic politics. Economic policy, economic empowerment, and the narratives associated with them have now become primarily about India's potential position relative to its rival, and one step further, relative to the world at large. Most other national goals have been made secondary to India's international empowerment, a stance with which all major political actors who have policy influence concur. It is this ideological shift that has lowered the risk of disruption despite upheaval, and will provide support for the future continuity of India's open-economy policy.

The manner in which this book conceptualizes the role of ideas aims to make our understanding of Indian political economy distinct in several ways. First, it treats continuity as a variable, not a given. Specific combinations of globalism and rivalry in policy-thinking affect the chances of the continuity of open-economy policy. By looking in-depth into a single case, India, we would be able to identify the different ways that the two have combined over time. This brings us to the second point: we need to treat ideas as more than a binary (existent or non-existent) and more than static epiphenomena. Ideas evolve, and the process of the evolution itself carries policy significance. In India's case, the perception that a historical mission was staying "unfulfilled" was derived from the ideational evolution of globalism and rivalry. India is an ideal case to investigate the power of ideas on economic policy because we can trace both globalism and rivalry as they grew from being marginal to powerful in their influence.

Third, the ideas of globalism and rivalry are fundamental to the practice of international politics and economics, as these ideas are connectors: they link the domestic to the foreign. Both are dependent on an awareness of self versus other, of territory, and of inside and outside. Consequently, they provide useful lenses to study how domestic demands affect or do not affect a state's perceived role or goals in international politics, and how economic globalization creates domestic political risks as well as opportunities.

Finally, treating globalism and rivalry as variables allows us to identify conditions under which domestic politics can either influence or be ignored in favor of policy continuity. The crucial assumption here is that continuity toward international economic openness may be hampered when left mostly to the swings of domestic politics. This would be the case especially through the period when openness is mainly an idea, and until the idea is established firmly as a state-level commitment whose rationale and basis are no longer under substantial threat. This situation is similar to one conceived by some theorists of democratic consolidation: a democracy, after transition from authoritarianism, can be considered consolidated when democratic institutions are no longer under threat – or as Giuseppe di Palma noted, when democrats can finally "relax."[47] The consolidation of India's open-economy policy began when policy debates were no longer about the principle of economic openness, but more about the specifics. In other words, they were no longer about the "why" but the "how." This transition happened roughly in the early 2000s, about a decade after open-economy policy was begun. This book contends that the reasons that India's open-economy policy could be ideationally consolidated are rooted strongly in the perception and construction of a dense strategic context in *addition* to a globalist mission.

Plan of the book

The next chapter begins the analysis by reviewing the political risks of India's open-economy policy. It has three objectives. First, it examines oppositional politics. One set of such politics focused on the *causes* of pursuing openness in India, charging that policies were promoted to cater to demands by international financial institutions like the IMF and the World Bank. Another set focused on the *consequences* of these policies on social groups and national ideologies. Second, the chapter points out why the dominant politics of causes and consequences both failed. The narrative of causes percolating in the popular imagination could not account for policy continuity; policymakers seemed unfazed. Likewise, even intense political activism based on the consequences of globalization could not stem the continuity of India's open-economy policy. The chapter concludes that material reasons do not explain why policymakers persisted with India's open-economy policy, especially in the formative decade of the 1990s. Third, the chapter alters conventional understanding about the significance of the external dimension in Indian policy-thinking. I argue that for pro-openness policymakers, external incentives were not tied to the dictates of international finance, as charged by the opposition and as indicated by India's balance of payments at that time. It was more fundamentally about India's emerging rivalries and its potential to play a strong role in world affairs. The chapter shows how both globalism and rivalry were tied to nationalist ambitions, and sets the stage for a deeper exploration conducted in the next two chapters.

From where did the perceptions of globalism and rivalry emerge? To answer the question, Chapter 3 traces the roots of India's international setting. It explores political and military rivalries in nationalist imaginations, going as far back as British colonial policies toward India's northern frontier. British and Indian policymakers had begun to view China as a worrisome rival, but India's context of strategic decision-making was not attuned to China's policy moves. Globalism also emerged as a strong current in Indian thinking from the colonial period, evolving especially out of India's anticolonial nationalist project. Because globalism became embedded increasingly into Indian policymaking, China's economic and military advances eventually came to be seen as natural and inevitable threats to India's bid for regional hegemony, and therefore urgent and policy-relevant. But until the 1980s, China was still perceived as primarily a military rival and not directly relevant to external economic policies.

Chapter 4 takes an in-depth look at the perception and construction of economic rivalry with China. I show how the evolution of India's economic globalism and rivalry began to provide a stimulus to "catch up" with China and emulate Chinese policies. This was aided by studies that had begun to come out from the 1970s, first comparing the two countries innocuously, but then progressing to convey a sense of relative loss for India and relative gain for China. After a period of rejecting the Chinese economic model as inappropriate or irrelevant, Indian policy circles began to take a closer look at China's growing economic strength. Continuing these inspections resulted in two important ideational changes in Indian policy circles. One was about the definition of globalism, which used to be expressed primarily in political and military terms in which economic policy served an instrumental and secondary role. The other was about the traditional dichotomy between self-reliance and economic interdependence. Instead of viewing economic independence as necessary for economic empowerment, Indian analysts, thanks to China's experience, began to see economic *inter*dependence as a source of security. Eventually, though fitfully, Indian globalism began to underscore the need to establish a fast-growing economy interconnected with the outside world as the best way to raise India's visibility and status in the hierarchy of states. The chapter ends with a survey of the emerging frontiers of India's economic rivalry with China.

This logic has been extremely useful to justify to domestic constituencies both outward orientation and policy continuity toward it. The final chapter mulls on the political value of marketing the ideas of strategic rivalry and globalism, pointing out how the logic of competitiveness and a global role eventually came to be accepted in society. The ideological alignment among disparate Indian administrations was not about the domestic (largely economic) role of the state, religion, or party affiliation. It was about an implicit, and later explicit, understanding of India's external dimension, and crucially related to concepts of power, rivalry, hierarchy and in world affairs. The narrative that promoted such an understanding established openness as an idea congruent with the evolution of Indian history, culture, and "mission statement." Challenges to openness were then increasingly marginalized, confined to debates about the effectiveness of particular economic policies rather than about the fundamental orientation of the Indian state. This was key to overcoming domestic opposition and continuing with economic openness in a country that for the previous forty years had remained substantially closed.

2 The politics of causes and consequences

> Some say the action in India began with the opening of the Suez Canal.... Others say the action began with the Boeing 707 and John F. Kennedy.... Still others say the action began when that long red line of loonies came straggling in by way of Afghanistan, the Northwest Frontier and the Punjab plains ... at last it is our turn to mass market.
>
> Gita Mehta, *Karma Cola*, 1994

Although India's trading links with the outside world go back at least two thousand years, they were never an integral part of its domestic economy until about fifteen years ago. The only other period that comes close was the height of British colonialism in the late nineteenth century, when the subcontinent was forced to supply primary products such as jute, cotton, and indigo, and to consume finished British goods. For most of its post-independence history, India emphasized domestic industrialization, especially the development of heavy industries. The aim, stated explicitly and frequently, was to achieve economic self-sufficiency through substituting imports with domestic production.[1] It accorded centralized planning a major responsibility for production and distribution, and tried to promote growth through extensive state investments and interventions.[2] As typical of import-substitution industrialization (ISI) regimes, it protected nascent industries by putting up high tariff barriers. Its import duties on consumer products were at times the highest in the developing world.

India's First Five Year Plan (1951–55) and Second Five Year Plan (1956–60) were both marked by "export pessimism." By the time of the Second Plan, India's economic framework was determined by a model created by P. C. Mahalanobis, a prominent economist. "[T]he closed nature of the economy was simply assumed" in the Mahalanobis model, which was strongly supported by Prime Minister Jawaharlal Nehru. "No balance of payments considerations entered into the calculations of the model."[3] The Third Five Year Plan (1961–65) was exceptional: it recognized contributions that exports can make to the economy. During that plan period, the government offered export subsidies, and devalued the rupee by 58 percent in June 1966. But neither the Fourth (1970–75) nor the Fifth (1976–80) plan included any chapter or significant section on foreign trade.[4] The overall intellectual and political climate was conditioned by the philosophy that economic independence entailed independence from imports, along a line that both Mahalanobis and Nehru emphasized consistently. As Nehru stated:

> No modern nation can exist without certain essential articles which can be produced only by big industry. Not to produce these is to rely on imports from abroad and thus to be subservient to the economy of foreign countries. It means economic bondage and probably also political subjection.[5]

The Sixth (1981–85) and the Seventh (1986–90) Five Year Plans sought to situate trade policies in a wider macroeconomic context, and considered trade beneficial insofar as it aids domestic industry. But while they extended the scope of "big industry" to include a greater role for private capital, they continued to accept that the goal of production was to meet domestic demand, and that "there is no possibility of export-led growth in an economy such as India."[6] In principle and practice, India was essentially an inward-looking economy, fundamentally different from the type of economic integration and openness to the rest of the world that is now taken as given. From this long tradition, how did a group of political leaders manage to change India's direction? In this chapter we want to understand the compulsions that key policymakers internalized and acted upon. We will begin by asking: what was the economic reality that they perceived? What type of information, facts, and data did they review and put together to construct their picture of India's economic health? We will then look at the public reaction to their policy measures. What were the crosscutting streams of explanations, accusations, defenses, and narratives about India's economy and its connections to the wider world? By the end of this chapter, we will have reconstructed the most immediate intellectual and political milieu of Indian economic policymaking in the 1990s. The next two chapters will then extend the analysis over the longer term, focusing specifically on the vital role played by the ideas of globalism and rivalry in impelling India's reformist policymakers to persist with their economic program. For now, the story begins with an impending bankruptcy.

Eyeing bankruptcy in 1991

During the 1980s, when many developing countries were languishing from a depression brought about by the debt crisis, India posted an impressive annual GDP growth rate of 5.5 percent.[7] However, the expansionary policies associated with central planning and populist politics in the previous decades had resulted in a substantial drainage of economic resources by the government. The government's consumption, as a percentage of GDP, grew by 7.2 percent annually between 1981 and 1991.[8] Consequently, the fiscal deficit grew substantially, as shown in Figure 2.1. The internal debt of the government grew from 35 percent of GDP in 1980–81 to about 53 percent of GDP by 1990–91.[9]

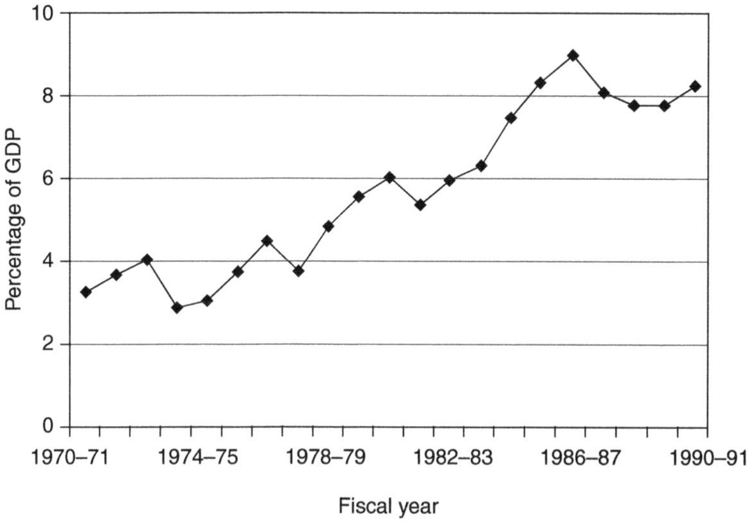

Figure 2.1 Fiscal deficit of the Indian government, 1970–71 to 1990–91 (as percentage of GDP) (source of data: Kirit S. Parikh, ed., *India Development Report 1997*, Delhi: Oxford University Press, 1997, statistical table 3).

Facing these fiscal pressures, and nudged on by a change in ideological setting, the government of Rajiv Gandhi, led by the Congress Party, initiated a package of economic reforms in the 1980s. The scope of those reforms was the domestic economy, and Rajiv Gandhi's policy change was targeted at trimming regulations on industry and private business, and on raising domestic, not external, competitiveness.[10] India's long-term economic health, however, was threatened not just by internal deficit, but also by mounting difficulties in its external sector. Since the Oil Crisis of 1973–74, prices of key commodities were decreasing in real terms.[11] Imports exceeded exports regularly, resulting in a steady increase in the current account deficit by 1991 (see Figure 2.2). The external debt increased from 12 percent of GDP in 1980–81 to about 23 percent of GDP by 1990–91. Debt service ratio during the same period doubled from 15 percent of export earnings to 30 percent.

As the Gulf War continued, remittances from Indian workers in the Middle East began to fall sharply, putting great pressures on India's foreign exchange reserves, which dwindled by mid-1991 to just about $1.2 billion, scarcely enough to finance two weeks' worth of imports.[12] It is this acute pressure on foreign reserves that was interpreted by the government as an unprecedented crisis. The government, headed by the Congress Party, noted gravely: "A default on payments, for the first time in our history became a serious possibility in June, 1991."[13]

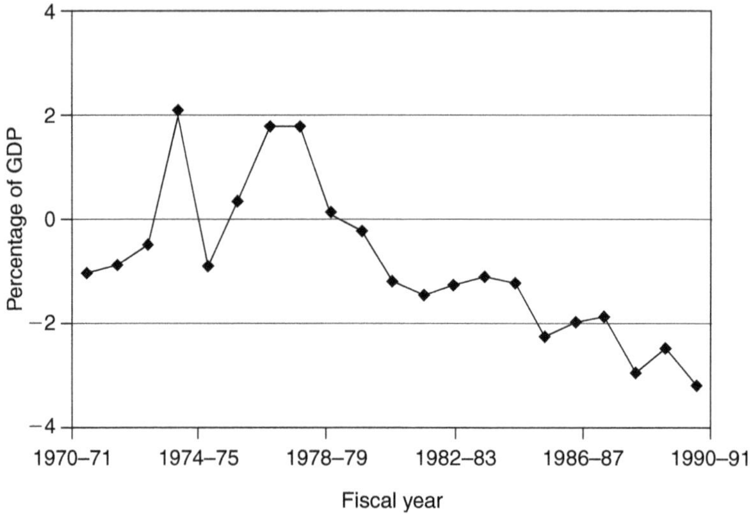

Figure 2.2 India's current account balance, 1970–71 to 1990–91 (as percentage of GDP) (source of data: Kirit S. Parikh, ed., *India Development Report 1997*, Delhi: Oxford University Press, 1997, statistical table 2).

Policy change: tactical response or strategic intent?

This crisis of 1991 occasioned a set of policy moves undertaken by a new government, representing what Achin Vanaik has called "dramatic ruptures with [India's] post-independence settlement."[14] The Congress Party, which traditionally had a centrist agenda, had just been returned to power earlier that year. The way the reformist inner circle of the government responded to the crisis surprised most other leaders of the party. While there were many in the party who did not view the situation as grave, those who agreed that there was an economic emergency thought that measures would be taken to shelter India from the world economy. The government's first move was to devalue the rupee by almost 20 percent in the course of three days. By itself, the move made sense, for devaluation would increase import prices, thereby discouraging imports and easing some pressure on India's dwindling foreign exchange reserves. Policy moves over the next few weeks, however, gave indication that the intent went deeper. The disincentive to import created by devaluation was offset within days, as the government lowered tariff and non-tariff barriers, encouraging especially imports of raw materials for export processing. It became clearer that the more important purpose behind the initial devaluation was not to reduce imports per se, but to encourage exports, that is, expose India to the world economy rather than shelter it. What was still not certain was whether the policy changes were tactical and temporary, or whether they foretold a strategic desire for closer integration with the world. Most Indian policy observers believed it was the former. The external world, from that perspective, was the source of India's economic hardship; deeper integration with it would only increase India's vulnerabilities.

The government, nonetheless, continued its policy path. It used executive ordinance to promulgate policies to encourage foreign direct investment (FDI) and foreign portfolio investment (FPI). The central policymakers began to lay out their agenda more vocally: in contrast to India's historical economic stance, the goal now was to achieve growth through a greater reliance on the world outside, particularly via foreign trade and direct investment. As Manmohan Singh, the finance minister at that time, explained to the parliament:

> The thrust of the reform process would be to increase the efficiency and *international* competitiveness of industrial production, to utilise for this purpose foreign investment and foreign technology to a much greater degree than we have done in the past ... so that the key sectors of our economy are enabled to attain an adequate technological and competitive edge in a fast changing global economy.[15]

The consequences of this new policy emphasis were not spelled out; nor were they foreseen in any systematic way. Though the extent of the predicament was disputed, it was generally accepted that the Indian economy was facing an acute external crisis, which necessitated adjustment of some sort. While a variety of historical and circumstantial causes were at play, what is indisputable is that the moment of policy change was triggered by the "arithmetic" of resource shortfall; it was a material urgency.[16] As Swaminathan Aiyer, a prominent columnist, wrote, the bottom line was that "bankruptcy drove the reform process, not ideology."[17]

In the first two years, the government also conveyed this point, detailing various aspects of the threat of bankruptcy that India faced. The government's public posture over the future of pro-openness policy changes was measured. Since both the probability of success and the nature of political backlash were uncertain, the government kept open the possibility, at least in public, that reforms might be reversed, and that the changes were tactical. But Aiyer was only half-right. There was a strong sense of ideology that drove the continuity of reforms, grounded in a strategic intent of fueling long-term economic growth and raising international competitiveness. In the initial years of reform, this deeper intent was mostly latent: it came through at times in key public speeches and interviews and other times from reading between the lines. When announcing the devaluation, the Finance Minister, Manmohan Singh, and the Governor of the central bank, R. Venkitaramanan, in separate statements, pointed specifically to competitive pressures from China in the export market.[18] The government's *Economic Survey 1991*, authored by the same policy circles, looked at the success of East Asia, asserting, "Much more rapid growth is possible [in India], as our neighbouring countries further east have demonstrated."[19] In a similar vein, Manmohan Singh justified the government's policies and disputed the apologists' view of the slow growth rate of India:

> [T]he world-is-in-a-recession attitude has created in our country a disastrous mindset.... If the world is in a recession, why are the Chinese exports booming? In 1973 our level of exports was the same as that of the Chinese. Where are the Chinese today, and where are the Indians?[20]

References to India's competitive position in the world and the sense of rivalry with China were neither accidental, nor temporary, nor mere rhetoric. They emanated from a strong ideological bedrock, the power and significance of which started to become more apparent from the late 1990s onwards. We will leave further exploration of the basis and evolution of this ideology to later chapters, and focus for now on the volatility that surrounded the initial years.

The story of the first decade of policy continuity is an epic one of "dominance and resistance," to borrow Partha Chatterjee's words. The government found itself frequently on the defensive against a two-prong attack from critics and activists. One set of charges focused on the *causes* of policy change and continuity, and questioned if the government is serving national interests by pursuing economic openness. The other set of charges targeted the domestic *consequences* of economic openness, and motivated politics around a wide set of issues from subsidies and welfare, to the role of the public sector, to the threat posed by increased foreign investment, social, economic, and environmental. The ensuing political commotion, reviewed thematically below, drowned the visibility of the strategic intent of the government's reformists, but, as this chapter will also show, failed to diminish its significance.[21]

Myths in the politics of causes

Allegations of India's "surrender" to pressures from the International Monetary Fund (IMF) surfaced immediately after the currency devaluation in early July 1991.[22] The government expected this. India's very first round of devaluation, back in 1966, was followed by hearty accusations of surrender to foreign powers, and ended up weakening its political leadership at that time, eventually causing heavy losses for the Congress Party in elections in 1967.[23] This time around, the Finance Minister continued to deny that the devaluation was part of IMF conditionalities.[24] The Fund and the Bank, nevertheless, strongly endorsed India's overall reform program. The first such endorsement came after the second round of devaluation in July 1991, when a Fund spokesman stated, rather cautiously, that depreciating the currency was "an appropriate measure under the circumstances."[25] These endorsements eventually became bolder as the years passed. In 1997, for instance, the IMF's Executive Board commended India "for pursuing policies that had set the Indian economy on a new course of modernization to meet the challenges of globalization."[26]

The government tried to counter critics by employing in its policy documents the classic rhetoric of "self-reliance." The government's *Economic Survey 1991–92* declared for instance: "The economic policies of the government have been designed to tackle the immediate crisis, but they emanate from a vision of a future … the basis of this vision is self-reliance."[27] Not convinced, the opposition denounced the government's annual budget by associating it with the "dictates" of IFIs. Confronting these accusations, the Finance Minister felt compelled to make a firm disclaimer in his budget speech in 1992:

> It has been alleged by some people that the reform programme has been dictated by the IMF and the World Bank. We are founder members of these two institutions and it is our right to borrow from them when we need assistance in support of our programmes. However, I wish to state categorically that the conditions we have accepted reflect no more than the implementation as outlined in my letters of intent sent to the IMF and the World Bank, and are wholly consistent with our national interests. The bulk of the reform programme is based on the election manifesto of our Party. There is no question of the Government ever compromising our national interests, not to speak of our sovereignty.[28]

This clear approach to address the primary concern of the critics was a refreshing break from the more tactful and nebulous explanations that Indian policymakers had provided in the past about changes in the economy. The critics were not appeased. The finance minister had acknowledged that there were "conditions we have accepted," which riled many critics, especially at a time when the IMF had a visible, and in India somewhat unpopular, role in the economic transition of the Communist Bloc. A violent industrial strike took place in September 1993 to protest policies that unions alleged would "enslave India to lending agencies such as the International Monetary Fund and the World Bank."[29] Critics of economic reforms contended that India's liberalization program contains the essential ingredients of the stabilization–adjustment–reform scheme that IFIs typically promote. As C. T. Kurien, a well-known critical economist in India, wrote: "Whether designed by the lenders or suggested by the borrower, the Indian attempt at stabilisation and structural adjustments … appears to follow the copy book."[30] Similarly, *The Economist*'s reports on India have been peppered with terms like "IMF-induced austerity,"[31] or "IMF-supervised reform programme."[32] The magazine was explicit in highlighting the role of the IMF: "The IMF persuaded India to turn its back on the policy of trade protection and import substitution that had been in place since the country became independent."[33]

In addition to pressures from IFIs, India, like any developing country, was subject to bilateral influence from the United States, the European Union and other industrial states that seek to tailor India's external liberalization in line with their individual interests.[34] There has not been any systematic study on how these pressures have changed as India began to open up its economy. However, the advent of the World Trade Organization and the World Economic Forum introduced additional channels through which pressures could be brought upon India. The United States, for example, succeeded in December 1999 in influencing India to lower trade barriers on more than 1400 products, after lodging an official complaint with the WTO's dispute settlement body.[35] The government acknowledged these pressures, but typically asserts that India does not agree to decisions that do not reflect "broad national interest," apparently amalgamated from the perspectives of "business associations, labour leaders, and political parties."[36] This cycle – allegations of dependence by the opposition and sections of the press followed by assertions of independence by the government – continued through the first decade of openness, including the budget for 2000–01.[37]

Surrender or independence?

Overall, from the documented evidence it is difficult to draw general conclusions about whether international organizations have held sway over Indian policymakers or whether the government has been in control of the process of opening up. Historically India, as a large developing country, has had a strong prior record of independence from external influence. Studies on India's relationship with international organizations and its role in multilateral forums conclude that India has hardly been a pushover against the demands of other countries and institutions.[38] India, in fact, led developing countries to organize themselves against the influence of globalizing or totalizing organizations that the rich industrialized countries seemed to control. India was at the forefront of the Non-Aligned Movement to counter Cold War politics, of the United Nations Conference on Trade and Development (UNCTAD) to counter GATT, of the Group of 24 and the Group of 9 to counter the Group of 7, and of the Group of 77, South-South cooperation, and the New International Economic Order to counter the resurgence of monetarism and the rise of neoclassical economic ideology.[39] India's emphasis on independence and propensity to lead was manifest again through the first decade of openness, including the 1999 and 2000 meetings of the WTO and the World Economic Forum. As the *Financial Times* put it, the Indian delegation left for the Seattle summit of the WTO, "mandated to resist firmly US and European Union attempts to enshrine core labour rights and environmental standards, as well as multilateral codes on investment and competition."[40] In both forums India led developing countries to resist demands to increase trade liberalization.[41] Murasoli Maran, the Commerce and Industry Minister, offered to lead the developing countries back into the negotiation process, provided that the rich countries agreed to reform the WTO and to remove "non-trade issues." Mike Moore, the Director General of the WTO at that time, concluded correctly:

> India is a major economic player and is an emerging superpower. No major international negotiation today starts unless India is present. In that sense, India is more than just India. Many developing countries look up to it for guidance and leadership.[42]

The experience of half a century of such independence and resistance, combined with a history of leadership within developing countries, has had a firm impact on the ethos and mindset of India's diplomats, administrators, and the policymaking elite. My interviews with Indian policymakers also produced consistent results, revealing a commitment to independence vis-à-vis IFIs.[43] Some secondary evidence, in addition, indicates that policymakers have resisted pressures from IFIs toward specific liberalization measures.[44]

Performance or ideology?

On the other hand, partly because of the discrediting of the traditional concept of development[45] and partly because of the positive empirical record of many other Asian countries, Indian policymakers recognized that previous models of development either had failed to deliver sustained high growth and eradicate poverty or had become a misfit with changed global economic circumstances. This recognition complemented both the ideology of IFIs and their material carrots and sticks offered through adjustment lending. As Jagdish Bhagwati wrote:

> The spread of reforms worldwide, before India was getting to them, meant that the IMF–World Bank conditionality could no longer be plausibly dismissed as ideological; it had been legitimated as a sensible prescription that only reflected what we had all learned in three decades of experience.[46]

Many of those who perceived India's policy reforms as "surrender" to IFIs reacted against the ideological stance of these organizations, that is, the so-called Washington Consensus, composed of privatization, deregulation, fiscal austerity, and liberalization of external flows.[47] Although all these ingredients were introduced in different levels of intensity into India's economy through various annual budgets during the 1990s, it would be erroneous to conclude that Indian policymakers were motivated by the *ideology* of the Washington Consensus. Their inspiration did not come from H Street in Washington, home to the headquarters of the World Bank and the IMF; it came from other sources, the influence of which was obscured by the fog of the dominant public narratives. They were motivated, as Bhagwati noted, more by the *performance* of certain countries than by standard crisis-response prescriptions from IFIs. Policymakers emphasized this point consistently in public, that their agenda was driven by performance-related motives. But in the tumult of change in the early 1990s, it seemed as though they were acting as agents of the interests of international capital, since their policy agenda contained some ingredients common to the Washington Consensus. These interests seemed ubiquitous and strong, and it looked like India was being coerced to implement the same type of changes that were being forced more dramatically on other transition economies, some of whom had historically close relations with India.

Sites of policy battles

This charge was partially correct: there was pressure from IFIs on the Indian government. But in its nature, nuances, and outcome, the pressure was significantly selective, and it was not decisive in India's continuity of openness. The point becomes clearer if we examine the issue in a disaggregated way, identifying the specific policy areas in which IFIs have been most interested and the sites of the major policy battles between the government and IFIs since 1991.[48] With regard to India's external economy, the two most significant obligations for the government were to maintain current account convertibility, which remains a commitment under Article VIII of the IMF's charter; and to remove direct import controls by 2003, which was a commitment to the WTO. India entered the IMF's Article VIII status in 1994, and joined the WTO in 1995. Needless to say, both are mainstays of a pro-globalization policy regime. Both of these obligations have directly affected India's external trade. They exist specifically to ensure that imports remain under a liberal, and possibly free, regime. But these policy commitments in the import sector were politically controversial to maintain. It was easy for opponents of openness to point to these and invoke protectionist sentiments or arguments that drew attention to national sovereignty. But precisely because import control is such a politically charged issue, commitments to keep imports free from control needed to be ensconced through international obligations such as these, so that they survive changes in government.

These formal obligations have linked India's import regime to the institutions that govern exchanges in the international economy, and in doing so, help support policy continuity toward import liberalization. But continuity of pro-openness policies in other crucial arenas of the external economy, namely, exports control or promotion, exchange rate, foreign direct investment, and foreign capital flows, has been generally the government's own responsibility, with periodic pats on the back from the IFIs. A look into the policy documents prepared by the World Bank and the IMF during this formative decade shows that these IFIs were trying to exert pressure in certain areas in which they felt the government's liberalization program was deficient. Interestingly, export promotion, exchange rate, and foreign flows are not the areas that have attracted the most concern from the Bank and the Fund. The fiercest policy battles were fought over domestic, not external, liberalization, and the four areas over which the Bank/Fund confronted the government most frequently were privatization, deficit reduction, public sector reform, and in the wake of the Asian Crisis, financial sector supervision.

The World Bank's 1994 macroeconomic analysis of India commended the liberalization efforts, but emphasized the need to reform public finance and to improve infrastructure. It also called for a broadening of the reforming policy-making process from the three major central ministries (finance, commerce, and industry) to the sectoral ministries and state governments.[49] The following year's report continued a similar policy emphasis. It urged for reforms in agriculture, and more investment in social sectors and infrastructure. It particularly pressed for "an urgent and appreciable improvement in public savings," observing that "a strong fiscal position has a central role in managing effectively the capital and current accounts of the balance of payments."[50] The Bank's Country Memorandum for 1996 took stock of the first five years of reform. It recognized the achievements of external liberalization, but noted that "fiscal imbalances remained the most important threat to India's long term growth." The report identified four major policy challenges for the future: (1) reducing fiscal deficit, (2) liberalizing agriculture, (3) improving infrastructure, and (4) ensuring "social justice." The 1997 country study on India kept up pressure on the government for fiscal reforms, banking and public enterprise reforms, and expenditure control at the state level.[51] The Bank's 1998 Macroeconomic Update re-emphasized the large public sector deficit (about 6 percent of GDP) as the major outstanding concern. Again, the report advocated fiscal reforms at the levels of central as well as state governments, overall tax reforms, and the need to strengthen the financial sector and to accelerate privatization. Other economic sectors, such as export promotion or foreign investment, were not central to the concerns of the update, and mentioned only in passing.[52] A visit by a specialized team from World Bank to the chief executives of the leading financial institutions also underscored the need for positive policy reform in these domestic policy areas.[53]

The IMF's assessments of India's policies since 1991–92 also directed most attention to the same areas. India negotiated a Stand-By Arrangement with the IMF in 1991, which financed the first two years of adjustment. When Indian officials began to negotiate financing under the Extended Fund Facility (EFF) in May 1993, the IMF put emphasis squarely on fiscal reform, changes in labor laws, and reforms of the banking sector.[54] In its 1993–94 annual report on India, the IMF urged the government to return "quickly and decisively to the path of fiscal reforms," with a "less distortionary and more revenue-elastic tax system" and lower interest rates.[55] The Fund's erstwhile Managing Director, Michel Camdessus, visited India after the announcement of India's 1997–98 budget. His official statement identified two major tasks "to enable India to move on to a permanently higher growth path." The first task was to tackle the fiscal deficit. The second was a set of complementary reforms, including financial sector, privatization, legislative framework, and finally, further trade liberalization.[56] Communication from the Fund in the late 1990s continued highlighting policy challenges in fiscal consolidation, subsidies, "profligacy" of state governments, public sector employment, and public sector management.[57] In May 1999, a high level team of eight IMF executive directors visited the country. Their report complimented the government on attaining growth and opening up the economy, though it noted that India still remained "a laggard," compared to the pace at which some other developing countries were lowering their protectionist barriers. It suggested that the government should focus mainly on reducing expenditures and fiscal deficit, and try to implement reforms in labor laws.[58]

The gist of the discussion above is that most of the formal pressure by IFIs on India through the 1990s, the decade during which policy change became policy continuity, was directed at reforms of the *domestic* rather than the *external* economy. The struggle over policy between the government and IFIs seemed stereotypical. IFIs criticized the government of intransigence in implementing what they considered to be necessary domestic policy reforms. The central and the state governments, on the other hand, gave them a patient hearing, but at times also opposed what they considered external meddling in domestic economic affairs. But on issues of openness, there seemed to be little conflict between the government and IFIs over either policy direction or policy implementation. The reason is that the government had been implementing policies toward external liberalization proactively and pre-emptively. IFIs, therefore, have had little reason to complain, dispute, or interfere, other than to encourage such policies with periodic applause and tie-ins with material benefits. On the issue of the openness of the external economy, IFIs have been concerned mostly with ensuring that foreign exporters have access to India's domestic market at prices close to the world price. To date, the specter of protectionism continues to elicit policy recommendations from IFIs, even though India's import openness has been progressively ensured through a web of norms, conditionalities, and treaty commitments to the World Bank, the IMF, the WTO, as well as to individual trading partners.

In sum, import control aside, Indian administrations in the 1990s were carrying out policies toward economic openness out of their own volition and, thus, very likely out of their own motive. To date, the Indian government has aggressively maintained a competitive exchange rate, promoted exports, and offered incentives to attract both foreign direct investment and foreign portfolio investment. All governments within the past decade and a half have been decisive about continuing pro-globalization policies in these arenas in spite of considerable political turbulence. IFIs have been quiet about liberalization in these areas precisely because the government, through its proactive and pre-emptive policy-making, obviated the need for their interference.

Limits of the politics of consequences

If one arena of dominance and resistance constituted the role of international financial institutions, the other – indeed the more turbulent one – was focused on the consequences, both perceived and actual, of economic openness on India's domestic political economy, and especially on organized interests. The remarkable aspect of this story is that the politics of consequences failed to stem the continuity of openness, despite being a tremendous driver of public debates, political resistance, social violence, electoral outcomes, and an unprecedented rate of change in governments.

Withdrawal from planning

The initial announcement of economic reforms in the summer of 1991 was met with a series of knee-jerk reactions from different parties. Opposition sentiments became particularly hostile when it was reported that the government had shipped forty-seven tons of gold to the Bank of England to raise about $600 million on an emergency basis. Aggressive opposition accompanied nearly every promulgation of major liberalization-oriented policies in the 1990s, including the first three Union Budgets (1991–92, 1992–93, 1993–94), the Eighth Five Year Plan (1992), the report of the Tarapore Committee on Capital Account Convertibility (1997), and the report of the Fifth Pay Commission (1997), which dealt with the government's fiscal health. In these documents, the government continued to emphasize that its priority was the eradication of poverty. But skeptics treated this as empty rhetoric, and noted that equal and at times greater emphasis was placed on "growth" stimulated by foreign trade and investment.

The Eighth Five Year Plan was significant. It appeared, almost a year late, to wide anticipation as the government's first official medium-term policy vision since the switch in economic direction in 1991. But in its fundamental approach, it was self-deprecating, as it emphasized the limits of economic governance through medium-term planning. It mandated the adoption of "indicative" instead of deterministic or centralized planning. Quantitative targets, a vestige of Soviet-influenced economics, were de-emphasized. Between the lines, however, this indirect approach also conveyed an additional limit, which the opposition discovered gradually through its experience of resistance: the government's withdrawal from direct economic management connoted also a reduced responsiveness to the politics of consequences. If private activity was to drive the Indian economy, the side effects of such activity should be managed privately. Labor problems, for example, would be negotiated primarily between workers and the owners of capital, without government mediation or restriction.

In orientation, plan documents in South Asia tend to have a more populist flavor than other types of policy documents, partly because plans can play with greater shades of gray by virtue of their longer-term perspective. The Eighth Plan was distinct also in this regard. On one hand, it emphasized indirectness in economic management by reducing the role of planning. This approach became further consolidated in the Ninth Plan, 1997–2002.[59] On the other hand, it was direct and forthright in promoting market mechanisms in the domestic economy and on its stress on the external economy to boost growth, much to the dismay of critics who had expected a greater social commitment from the government after the initial year of economic reforms. The Eighth Plan repeated, over and again, the need for "globalization" of Indian trade and industry. It identified that one of the main tasks of the government was to "move our trade policy towards greater openness and to reap the full benefits of international trade."[60]

Industrial resistance

The Plan, however, was careful to temper the pace: "Indian industry must be readied to face international competition in a phased manner."[61] Programs were subsequently undertaken to rally support for the government's policies.[62] Out of 243 major public sector units (PSUs), the government identified nine as potential "global players." The government began to encourage large private businesses to incorporate higher managerial and production standards to compete with

TNCs and even expand operations abroad.[63] But overall, Indian policymakers tried to assure the opposition that "gradualism" was their stance toward the pace and extent of globalization, even though they continued to implement policies rapidly, especially in contrast to the slow and haphazard pace of liberalization in China, a country which began to feature prominently in Indian policy discourse.[64]

The government found allies in peak industry organizations like Assocham (Associated Chambers of Commerce and Industry), who urged that open-door policies were conducive to raising the competitiveness of Indian business. Businesses were especially enthusiastic about the reduction of domestic red tape or "internal liberalization." But most firms that were not already engaged in export-oriented businesses were extremely wary of foreign competition.[65] The opponents of open-economy policies included not just small firms but large conglomerates like Godrej, a consumer goods giant, or Bajaj Auto, one of the largest manufacturers of scooters and mopeds in the world. Rahul Bajaj, the chairman, declared that Indian industry was being "wiped out."[66] Many other important business leaders joined force to express similar sentiments.[67] K. K. Birla, the President of the Federation of Indian Chambers of Commerce and Industry (FICCI), let it be known publicly, which did not endear him to the authorities, that the reforms "were not in the best interests of the country or industry."[68] Freddie Mehta, a prominent director of Tata, commented: "Indian industry in the coming years will see a few dramatic winners and a large number of losers. The staying power of Indian industry is not comparable to that of global players."[69] The Executive Director of the Industrial Development Bank of India noted: "Hasty steps towards globalisation without ensuring a level playing field have led to the eclipsing of Indian industry. We should have exercised extreme caution in liberalising the economy."[70] In face of external competition, Tata, the largest business group in India at that time, began a major consolidation move to integrate its eighty companies and 272,000 employees into thirty larger entities. Indal, the huge Indian Aluminum Company, faced considerable losses and the prospect of substantial layoffs after tariff liberalization introduced foreign competition in the local aluminum market.[71]

The most influential of these businesses formed a pressure group, known as the Bombay Club, and began to organize, in addition to private lobbying, seminars and sessions to publicize the deleterious effects of the opening up of the Indian economy. The main agenda of this group was protectionism, especially for large capital that had enjoyed from the state direct and indirect patronage, such as joint ventures, or the license raj and the consequent high barriers to entry. This group found a willing audience in the BJP and other parties that were in opposition at that time. Together they succeeded in compelling the government to withdraw the Insurance Regulatory Authority Bill in 1997, which would have deregulated the insurance industry and allowed foreign companies a presence in the local market.[72] This withdrawal was the only major departure from India's pro-openness policies since 1991.

By the mid-1990s, the government was in danger of losing some of its earlier supporters in business, as foreign investors and multinationals began to flex their muscle in an increasingly liberal economic environment. In March 1996, Tarun Das, the Director-General of CII (The Confederation of Indian Industry) assailed the opportunistic behavior of multinational corporations. Some observers noted that CII was changing "from being an ardent supporter to becoming a staunch critic." Assocham President H. Somnay also expressed concerns about the increasing perks available to foreign investors, and there was pressure on the government to reverse its policies and reduce the ceiling on foreign investment from majority ownership back to minority ownership.[73] When a new government came to power in the mid-1990s, the Prime Minister, Inder Kumar Gujral, struck a conciliatory note to Indian businesses:

> I share your discomfort. The country must strike a golden mean between opening up the economy to foreign investors and providing [a] level playing field for the domestic entrepreneur. We will not allow 16th century capitalism where any outsider can come and overwhelm you. We will look after you and give you benefits of paternity. Outsiders are welcome but not to take over, not to drown you.[74]

Gujral repeated this type of commitment, but did nothing concrete. Open-economy policies continued and eventually further sectors of the economy were opened up to foreign investment. This is akin to the promises and betrayals that marked much of the politics of economic reform, as detailed in Rob Jenkins's study.[75]

Organized labor, especially in the public sector, was another formidable adversary of the government's openness policies. Nationwide industrial strikes were organized in November 1991, June 1992, and September 1993 to protest the government's policy reforms.[76] The Centre of Indian Trade Unions (CITU), along with other parties of organized labor, condemned the absence of labor issues in the foreign investment legislation proposed by the government.[77] Especially at stake was the debate over "exit policy," that is, the right of factories to lay off workers and close down.[78] CITU was also one of the major organizations that sued the Enron Corporation, challenging its $2.5 billion flagship investment project of power generation (Dabhol power plant) in Maharashtra.[79]

Rural risks

Much of this type of opposition was built on an eclectic mix of ideology, spanning socialism, nationalism, and rentier capitalism, and even neo-dependency approaches that together argued that the pursuit of open-economy policies driven by the Washington Consensus would come at the expense of adverse consequences to welfare, poverty, human rights, and the environment.[80] The cutback in the economic role of the state, especially the role of industrial and social planning, was the cause of severe grievances, notwithstanding the fact that the reformist prime minister and the finance minister were essentially social democrats, not neo-conservatives.[81] The central government's capital expenditures fell from 6.8 percent of GDP in the second half of the 1980s to 4.6 percent in the first half of the 1990s.[82] Part of this reduction was achieved through the withdrawal of subsidies, especially on imported kerosene and foodstuff. These withdrawals have been a major cause of turmoil against pro-globalization policies.[83] The major brunt of these changes, as the critics rightly expected, fell on the poor, especially the rural poor. The World Bank estimated that in the first year of reform, the incidence of poverty in India increased from 36 percent to 41 percent, and attributed at least a third of this increase directly to the austerity measures of the government.[84] The 1970s had a higher rate of decline in poverty than did the 1990s.[85] Militant rallies were held at frequent intervals in different parts of the country, denouncing globalization and the increase in prices of essential commodities. In several important instances those rallies were organized nationally, in January 1992, October 1993, and autumn 1997.[86]

Farmers in particular identified WTO as a foe that represented all that was wrong with globalization. Prices of several key crops dropped significantly as the government eased quantitative restrictions, which accelerated after India joined the WTO. By 2001, cotton prices fell from $60 to $20 per 100kg; the price of rice halved; that of groundnuts fell by approximately two-thirds. This fall in prices occurred without an increase in supply. In fact, growth in foodgrain production decelerated from 3.5 percent in the 1980s to 1.7 percent in the 1990s.[87] The closer a region was to ports, the more vulnerable market prices became to the effects of external trade.[88] Additionally, the right to sow seeds became a particularly contentious issue in rural India. India's accession to WTO's intellectual property rules "made seed-saving a crime": farmers would have to re-purchase seeds from multinationals such as Monsanto every year, instead of collecting seeds from their previous harvest.[89] Similarly, within a few months of opening up soybean imports, this began to drive out mustard as the source of edible oil. Before 1998, 68 percent of edible oil in India was pressed through small-scale crushers using local technology. This type of processing was banned in 1998, around the same time that soybean imports were deregulated, resulting in large job losses in the local edible oil industry.[90] There was also vibrant resistance to the advent of genetically modified crops and foodstuff in the wake of India's membership of the WTO.

Given the assault from multiple fronts, especially the reduction in income, and at times, a failure in the ability to sell, farmers by the end of the 1990s began to commit suicide in several well-publicized waves. In a particularly tragic incident in 1998, 500 mostly marginal cotton farmers in Warangal District of Andhra Pradesh committed suicide by drinking pesticides and insecticides.[91] A "Monsanto, Quit India" movement began in 1998, formulated along the lines of Gandhi's original Quit India movement against the British, but directed at multinational agribusinesses. In June 1999, several hundred farmers traveled to Geneva to protest in front of the WTO. The All-Indian Kisan Sabha (Farmers' Forum) rallied thousands in mid-2001 in several protests against the WTO and the consequences of openness. In October 2001, thousands of farmers protested in Bangalore against food imports and withdrawal of subsidies. In October 2005, more than 50,000 farmers from fourteen states protested in Mumbai against the WTO.[92]

The increase in trade and multinational presence also unified several large environmental groups across rural and urban India. They lent their support to a variety of causes in solidarity with other opponents of the government's globalization policies, who were seeking to send Coca Cola, Pepsico, and Monsanto out of India.[93] Such opposition manifested itself frequently, but especially on the eve of major forums, like the WTO Ministerial Meeting in Seattle in 1999 and the World Economic Forum at Davos in 2000.[94] In one of the most publicized cases of environmental activism, the World Bank was forced to withdraw funding for building a $3 billion dam over the river Narmada.

Tensions in political parties

Political organization against openness in the 1990s benefited from the rise of Hindu nationalism, especially in the initial power of BJP (before it became more moderate) and its more extreme sub-groups. Despite Rajiv Gandhi's popularity in the 1980s, the Congress Party was in gradual decline since Indira Gandhi's imposition of a state of emergency. Hindu nationalism was becoming more appealing to the masses as a viable alternative at the federal level to Congress and other centrist parties. Socialist and communist parties exerted force at the state level, but they took a strong hit with the dismantling of the Soviet Union in 1991. The near-simultaneous opening up of the economy indicated fissures in India's overall ideological bedrock. In this atmosphere, "aggressive cultural self-assertion, religious or ethnic, becomes a form of consolation," for which BJP provided a perfect vehicle.[95]

BJP pursued an intelligent, if contradictory, anti-foreign approach that earned it political capital in both urban and rural areas. In the urban areas, BJP's main allies were protectionist small and large businesses that were threatened by foreign competition, as mentioned earlier in reference to the Bombay Club. A large-N post-election survey in 1999, for example, showed that 69 percent of BJP's votes came from the "upper strata," composed of high-caste or high-income groups.[96] In the rural areas, BJP's grassroots affiliate, the saffron-clad RSS (Rashtriya Samajsevak Sangh), egged on sentiments against the advent of a Western-style consumerist culture and against multinational agribusinesses, the combination of which threatened both rural traditions and livelihood. This got the BJP support from a wide swathe of farmers and traders. In the mid- to late-1990s, RSS threatened to raise a *swadeshi* (nationalist) army to drive out foreign corporations, a move that was backed by small retailers and traders across the country.[97]

In both urban and rural constituencies in the early 1990s, BJP and RSS also portrayed Muslims as the original foreign invaders who began poisoning national culture. The fervor created by them culminated in the destruction of the Babri Mosque in Bihar in 1992 by Hindu extremists. BJP's nationalist approach against globalization, and indeed all that is foreign, helped it gain political power rather speedily. In the late 1980s, BJP had only two parliamentary seats in the Lok Sabha (India's lower house), compared to Congress's 409. By 1996, it emerged as the largest party in the general elections, with 162 members in the Lok Sabha. After a series of communal riots in India, starting from the Babri Mosque fiasco, BJP began to distance itself from RSS and from explicit Hindu-nationalistic rhetoric. The party's rift continued over the role of multinationals. The nationalist faction, with strong support in the rural areas, was strongly against foreign investment. S. Gurumurthy, one of the chief leaders of the nationalist faction, denounced the government's pro-investment stance: "Like Nawabs and kings who shamelessly welcomed and paid obeisance to East India Company, politicians and media are welcoming Rebecca Marks [the CEO of Enron Corporation at that time]."[98] Nationalism and capitalism continued to have an uneasy marriage within BJP until about 2004, when the Indian electorate voted it out of power, perhaps seeing through the divergence between its nationalist rhetoric and pro-market and pro-openness policy. RSS meanwhile has continued its mobilization against almost everything that is foreign, and continued to receive support from rural areas.

The major political parties, in both the parliament and internal debates, went through great turmoil in staking out their positions for and against policies toward globalization. The most potent opposition was occasioned by India's acceptance of the final Dunkel Draft[99] of the Uruguay Round of GATT negotiations in 1993, to take effect through India's accession to the WTO in 1995. Parliamentary debates around India's joining the WTO were fiercer than any other issue in the 1990s. Opposition parties and nationalist groups, like the Shiv Sena and the RSS, allied with local protectionist business groups like the Bombay Club, highly visible public-sector trade unions, farmers' organizations, and environmentalists.[100] The former prime minister, V. P. Singh, equated the acceptance of the Dunkel Draft to economic slavery.[101] George Fernandes (Samata Party), who would later become BJP's Defense Minister during India's nuclear tests, charged the government with "selling out national interests to Western funding agencies."[102]

The compromise solution for the internal divisions in most parties was to encourage foreign investment but retain a large social role of the state.[103] Especially in the 1990s, all parties were especially shy about reducing public sector employment or reforming and closing unproductive or outdated factories.[104] Facing strong pressure, Finance Minister P. Chidambaram asserted in 1996 that no government employee would be retrenched as part of the austerity measures.[105] When the gigantic report of the Fifth Pay Commission came out in August, 1997, advocating fiscal reforms within the government, strong resistance was voiced not only from other parties but from important divisions within the government itself. Traditionally reticent, the Army expressed dissatisfaction over the pay scale. 1.7 million workers of the Indian Railway threatened to strike.[106]

India's vibrant left-leaning intellectuals bolstered political arguments against openness, especially in the 1990s. Academic economists have always enjoyed a place of honor in Indian policymaking, and many have gone back and forth between academic vocations and policy assignments.[107] Their attack on the consequences of economic openness was multi-dimensional, beginning with the assertion that the domestic resource limitations were exaggerated; that contrary to the claims by the government, India's economy was not on the verge of a collapse sufficient to justify extensive reforms.[108] Prabhat Patnaik contended that the priorities placed on international capital would lead to de-industrialization and unemployment.[109] Dependency and neo-dependency approaches saw foreign capital and trade as a rent-seeking menace,[110] an agent of neo-imperialism,[111] a threat to national autonomy,[112] a dilution of distributive justice,[113] and a threat to domestic industry and labor. As an editorial in the *Economic and Political Weekly* put it: "The liberalisation and globalisation process ... has emasculated Indian business enterprise, both in the public and private sectors, and driven out of gainful employment 'surplus' workers in organised industry in sizeable numbers."[114] The WTO was condemned widely as flatly antithetical to national interests.[115] GATT's propositions about Trade-Related Investment Measures (TRIMs) came under sharp criticism.[116] Heated condemnation also centered on the promotion of intellectual property rights, especially patents and rights over common biological resources.[117]

Instability in governance

All told, the social dislocation and the intellectual and political resistance only exacerbated the fragility of governments at the helm of Indian power. The reforms were begun in an extremely tenuous political and economic environment. In the beginning there were, "for all intents and purposes, only two politically active reformers, the Prime Minister and his Finance Minister."[118] The first set of reforms led by these two men were orchestrated carefully and intelligently to minimize disruptions from interest groups. Both in words and deeds, the government emphasized that gradualism was its mantra with regard to the pace of reforms. James Manor describes its go-slow policy in the first half of the 1990s:

> One interest group would be faced with an unwelcome new policy, but then it would be left alone for a considerable time (often with a few political concessions to ease the discomfort of liberalization) while the reformers made changes that affected other interests ... [The Prime Minister also] staunchly opposed confrontational action of any sort ... he was determined not to outrage any major interest group. Unionized workers had the ability to mount disruptive agitations across urban India.[119]

A similar argument is made by Jenkins, who argues that much of the changes that the government made were cloaked in languages of accommodation, and that underhand tactics – Jenkins uses the term not pejoratively but as an objective observation – marked the reformist politicians' approach toward politics.[120] But while the government was continuing gradually with its open-economy policies, it was also allowing the opposition to organize itself against it. The advantages of gradualism were likely deflated by the non-confrontational policy; the opposition took full advantage of the space offered to them, as shown earlier in this chapter. Most other political leaders in the first few years of reform were haphazard in their agenda and stances, and "many ministers were probably quite reluctant to agree to many of the changes they [the Prime Minister and the Finance Minister] promoted."[121] Given its increasing unpopularity, the government raised spending before the 1996 elections in order to increase support, but to no avail.

The consequences of economic adjustment were felt not only in rural sectors, but also on the economy as a whole. Average GDP growth in the first five years of policy continuity (1992–96) was 5.3 percent, compared with 5.9 percent in the five years immediately prior (1986–91). In 1981–85, the average GDP growth rate was 5.7 percent.[122] The Congress Party, pioneer of reforms, suffered major electoral defeats. Congress lost in three (Andhra, Karnataka, Sikkim) of the four states in which elections were held in November and December 1994. In the late 1980s, Congress controlled 409 out of a total 538 seats in the Lok Sabha. By early 1991 it had 197, by the late 1990s it had 139, and by 2001, its number of seats fell to 118. Much of the central party leadership blamed the liberalization policies.[123] By 2000, there were five changes of government, the average tenure of each being just two years, as shown in Table 2.1.

Mala Lalvani has studied this type of political instability in India, especially the high frequency of changes in government *between* elections. Analyzing the influence of irregular changes in state government on the state economy (measured by growth in gross state product), between 1981 and 1999, Lalvani finds

Table 2.1 Changes in India's governments, 1991–99

Year	*No. of government*	*Event*
1991 (June)	1	Congress wins elections; forms minority government.
1993 (July)		Congress survives a no-confidence vote by fourteen votes.
1994 (January)		Congress secures majority.
1996 (May)	2	No majority in general elections. BJP wins largest share of seats and forms a government.
1996 (May)	3	BJP government falls after thirteen days. United Front coalition forms a government.
1997 (November)		Congress withdraws support from UF. Government falls.
1998 (March)	4	No majority in elections. BJP forms coalition government.
1999 (April)		BJP government falls.
1999 (October)	5	BJP wins elections; forms government.

that these irregular changes had become frequent and had adverse effects on economic growth and fiscal health of the states.[124] In the 1990s, most of the 25 state governments were lukewarm toward openness, especially during the first five years. Many of them were in the dark about the policy goals of the central government, partly because the central government did not engage them in explanatory dialog. As Manor remarks:

> [Prime Minister Rao] never sought to "sell" reform (until desultory attempts during state elections in 1995), even among his party colleagues in the supposedly crucial early years. In 1993, only one of the cabinet ministers from the prime minister's own party in the state of Karnataka had the remotest idea of what the central government was up to, a minister who had studied economics at Cambridge.[125]

In some ways this policy was successful, in particular because it was efficient since it did not invite opposition before policies were enacted. The government ensured that the reaction from the states was focused more on consequences rather than causes. It was in the mid-1990s that state governments began to finally understand the depth of the central government's intent. But India's federal system allowed the central government to "manage dissent" effectively because the system helped "quarantine political resistance to reform within the confines of state-level political systems."[126] On the other hand, the system also exacerbated the complexity of managing reforms because the states did not just act as conduits or a shelter for the central government, but themselves were resisters. They opposed the policy initiatives of the central government on multiple grounds. Some states like Kerala and West Bengal were ruled by the Communist Party of India (CPI), and hence resisted globalization ideologically. The Congress Party, the pioneer of globalization policies, had been continuously out of power in some of the key states, such as Tamil Nadu since 1967 and West Bengal since 1977. In addition, the states disapproved the lack of material incentives. Although the states were urged to provide infrastructure support, subsidies, and tax incentives to exporters and foreign investors, they did not have direct access to the foreign exchange earned, which accrues to the central government.[127] States were unwilling to allow labor force adjustment. Guhan, who did the authoritative study on center-state relations during the early reform process, concluded that support from the states in response to federally undertaken openness has been "grudging at best and non-cooperative at worst."[128] The significance of such political instability in India was not lost on either academics or investors, especially when compared to China's relative stability. As British investment banker Peter Tose, a key figure in China's overseas listings boom in the 1990s, remarked famously in 1997: "India's problems can be summed up in one word: democracy."[129]

Noise, stealth, and tenacity

So far, I hope, I have been able to demonstrate in detail the public noise that has accompanied India's open-economy policy, organized roughly around the narratives of causes and consequences. In the 1990s, the political atmosphere was charged, loud, unstable, unpredictable, and highly active. Given the strong political resistance and an electoral situation in which no party has been able to command national power since 1991, and especially since 1996, it hardly seemed politically rational for Indian governments to continue openness at significant social cost. This argument has been made, among others, by Eswaran Sridharan. Using a rational-choice perspective, Sridharan predicted that "[f]or a coalition government to undertake an economic and social policy package that has short-term political costs but only long-term gains will be very difficult."[130] In view of all this, the Finance Minister admitted to the *Financial Times*: "With all the problems we have had, it is a miracle the [liberalization] programme is still intact."[131]

Despite their trepidations, what reformist leaders showed was sheer tenacity. Regardless of party, they have largely ignored domestic outcries, even mobilization, for protectionism. One thing that the "hung" parliaments of India have not been inactive about is the continuity of reforms.[132] The influential nationalist newspaper, *The Hindu*, felt certain on the eve of elections in 1996 that "political changes would not stop India from going ahead with the new economic policy."[133] The new governments that have shared power since then have explicitly reaffirmed this conviction. After the BJP won the elections in 1996, the Finance Minister, Jaswant Singh, promised to pursue the same globalization path.[134] The BJP government fell a few days later, but the new Prime Minister, Deve Gowda, asserted: "Reversing economic liberalization is ruled out."[135] In February 1999 at the Davos World Economic Forum, the government reasserted its commitment to openness despite the troubles India was facing.[136] After another short-lived BJP government fell, L. K. Advani, the Home Minister, assured that the BJP would pursue globalization with greater intensity if returned to power.[137] BJP was returned to power, and it kept that commitment.

Such resilience is remarkable in a country like India, where policymakers at any given time find their decision-making process complicated by demands from a motley array of domestic factions – economic, religious, ethnic, regional, and political.[138] Firm control of the government by a single party could have been one source of such tenacity. The ad hoc industrial reforms that Rajiv Gandhi's government had attempted earlier (1985–89) were implemented when the Congress Party enjoyed almost a three-quarter majority in the Lok Sabha. The government of Narasimha Rao, which undertook the reforms in 1991, did not even have a simple majority until 1994, which they lost within two years to BJP. But the subsequent coalition governments, however shaky, have continued globalization proactively, in some instances surprising even the international financial institutions by their pace and extent of reforms. In the elections of May 2004, BJP was defeated, and a key reason for an electoral defeat in India once again was voters' rejection of aspects of the government's economic platform. Congress Party, which ran on a more populist agenda in contrast to its stance in the early 1990s, was returned to power as the surprise victors. It has been trying to keep control over a daunting yet familiar task of retaining the support of leftist parties that demand less attention on the external sector and more on poverty and social equity. Any significant reversal of India's economic orientation, nonetheless, is unlikely. The politics of consequences essentially have failed to have any significant impact on the continuity of openness.

Rob Jenkins provides a groundbreaking explanation of the process by which reformist policymakers persisted. He argues that Indian politicians frequently resorted to broken promises, betrayals, and other forms of obfuscation to push their reformist agenda and widen their network of supporters. These tactics could be pursued without significantly damaging their credibility due to the flexibilities allowed by India's political norms, one of which is to permit politicians to change colors as circumstances change. Reformist politicians often "cloaked" their policy changes in vague terms and were not forthcoming about their intent. They also resorted to "stealth," enacting liberalization gradually, without fanfare, and trying to catch potential opposition unawares. As to why politicians were motivated to continue economic liberalization, Jenkins proposes an approach centered on rational incentives. Features of India's democracy, including federalism, protected central politicians to some extent, and allowed them to introduce economic change without jeopardizing their chances of political survival or their ability to continue with their familiar "old-style politics." And economic reforms also allowed them to cultivate new sources of patronage and at times "new methods of obtaining illegal income in a liberalising economy."[139]

While it is the only thorough explanation available for policy continuity in India, Jenkins's perspective leaves several important gaps. First, the incentives that Jenkins points out are essentially incentives of everyday political survival, and they can apply to earlier episodes of liberalization as well. But they cannot explain why the earlier episodes were discontinued while the post-1991 pro-openness policies were continued. Second, to argue that politicians pursued a path because it did not jeopardize their survival can neither adequately distinguish between alternative paths nor problematize agency. Open-economy policy was not the path of least resistance; it was certainly one of the more risky choices in the Indian political atmosphere. A motive rooted in the rational incentive of survival can explain well how politicians endured resistance to their agenda, but cannot explain why they chose to persist with high risk policies when other easier options were available. Survival is not equivalent to continuity; policy continuity of the sort undertaken in India required committed and proactive *agency*. Third, in emphasizing stealth, Jenkins discounts the *noise* of politics that was ubiquitous in India in the 1990s. There were cases of introducing policy through stealth, as Jenkins notes correctly, especially in the domestic economy – but stealth could only be short-lived, since India's media as well as political, industry, and intellectual interests of all hue kept constant vigilance on nearly every policy move, as detailed earlier in this chapter. After all, our subject of study is, as Vincent Cable pointed out eloquently, "a country where the level of political consciousness is such that factory occupations and demonstrations can be organized in protest against a sub-clause of a draft document in GATT negotiations in Geneva."[140] Stealth was the exception, not the norm. Finally, Jenkins forcefully discounts ideas or vision, either as motives for policy or as instruments of political utility: "they did not capture anyone's imagination."[141] While recognizing the contribution of Jenkins's study, this book makes a case for the converse, that certain ideas, constructed and cumulated over time, in fact were extremely powerful motivators for the continuity of policy despite tremendous resistance.

Elements of an explanation

This chapter attempted to re-enact the risky political-intellectual environment in which India's open-economy policy was launched and sustained. What is remarkable about this story is not the change in policy per se. The earlier external crisis in India, in the wake of the oil shocks in 1979–81, also compelled adjustment, financed through heavy borrowing from the IMF. But crisis response in the 1970s and the 1980s was not accompanied by any significant current account adjustment, let alone resolute policy moves to open up the economy, boost exports, solicit investment, or liberalize imports.[142] Compared to previous episodes, crisis-led economic reform after 1991 has been remarkably distinct for its *continuity*. The government's core circle of reformists, including the Prime Minister, Finance Minister, and Commerce Minister, did not just seek to correct the balance of payments problem of 1991; over the next few years, they strived to extend openness to virtually every sector of the economy, stirring every form of organized political interests in the country.

These political interests clashed passionately with the government and with one another over the causes and consequences of globalization, making policy continuity both difficult and vital. A dominance-resistance narrative characterized each. The politics about causes focused much attention on the supposed dominance of international financial organizations and international capital, which were basking in the triumphant climate of the immediate post-Cold War years. The government's liberalization effort was said to be a representation of the Washington Consensus and broader policy trends worldwide. From this perspective, policy continuity was a function of direct conditionalities and indirect socialization by IFIs. True, many policy battles that have shaped openness in India have been fought and negotiated between the Indian government and IFIs. But contrary to conventional understanding, most of these battles were fought around issues of domestic, rather than external, liberalization. India's successive governments have proactively opened up the external economy by themselves.

The politics of consequences were even more turbulent than the debate over causes. Here, too, we can draw an interesting comparison with an earlier episode of liberalization: India's first currency devaluation, in 1966. Widely assailed for its alleged "foreign authorship," it caused "a radical revolt" especially when prices of essentials began to rise. There were strikes, lockouts, demonstrations, and a massive march to the Parliament, in spite of Prime Minister Indira Gandhi's attempts at appeasement. The consequences of this policy were a political watershed, which Baldev Raj Nayar describes as follows:

> [T]he Congress Party, even though returning to power at the centre, met with an electoral disaster which put an effective end to the one-party-dominant system characteristic of the Indian polity. Many of the top leaders of the Congress Party were defeated. The party was ousted from power in eight states, while at the centre its majority was reduced from 361 to 283, even as it now faced a more self-confident and increasingly obstreperous opposition. The Congress Party's electoral disaster in 1967 led to an internecine conflict within the party which finally eventuated in a split in 1969.[143]

In face of this turmoil, the government reversed its economic liberalization program. It also initiated a move toward nationalization of private capital, in order to show its commitment to strong economic management and independence from capitalism, both domestic and foreign. This entire series of political disruption was triggered by a single policy event, the devaluation of 1966. In contrast, India in the 1990s went through steady liberalization in almost every sector of the economy. The accompanying vicissitudes and violence in the domestic polity have been unprecedented. But they did not arrest the continuity of openness in any substantive way.

So we are confronted with a dual limitation, even failure, of the dominance-resistance framework that structured much of the political response to policy continuity in the 1990s. At one level we have a failure of conventional narratives in interpreting and explaining the source of policy continuity, mostly in terms of external financial interests. At the level of consequential politics, we see, broadly speaking, a failure of the political resistance to the continuity of openness. In particular, the irrationality of a democratic government to not just survive, but *proactively* continue openness in face of severe opposition and fragility of power presents us with a puzzle. What might explain continuity, if it is rooted in neither domestic political pressures nor global financial influence?

Given that policies have continued in spite of political, institutional, and intellectual *dis*continuities, we can assume that something must have existed to provide a sense of unity, something that is situated beyond the platforms of specific political parties or governments. One key to the puzzle therefore may be in common motives and a unifying current within the state itself, which may bridge divides among the agendas of different parties in power. Furthermore, if domestic politics have not been able to arrest the continuity of economic openness, there may be reasons to investigate pressures from international politics. Specifically we will need to look into what it is within international politics that may privilege, in the mindset of policymakers, the external economy over domestic political needs.

These "keys," so to speak, have been present in the actions and rhetoric of reformist politicians throughout the 1990s and the current decade. As early parts of this chapter pointed out, much of these were drowned out by the noisy politics of causes and consequences, but they become apparent if we situate India's policies in the context of its perception of China and the world at large. To understand why and how India's wider international context have influenced the continuity of economic openness, we will need to first cast attention to many decades before 1991, and understand the historical evolution of India's perception of itself and its rivalries. The next chapter undertakes this interpretive historical analysis.

3 Roots of globalism and rivalry

> A great Empire, the future military strength of which no man can foresee, has suddenly appeared on the North-East Frontier of India … China, in a word, has come to the gates of India, and the fact has to be reckoned with.
>
> *The Morning Post* (London), 28 October 1910

> The fact is, and it is a major fact of the middle of the Twentieth century, that China has become a great power – united and strong. By that I do not imply that because China is a great power, India must be afraid of China or submit to China. … Not at all … China, which is a great power and which is powerful today, is potentially still more powerful. Leaving these three big countries, the United States of America, the Soviet Union and China, aside for the moment, look at the world. There are many advanced, highly cultured countries. But if you peep into the future and if nothing goes wrong – wars and the like – the obvious fourth country in the world is India.
>
> Jawaharlal Nehru, 30 September 1954

Many were surprised by Indian Defense Minister George Fernandes's sharp comment about China right after the Chinese army chief's historic visit to New Delhi and right before India's nuclear tests in May 1998. Most outside analysts around that time had assumed that India's tests were targeted against its archrival, Pakistan. But Fernandes publicly identified China, not Pakistan, as India's "threat number one."[1] Critics denounced his observation as hotheaded or shallow. Some claimed that he launched his invective without knowing that nuclear tests were imminent.[2] To ease tensions, policy doves tried to brush aside the defense minister's comments as idiosyncratic, as an accidental slip rather than a reflection of the government's official sentiment.

Fernandes's observation, nonetheless, reflected a deeper and more systematic evolution of Indian policy thinking and perceptions. In important ways, Indian strategic thinkers had for decades imagined a multi-dimensional and historical rivalry with China, going as far back as the turn of the century, as shown by the opening quote from *The Morning Post*. But it was essentially perceived as a longer-term potential rather than an immediate concern. Incessant attention by academia and the media to the Indo-Pak axis, in addition, obscured until recently the importance of competition between India and China, a rivalry that in the eyes of some policymakers is in many ways more fundamental and natural. The neglect of China was also a result of the tendency to characterize India's traditional stance on foreign policy as "idealist." Especially the first two decades of India's postcolonial history are said to be experiments in idealism, manifested as much in Jawaharlal Nehru's emphasis on non-alignment as it was in the proto-socialist policies pursued in the economy and the rhetoric of grassroots democracy and cottage industries. The prevalent perception among policymakers at that time was that India and China were advancing at the same slow and steady pace toward economic development and empowerment, each on their own. By the late 1990s, the key spokespersons and policymakers in the government became increasingly vocal about the immediacy of the rivalry with China in almost every arena. This was not merely rhetoric; there was an acute perception of "falling behind" China in a permanent way, a perception cultivated in part by media hype.

Although geopolitical conditions can pit two countries as seemingly natural competitors, rivalry is most significantly a matter of perception. It is difficult, indeed counterproductive, to try to analyze rivalry without discussing how it is socially and politically constructed. Between India and China, certain parameters of rivalry are defined by competition for material resources, for power and plenty, combined with geopolitical circumstances. These are the hard and tangible facts, so to speak, such as mountain, sea, oil and gas, war, or export products. But the policy-relevance of such tangibles is interpreted through subjective and historically mutable lenses. Geopolitically, for instance, India and China, much like the United States and Canada, have shared a long territorial border between them – that much is a material fact. But the importance of that border, and by extension, the importance of territorial competition, has changed over time. Similarly, the "facts" that China's economy grew annually at 10.2 percent between 1980 and 1990 while India's economy grew at 5.8 percent remain unrelated pieces of statistics until and unless one country perceives the other to be a rival. Once rivalry is imagined and constructed, it becomes easy, almost automatic, to interpret from the juxtaposition of these data a relative loss of India's competitive position to China during that decade. Such a reading of data might then encourage the promulgation of appropriate policies to accelerate India's growth rate. In other words, the perception of rivalry determines whether comparative material trends among states warrant a policy response. Scanning material conditions alone without examining the historical dynamics of perception makes it difficult to theorize strategic policy response.

This chapter and the following chapter together show how material events and subjective interpretations have combined to construct, from an Indian policymaker's perspective, an image of China as a rival that by the 1990s required a multi-dimensional and strategic policy response. The construction of this image has been contingent on three factors. First of all, it has been linked to how Indian policymakers have perceived India itself, especially its role in the regional and international order. Second, it has been conditioned by landmark events in India-China relations – most importantly, a border crisis between 1958 and 1962. Third, it is connected to changing economic circumstances that have begun to introduce new and more intense interpretations of competition between the two countries. This chapter discusses the first two of these three factors. It recounts events that have shaped, from the perspective of India's globalist policymakers, the military, political, and technological dimensions of rivalry between the two countries. In addition to the significance of the 1958–62 crisis, which became a turning point in relations between the two giants, the chapter also highlights the effects of China's nuclear tests, the buildup of the army and the navy in the 1980s, and India's nuclear tests in 1974 and 1998. Intertwined with the discussion of these events is a historical narrative on India's self-image and the emergence of globalism in Indian policymaking circles. Chapter 4 extends the analysis to focus specifically on the perception of economic rivalry and its effect on the type of strategic policymaking that encouraged the continuity of external openness.

"The gates of India": roots of rivalry

China and India are ancient, neighboring civilizations. But rivalry between them is mostly a product of the twentieth century. It was rooted in the demarcation of boundaries, which provided colonial Britain with the basis for practicing aggressive foreign policy toward other powers. Neither China nor India could fully anticipate at that time how boundaried territories would later assume a level of material import and symbolic meaning that would make competition between the two seem innate. It was after World War II that these two countries, in possession of sovereign territories and empowering rhetoric, began to engage fully in the trappings of modern international relations and to participate in the elaborate construction of rivalry on which much of international politics rests.

From a frontier of separation to a "pink territory"

Until technology permitted aerial traversing of the Himalayas, the mountain range served each country as an impregnable barrier to invasion from the other. In fact, argues historian Dorothy Woodman in her masterful study of the range, the Himalayas had been historically and culturally much less important to China than they were to India, as the mountains were close to the centers of Indian civilization, but far away from the heart of Chinese civilization. For India the Himalayas were the fount of cultural myths and spirituality, and perceived to be the provider of security. Early Chinese maps, in contrast, did not even feature the mountains.[3]

In the sixteenth and seventeenth centuries the Mughal rulers of India began to expand systematically into the mountains, and the Chinese also began to impinge southwards on Tibet. But severe topography still made territorial competition or conflict futile. The mountains were such a buffer that the two countries, though neighbors, hardly shared a common border. In historian

Neville Maxwell's words, the countries enjoyed "a sovereignty that shaded off into no-man's-land, giving a frontier of separation rather than contact."[4] The ambiguity did not matter much before the mid-nineteenth century, when various tribes, cults, and communities lived isolated in the Himalayas with de facto independence. The area became politically significant as the colonial powers began to clearly divide and demarcate the world among themselves, and as the emerging forces of modern nationalism encouraged the unification of diverse groups and localities under a national banner within a clearly specified territory. Eventually out of the imaginations of imperialism and nationalism,[5] appeared, at least on paper, a boundary between India and China, stretching 2400 miles through mountains, making it the fifth longest border in the world. This is not to say that a formal boundary would never have been created otherwise. But, as Sunil Khilnani wrote in *The Idea of India*: "It was the British interest in determining geographical boundaries that by an Act of Parliament in 1899 converted 'India' from the name of a cultural region into a precise, pink territory."[6]

Growth of the British East India Company's trading and political activities into the Himalayan region in the nineteenth century had begun to cause apprehension in Russia and China about the potential danger of increased British influence in central Asia. For China, the Opium Wars had already cast the British East India Company as a group of predatory traders. The suspicion of China and Russia – not far misplaced – that British motives were expansionary, precipitated territorial rivalries among the three powers over control of the Himalayas. The British administration's approach was rooted in "balance of power," a type of *realpolitik* that was accepted as a common principle of foreign policy at that time. British strategists imagined various possibilities and routes of enemy attack, and formulated their response by either tightening or loosening their network of alliances with other powers. For instance, when Britain felt threatened by czarist expansion around India's northwest frontier, it treated China as an ally. Conversely, when China loomed large over India's northeastern province of Assam, Britain wooed Russia and agreed to respect its sphere of influence in Persia and Afghanistan as quid pro quo for Russia's noninterference in Tibet, which the British treated as its own sphere of influence and a buffer against China.[7] These machinations eventually magnified the importance of the India–China border.

After Russia's defeat in the war against Japan in 1905, Anglo-Russian territorial competition abated, and China emerged as a more imminent threat in British eyes. Sir Halford Mackinder, who was an influential strategic theorist at that time, widely underscored the importance of geopolitics,[8] and British India's potential for conflict with China made sense from a geopolitical standpoint: China was not only a large neighbor but also at odds with British foreign policy. Given such interpretations early in the twentieth century, a "forward school" in British policy circles advocated engaging China aggressively in *realpolitik*. The need was seen as more pressing between 1900 and 1910, when Manchu dynasty itself adopted a more assertive policy toward Tibet. Lord Hardinge, the British viceroy in India, formulated an engagement strategy around 1910. It specified that in case of a Chinese attack over land, Britain should retaliate over sea because of its naval superiority. It also urged the construction of patrol bases in strategic locations along the Indo-Chinese border. But financial constraints as well as logistical difficulties in administering the treacherous terrain ultimately prevented the colonial administration from acting concretely on the propositions of the forward school.[9]

A line almost forgotten

The British colonial administration eventually undertook to demarcate the boundary to the extent feasible. The administration's call for a clear "linear boundary" strengthened as local insurgents, such as the Dogras, perched in the mountains, began to irritate the administration with forays into what was considered clearly imperial land. After a few abortive attempts at involving Chinese and Tibetan emissaries in diplomatic conferences – the most famous of those being the Simla Conference of 1913 – the British concluded secretly an agreement with Tibet to delimit the boundary. That boundary came to be known as the McMahon Line, named after Captain Henry McMahon, who represented Britain at the Simla Conference. The line, drawn on two sheets of paper, and sent by mail to the Tibetan plenipotentiary, pushed the existing Indian boundary, which was vague to begin with, about sixty miles northwards, to the advantage of the British. It was an effort "to commit the Chinese to accept the Himalayan crest – India's vital rampart of defense – rather than the Himalayan southern base as the northeast boundary between India and Tibet."[10] China was not a party to this agreement, and not privy to the creation of the McMahon Line.[11]

For the British, the McMahon Line did not seem that important in the early years. In effect, it was forgotten until 1935, when a deputy secretary accidentally stumbled upon the documents. Upon this rediscovery, the British undertook to update the imperial gazetteer and maps to show the Line as the official boundary between India and China.[12] By World War II commercial atlases began to conform. When India became independent in 1947, it inherited all the "rights and facilities" that the British enjoyed with regard to Tibet. But technically India's proper boundary was with China, for Tibet was not recognized internationally as fully sovereign. The colonial administration, however, had concluded the McMahon agreement with Tibet, which they considered a suzerainty of China with de facto independence. This approach was not unique. As David Strang argues, the "collective delegitimation" of sovereignty over non-Western lands was routinely part of the European imperial mindset, whereby land outside the European state system was considered "unclaimed," regardless of whether it was inhabited or not. "Non-Western polities lacked legitimacy," whether juridical or de facto.[13] In simple terms, the colonial administration did not care. Regardless of these complications and historical ambiguities, Jawaharlal Nehru, India's first Prime Minister and the major architect of its foreign policy, was asserting India's claim in no uncertain terms in the parliament by 1950:

> Our maps show that the McMahon Line is our boundary and that is our boundary, map or no map. That fact remains and we stand by that boundary, and we will not let anybody come across that boundary.[14]

In addition to the McMahon line in India's northeast, the British had drawn up three other boundaries in India's northwest – the Ardagh–Johnson Line, the Macartney–MacDonald Line, and the Trelawney–Saunders Line – out of which independent India chose, for mostly administrative reasons, the most expansive (the Ardagh–Johnson Line) as its boundary.[15] The fact that China never recognized this mountainous border as legitimately drawn precipitated a series of territorial conflicts, culminating in a war in 1962. Before examining the significance of the war, we need to ascertain why India was also becoming increasingly assertive, rather than conciliatory, about territorial rights. As evident from Nehru's comments, quoted above, Indian leaders fully subscribed to the norms and pretensions of territoriality and sovereignty that form the core of the Western approach to international relations. While such acceptance can seem contradictory or at least uncomfortable for a country aspiring to free itself of the shackles of Western approaches, it in fact was not viewed as such by Nehru and his cohorts. They intended to integrate India fully into the modern international system, for they felt that the only way to prove that India was on a par with the West was through a rapid integration into modernity. Driven by that intention, they became as sensitive to the concept of territorial inviolability as the British colonial administration had been. But they did not show just sensitivity to or acceptance of the norms of sovereignty, they went much further: they were strongly assertive about their perceived rights and entitlements as a nation – and this was rooted ultimately in their perspective on India's role in Asia and the world.

"Fate has marked us for big things": roots of globalism

On the eve of independence in 1947, Nehru, in his famous "tryst with destiny" speech, foresaw the "awakening" of a potentially major regional and global power. He proclaimed: "The achievement we celebrate today is but a step, an opening of opportunity, to the great triumphs and achievements that await us."[16] Conversely, Great Britain was lamenting a vital economic and strategic setback, as it yielded control of its prized colony. As Winston Churchill noted, "[t]he loss of India would be final and fatal to us. It could not fail to be part of a process that would reduce us to the scale of a minor power."[17] Churchill's idea of a great loss and Nehru's impression of a grand awakening are hardly surprising, for India's potential for economic and political power was apparent – if not materially, then certainly in the imaginations and convictions of the national elite. It was a vast country, rich in natural and human resources, an ancient civilization occupying a prominent geopolitical space. This notion of grandeur, of being or becoming a great power, was an integral part of India's emerging nationalist and anticolonial movement. In spite of the traumatic consequences of partition, the crushing poverty in the countryside, and all the attendant problems of postcolonial development, this belief inhabited the Indian policymaking elite. Even India's failings were grand-scale, observed Nehru in his inaugural speech.

Globalism in the early nationalist project

Nationalism in India confronted a remarkable diversity of race, culture, language, and religion; it was "a quandary – the tantalizing possibility of a principle of unity but its evident empirical lack."[18] The nationalist project experimented to accommodate several polarities: unification versus diversity, centralism versus federalism, secularism versus theocratic tendencies, globalism versus autarky, idealism versus realism. The project was spearheaded by a small elite to whom the British eventually transferred power, and most of who, through formal Western education, were versed in post-enlightenment ideas about the modern state and the rational organization of domestic and international society. Their exposure to the West, coupled with the ideational and ideological currents in nationalist narratives (literature, art, historiography), made the nationalist elite *globalist* in its outlook. Globalism, as a result, became the least contentious among the divergent currents within Indian nationalism.

Ideationally the nationalist elite viewed India as a great, ancient civilization. British colonialism contributed to this belief immensely. India had never been united to the extent that it came together under British rule, and that made possible concepts like "All-India" or "Bharat-varsha," encompassing a truly large swathe of land and population between Afghanistan and Burma. Once India could be imagined in whole and in unity, nationalist thinkers could easily identify India's past, present, and future influence and significance. In their perspective, reaching out for regional and eventually global influence was inevitable. Examining myths, folklore, art, architecture, trading links, science, language, and rituals, nationalist historiography imagined an internationally influential civilization, whose religious and cultural marks extended from Persia in the west to Indonesia in the east.[19] Because of India's size, "commanding position in the Indian Ocean," and geopolitical location between the Near East and the Far East, foreign strategists within the incipient nationalist movement in the late nineteenth century began to believe that "India must have a say in all developments affecting Asia."[20] They pointed to the early influence of India on kingdoms in Southeast Asia through the spread of Hinduism and Buddhism, and spoke about a Greater India, based on civilizational kinship. The emigration of a large number of Indian laborers to work in other British colonies in Southeast Asia, Southern and Eastern Africa, the Caribbean, and the Pacific also established for India a concrete presence worldwide. The most famous of the emigrants, of course, was Gandhi, who spent twenty-one years in South Africa.

In the vibrant and grand intellectual environment inhabited by the nationalists, isolationism was not an attractive school of thought. The nationalists not only imagined an internationally influential India, but were also well aware of theories of capitalism and Marxism, which had begun to highlight, from different angles, the interconnections among nations. As a result, prominent Indian intellectuals espoused cosmopolitan views, even while they advocated a breaching of colonial ties. As Bimla Prasad noted,

> The great leaders of Indian thought in the nineteenth and twentieth centuries like Raja Rammohan Roy, Swami Vivekananda and Rabindranath Tagore looked far back to India's past, but stressed the unity of all universe and showed keen interest in the world outside ... Bal Gangadhar Tilak and Mohandas Karamchand Gandhi based their teachings on old Indian currents of thought, but never advocated isolation from the rest of the world.[21]

Ideologically the nationalist narrative defined itself in opposition to foreign imperialism, and imbued itself with powerful doctrines about peace and nonviolence. Its international ramification therefore included support for self-determination, pacifism, and cooperative means for resolving international conflicts. These were considered indigenous Indian values, which should be reflected in foreign relations, and disseminated to counter the more confrontational and imperialist norms that were the hallmarks of traditional politics among great powers.

The Indian National Congress, which was the most prominent political organization leading the nationalist movement, reflected these ideational and ideological currents of globalism in its politics. From its inception, INC was aware of the increasingly large Indian diaspora, and since the 1890s it began to pass resolutions and lobby the administration for upholding the rights of Indians in other British colonies. INC's foreign policy reflected distaste for the kind of power politics that was, in its view, Western and imperialist. In the 1890s the Seventh National Congress warned the British against expanding farther north, as it "might lead to a clash with China which would disastrously increase India's financial burdens."[22] INC also opposed the rising military expenditure on account of Britain's perceived threat from Russia in the northwest. The Eighth Congress indicated that this rivalry pertains to the great powers of Europe, and India should not be forced to bear most of the financial burden.[23]

Although INC and Mahatma Gandhi supported Britain in World War I, India's costly contribution to the British effort brought home the realities of power politics in a poignant way. Its foreign policy afterwards became more normative and pacifist. Influenced by Wilsonian rhetoric of self-determination, Congress began to "place the demand for Indian freedom in the context of a world setting and before the whole world, not as heretofore only before the British people."[24] The more radical leaders of INC began to look ahead to India's emergence as a major recognized power. One of the most influential leaders, Bal Gangadhar Tilak, wrote a letter to the president of the Peace Conference in 1919, urging for India's admittance to the League of Nations:

> With her vast area, enormous resources and a prodigious population she [India] might well aspire to be a leading power in Asia, if not in the world.

> She could, therefore, be a powerful steward of the League of Nations in the East...[25]

In 1920 Congress adopted *swaraj* (self-government) as its main political goal. In 1929 it redefined *swaraj* as complete independence. Following this move the mainstream of INC began to concur with Tilak's views, envisioning India's normative globalism as a powerful force distinct from realist British foreign policy goals. The nationalist movement by this time had gained full momentum. Thanks to the printing press, narratives extolling India's glorious past and unified destiny were distributed widely to an enthusiastic audience.[26]

The wider spread of nationalist concepts also gave rise to increasing debates, and there was at times tension between isolationism and globalism. In most cases the dominant and conclusive current was globalist. Rabindranath Tagore, India's Nobel Prize-winning poet, questioned, for instance, whether the rising movement of non-cooperation would ultimately mean that India would isolate itself from the rest of the world. Gandhi assured him that to the contrary, it would send messages of pacifism around the world, and that India needed a strong foreign policy to interact with other nations and disseminate such values.[27] Gandhi's ideal was reminiscent of Kantian cosmopolitanism: he anticipated a world federation of interdependent, interacting states, sharing pacifist norms and values. Gandhi's activism and moral messages in his anticolonial movement gave Indian foreign policy its moralism and historic themes of justice against larger powers.[28]

After World War I, INC began to forge closer links with other anticolonial movements in Africa and Asia. It expressed sympathy and support for Turkey. It interpreted Japan's victory over Russia in 1905 and China's revolution in 1911 as strong indications of the rising power of Asia.[29] It held independent China in high regard, and proclaimed solidarity with Chinese efforts to install social justice and fight a common enemy. It repeatedly condemned the use of Indian troops in Britain's wars against China, and urged Indians to disobey and not fight the Chinese. Congress leaders as well as Gandhi were urging Asian nations to cooperate based on their common civilizational bonds, especially toward the fight for freedom. In 1928, the Congress officially declared that the Indian struggle was part of a world movement against imperialism, and that India, consequently, could not afford to remain isolated from developments around the world.[30]

Nehru's aspirations

Jawaharlal Nehru was at the epicenter of both the nationalist project and the politics of the Congress Party. He returned from Europe in 1927 with a fresh view about India's position in the world, and declared to Congress his goal: "independence with full control over the defence forces of the country, the financial and economic policy and the relations with foreign countries."[31] Instrumental in designing and discharging the foreign policy of the Congress Party in the 1930s and 1940s, he became the virtually uncontested architect of independent India's international relations. As Michael Brecher noted in his biography of Nehru:

> In no other state does one man determine foreign policy as does Nehru in India … he has impressed his personality and his views with such overpowering effect that foreign policy may properly be termed as a private monopoly.… No one in the Congress or the Government, not even Sardar Patel, ever challenged his control in this field.[32]

The acceptance of globalism over isolation was aided by ideational images of ancient India, ideological values of the nationalist movement, and practical exigencies that Indian National Congress faced. But what entrenched globalism in active foreign policymaking was Nehru's single-handed dominance of the theory and practice of India's international relations. Under his leadership the globalist project had become a major objective of the nationalist struggle, and that leadership continued visibly after independence. As Khilnani noted: "Nehru understood independence as an opportunity to establish India as a presence on the world stage."[33] Nehru's aspiration was to turn around the image of colonial subjection and despair by transforming India into a prominent actor in international politics with a glorious past and an independent voice. He wrote in 1939:

> A free India, with her vast resources, can be a great service to the world and to humanity. India will always make a difference to the world; fate has marked us for big things. When we fall, we fall low; when we rise, inevitably we play our part in the world drama.[34]

Over the decade following independence, Nehru and his contemporaries reveled in India's potential grandeur. This is evident in numerous speeches in the Parliament and in policy statements. In a famous debate on foreign policy in the Constituent Assembly in 1947, he remarked:

> India is a great country, great in her resources, great in manpower, great in her potential, in every way. I have little doubt that free India on every plane will play a big part on the world stage, even on the narrowest plane of material power.[35]

Again, in a speech to the Constituent Assembly in 1948, he laid out his firm conviction about India's potential:

> India even today counts in world affairs … we are going to count more … it is not a question of our viewpoint … it is merely the fact that we are potentially a great nation, and a big power.[36]

This type of observation was frequent as India's foreign policy began to take shape. Here is another example from 1949:

> [I]n regard to any major problem of a country or a group of countries of Asia, India has to be considered.... She cannot be ignored, because ... her geographic position is a compelling reason. She cannot be ignored also, because of her actual or potential power and resources. Whatever her actual strength may or may not be, India is potentially a very powerful country...[37]

Idealism as a realist instrument

Globalism, in short, had become part of the creed of early Indian nationalists. But it contained an important contradiction. On one hand, globalism was the avenue to disseminate around the world what were considered Indian values. It was a means to reproduce the prominent role that the subcontinental civilization once played in shaping cultures and religions far beyond its borders. Achieving this idealist enterprise, however, required a practical stance in everyday international relations, so that India would be recognized as a competent player, not a hapless developing country with utopian dreams. How was this paradox resolved?

It was not – not in the Western sense of "resolution" anyway. By my reading, contradictions in India's globalist policies were accepted. Like its nationalism, India's globalism was in many ways fragmented, practiced in multiple domains and pulled in different directions by divergent ideologies. Even with its contradictions, globalism made sense to Indian policymakers. This is akin to Partha Chatterjee's understanding of the fragmented nature of Indian nationalism. Anticolonial nationalism, Chatterjee argues in *The Nation and Its Fragments*, created both a material and "spiritual" domain of sovereignty. In the material domain, anticolonial nationalism confronted imperialism by asserting sovereignty but replicating Western ideas and institutions, such as a modern state and its attendant concepts, such as sovereignty and territoriality. This was necessary because Western ideas and institutions had proven their superiority in the material realm. The spiritual domain, by contrast, emphasized the preservation of culture, and sought to "fashion a 'modern' national culture that is nevertheless not Western."[38] Unlike the material domain, the spiritual domain involved original national imaginations among the marginalized, the subaltern, women, local communities, and ethnic regions. Conventional histories that focus on the centripetal politics of nationalism miss the parallel emergence and practice of these fragmented nationalisms.[39]

The duality in India's globalist policies is similar. On one hand, the policymaking elite wanted India's globalism to be non-Western, exalting a set of values uniquely Indian. For instance, Swami Vivekananda, an influential spiritual leader in the nationalist movement, envisioned "the spiritual conquest of the world by India in order to save humanity."[40] But contact, and possibly conflict, with other powers would require engaging in diplomacy and politics informed by realism. Instead of picking one over the other in its foreign policy, the Nehruvian mainstream pursued both. As Nehru clarified in the Parliament in 1950:

> It is in a spirit of realism that I want you to approach the question of our foreign policy.... Idealism alone will not do. What exactly is idealism? Surely it is not something so insubstantial as to elude one's grasp! Idealism is the realism of tomorrow. It is the capacity to know what is good for the day after tomorrow or for the next year and to fashion yourself accordingly.[41]

Nehru's vision for India's defense, for instance, incorporated a realist framework with idealist goals. He thought that because of India's geopolitical position and importance, the world powers would not let any single country conquer or dominate India. The conquest of India would give any one power a huge strategic advantage in world affairs, just as the British had profited from India. So any attempt to dominate India would be balanced by the intervention of other powers. The ideal of non-alignment served this strategic position. Non-alignment was the major foreign policy decision immediately after independence. The refusal to join either power bloc is rooted in a "fierce determination" to be fully independent, which in turn was fed through India's globalist perception of itself. Because India needed to have a strong outward projection, it was imperative that such projection reflects what is Indian, not tainted by the interests of other powers.[42] Non-alignment was the result. As Baldev Raj Nayar points out:

> It is precisely India's perception of itself as a potential great power – however distant the prospect may seem – combined with the recognition of its present weakness [e.g. developmental problems] that led to the policy of nonalignment in the first place.... Given the perception of India's potential, a satellite role was clearly unacceptable.[43]

This line of thinking, that idealism and realism are complementary for a country with globalist ambitions, continued well after independence. Various foreign ministers of India have continued this idea in their agendas.[44] India saw itself as unique in pioneering a type of foreign policymaking that promoted normative values. The value-orientation or idealism in India's foreign policy was not utopian. It was instrumental: it was the means to achieve a distinct, independent position and voice in the world. Like the way India's nationalism, based on non-violent civil disobedience, gave the country respect and renown, its globalism, based on pacifism, non-alignment, cooperation, and democratic self-determination, was to propel India into global prominence. Considered timeless, these values could not be shed from policymaking, for they constituted the persona of India's great, ancient civilization.

The war: globalism questioned, rivalry confirmed

The evolution of Indian policymakers' perception of China reflects the tension between idealism and realism within India's globalism. While reveling in India's grandeur, Nehru realized the existence of another potential great power to the north, as the opening quotation of this chapter conveys. In the eyes of the hawks in India's policymaking circle, the two shared a natural potential for conflict. While Nehru identified both China and India as potential great powers, he thought that China, as a developing country like India, would be far too preoccupied with its internal economic and social problems to aspire to military hegemony.[45] Moreover, both he and his foreign policy advisors, notably Krishna Menon, held fundamentally salubrious perceptions about China, shaped by the official stance of the INC in the 1930s and the 1940s. They envisioned China as an Asian compatriot forging an independent, non-aligned path of the kind India championed. INC held China in admiration, as a partner in solidarity against Western oppression and capitalist exploitation.[46] There were, in addition, pragmatic reasons for their perception of China. Nehru prioritized economic development as India's and China's pressing concerns and did not believe that disturbing peace on the border was necessary,[47] which resulted in either a somewhat appeasing or at times neglectful stance toward China's concerns. They also thought that India and China through mutual cooperation could handle the regional affairs of Asia, thus obviating the spread of the Cold War into the continent. Their image, as Michael Brecher noted, "was widely at variance with Peking's real posture towards India."[48] This posture, Nehru recognized a little too late, was aggressive and expansionist.

The trap of an imperial treaty

India's quest for normatively guided globalism met its greatest challenge around the late 1950s. Asserting that it never recognized the McMahon Line, China began to push southwards, into what India considered its own land. The first Chinese action that upset India was the invasion of Tibet in October 1950. Like the British, Indian strategists considered Tibet a necessary buffer zone for India's defense. After the invasion, China indicated that Tibet was its territory and that it would no longer honor "unequal treaties" imposed on Tibet by "imperialists."[49] Recognizing that their country could not afford a prolonged confrontation, Indian leaders sought a treaty with China affirming peace and cooperation. At the same time, the United States was planning to begin what was to be a protracted injection of military aid to Pakistan; this also prompted India to adopt an accommodating attitude toward China. In 1954, the two countries signed a treaty in which India recognized China's authority over Tibet, and purported to mutually uphold *Panchsheel*, or five pillars of coexistence. It emphasized mutual respect for territorial integrity, mutual non-aggression, and non-interference. Nehru considered it a major foreign policy achievement, but the treaty did not mention anything about the sensitive McMahon Line.[50] Indian policy circles had assumed that if not for anything else, China would respect the border out of tradition, custom and usage.[51]

From 1955 Chinese troops began to cross the border – that is, what India considered the legitimate border – in regular intervals, resulting in a hostile exchange of diplomatic notes between Delhi and Peking. Relations deteriorated in 1959, when China shelled the Dalai Lama's residence in Tibet, after which he was given political asylum in India. This was an affront to China. As Stanley Wolpert notes in hindsight: "China never forgave Nehru for sheltering the twenty-four-year-old Dalai Lama, contributing to China's invasion of India three years later."[52] Meanwhile tensions along the border increased, as Chinese intrusions into Indian territory became more frequent. Nehru exchanged a series of letters with Chou En Lai, the Chinese Premier, protesting the intrusions, and attesting to the validity of India's existing borders. Premier Chou rejected the line demarcated by the British, and China's official news agencies began to label India as "reactionary" and "expansionist."[53]

China mounted a full-scale invasion along India's northeastern frontier in October 1962. It routed the Indian army and went on to occupy about 14,000 square miles of what used to be British Indian territory in the northwestern frontier. Within a week of fighting India had lost more than 5000 soldiers.[54] China declared a unilateral ceasefire after a month and specified troop withdrawal twenty kilometers behind the line of actual control (LAC), as it existed in November 1959. This meant that India still had the McMahon Line as the border in the northeast, but China would hold on to its captured territory in the northwest. The declaration almost coincided with the end of the Cuban Missile Crisis, which proved a double relief for Nehru and much of the world.

Pretensions and capabilities

The 1962 war with China prompted several significant realizations on the part of the shapers of Indian foreign policy. It changed their perception of China starkly; decades later it would serve as the main prism through which Indian nationalist thinkers would interpret the implications of China's economic advances. First of all, China was not just another developing country that had suffered at the hands of imperialism and was now trying to promote a kinder, gentler world order, like India was. China and India were not even pursuing their own respective paths toward power and plenty by their own respective designs, in isolation. They were competitors. Nehru now firmly believed that China was seeking Asian hegemony at India's expense, if not by physical domination then certainly by forcing "a mental surrender."[55] As he acknowledged after the war:

> It was a little naïve to think that the trouble with China was essentially due to a dispute over the same territory. It has a deeper reason. Two of the largest countries in Asia confronted over the vast border. They differed in

> many ways. The test was whether any one of them could have a more dominating position than the other on the border and in Asia itself.[56]

Second, Indian policy thinking became more "rational," in the sense that Indian policymakers were more inclined now to think of international relations as an arena in which decisions would need to be guided by a modicum of detached cost-benefit analysis and relative gains. This was a break from the evolution of India's foreign policy, which till then was basically a continuation of the politics and philosophies of its anticolonial movement. The bitter experience with China exposed the need to institutionalize *strategic* thinking and policy coordination. It was felt that India needed long-term strategic planning around its vital domestic and regional interests and resources, which was missing in the early days of Indian foreign policy. The Emergency Committee of the Cabinet, which was formed during the war, became the "key consultative body" in the postwar period. The Ministry of Defense and the Ministry of Finance began to cooperate with each other in supplying information and formulating policy.[57] While initially this type of thinking related more to security affairs, it was eventually considered successful, and it later began to affect how India approached international economic issues. The increase in the stature of analytic and strategic thinking began to enhance, even though slowly, the policy role of technocrats. Although Nehru remained the major decision-maker for China-related policy, his authority slipped after the war, and he became more open to suggestions from others.[58] The wider policy circle began to concur on the inescapability of rivalry with China. This began to give rivalry, and policies emanating from it, greater political meaning and power than idealist thinking emanating from Nehru's aspirations. In *India and the China Crisis*, a detailed study of decision-making during the war, Steven Hoffmann contends that the misgivings India had about China becoming an assertive rival were now confirmed and transformed into "a coherent and long-lasting belief system":

> The most important of the now-confirmed Indian beliefs was that China, long hostile to India for ideological and national character reasons, wanted to hold the premier position in Asia … India had to be reduced to a position of subordination or subservience. Furthermore, the Chinese could gain an edge in an Asian power rivalry by demonstrating India's military weakness. They had therefore acted in 1962 to eclipse India in international standing and prestige.[59]

Third, although India lost a large chunk of territory, Indian policymakers did not interpret the loss as a blow to India's inherent great power status. Nehru remained giddy with India's prospects with regard to international affairs. Globalism remained unscathed as a strong undercurrent in the turbulent waters of Indian foreign policy in the 1960s and 1970s. Nehru was not alone. Such feelings permeated in wider policy circles as well, and thus began to obtain greater ideational legitimacy. Indian strategists obviously assigned China the entire responsibility for the war. They were not swayed by alternative interpretations, such as that by political historian Neville Maxwell that India was to blame for the war for being intransigent about a border that was never clearly legitimate. To the extent that Maxwell's claim is true, India's globalism is mainly responsible for India's inflexibility about negotiation. Essentially, as Achin Vanaik put it, the government had "readily assumed the mantle of colonial Britain's subcontinental pretensions."[60]

Finally, Indian foreign policy circles no longer held any illusion about the need to aggrandize material power. In the mindset of the globalist policymakers, India's only major mistake was an oversight about having a strong northern defense. This oversight was unpardonable for a state claiming a great power status. This, Baldev Raj Nayar points out, was the crucial lesson that policymakers drew:

> India had obviously behaved irresponsibly as a major power, devoting to defense a mere 2 percent of its gross national product.... For India, the real message of the border conflict was that the country's role pretensions were inconsistent with its capabilities.[61]

Indian foreign policy began to emphasize the need for *realpolitik* to engage the other great – and possibly, more aggressive – power, China.[62] The United States was already helping Pakistan to develop its armed forces, with a program of military aid begun in 1954. There was no reason for India not to follow suit. It adopted as a major policy objective a program to develop an adequate military industrial complex and invest in science and technology. Nehru and his policy supporters began to claim that military expenditures actually complemented development policy; that agriculture, transport, energy, education, and health were all important sources of military strength. Accordingly, Nehru told a meeting of the National Development Council that 85 percent of India's development program was somehow connected to defense – a pseudo-mercantilist turn in stance![63]

India doubled its defense spending in early 1963. The expenses would allow raising six additional mountain divisions, a rapid modernization of defense, and long-term strategic planning. The mountain divisions were raised within seven years. By the late 1960s, five-year defense plans were being devised. The parliament was sympathetic to these goals.[64] A large defense allocation was said to be a permanent, expected feature in subsequent Indian budgets.[65] India still could not match China's increases in defense spending. After the initial raise, India's defense spending remained at a fairly constant level (in real terms) throughout the 1960s, as shown in Figure 3.1.

Expansion of regional rivalry

India's program for an integrated strategic and competitive vision was a direct outgrowth of the war with China. The war had implanted an acute sense of insecurity about China's expanding sphere of influence as well as its rising military budget. It did not alter India's globalist aspirations, but ensconced the need to

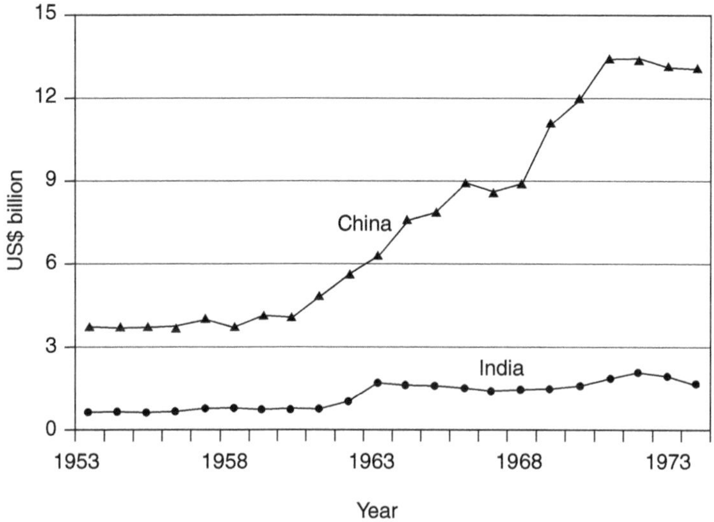

Figure 3.1 Defense spending in China and India, 1953–74 (in constant 1970 US$ billions) (source of data: Stockholm International Peace Research Institute, *SIPRI 1975 Yearbook*, Cambridge: MIT Press, 1975, pp. 120–121).

increase material power. The war, in addition, shattered any faith India had that other developing countries would share its notions about peaceful international relations. Nehru and other strategists were disappointed at the ambivalence of other non-aligned nations.[66] Consequently, Indian *realpolitik* in the 1970s and 1980s involved greater attention to containing the countries in South Asia that were susceptible to an expanding Chinese ambit of influence.

From perception to assertiveness

India accepted China's ceasefire line in 1962 as de facto, not *de jure*, a position that has continued to date.[67] Because of the uncertainty of the border and insecurity about Chinese ambitions in an era when China was asserting itself in Southeast Asia, territorial competition and security continued to be the centerpiece of India's China strategy through Indira Gandhi's prime-ministership in the 1970s.[68] At the same time, Indira Gandhi did not seem to have reflected on India's globalism as philosophically as did her father, Nehru.[69] But she adopted a relatively more hard-line approach toward China and "made no bones in her public statements about China being a major destabilizing and subversive factor in Asia."[70] The hard-line was due to her stronger belief in realpolitik, a rising insurgency in the border areas, China's support of Pakistan, as well as India's growing defense capabilities.

The India–Pakistan war of 1965 brought India and China close to another conflict, in which China threatened to strike at India along the Himalayan front. Strong opposition from both the United States and the Soviet Union defused this dangerous threat. The Soviet Union sponsored a peace settlement in 1966.[71] A major border skirmish took place in 1967, and three Indian diplomats were beaten up in Beijing that year.[72] China's overt support for Pakistan during Bangladesh's independence war in 1971 was also a cause for concern among Indian policymakers. They were further unnerved by the US's stance during this time. Although the US supported India materially and ideologically in 1962, they warned that they would not come to India's aid should China intervene in Bangladesh.[73]

Importantly, the election manifestos of all major Indian political parties between 1967 and 1972 included an aggressive competitive stance against China, portraying it as a major threat.[74] The dismemberment of Pakistan, India's successful intervention in Bangladesh, and the thawing of US–China relations in the early 1970s encouraged a move toward rapprochement throughout the decade. There was, however, another round of border battles in 1975. Diplomatic relations that were severed after the 1962 war were finally fully restored in 1976, and Atal Behari Vajpayee, then Foreign Minister, visited China in 1979. But China launched an attack on Vietnam while he was visiting, and that, needless to say, only enhanced India's general sense of insecurity about being China's neighbor.[75]

China and India undertook to "normalize" relations during the 1980s, especially with Rajiv Gandhi's prime-ministership. Eight rounds of diplomatic talks were held between 1981 and 1987, but territorial disputes remained largely unsolved.[76] The closest that the two countries have come to war since 1962 was during the winter of 1986 and the spring of 1987. In December 1986 India declared the Northwest Frontier Agency (the administrative unit along which runs the McMahon Line) a full-fledged state, named Arunachal Pradesh. China protested strongly that the territory is disputed, and demanded territorial concessions. Another war seemed imminent as both countries began to amass troops along the border, with India placing as many as 200,000 soldiers on its side by spring 1987. A flurry of diplomatic activities ensued to abate the tensions by summer 1987.[77] As an effort toward reconciliation, in 1993 and 1996, India and China agreed to try to increase "peace and tranquility" along the length of the border.[78] India's president K. R. Narayanan visited China in 2000. Following the trip, for the first time the two sides exchanged their respective maps of a 545 kilometer long section of the border to facilitate better mutual understanding.[79] This encouraged a program to delineate the LAC (Line of Actual Control).

Regionalism as a part of globalism

With its effort to increase capabilities, discussions of India's power and status spread beyond foreign policy rhetoric and infiltrated academic discourse, especially in the literature on the nebulous middle powers. Peter Lyon, for instance, asked in 1968: "Is she [i.e., India] the last and least of the great Powers, or is she the first of the lesser Powers?"[80] Some, like Baldev Raj Nayar, pointed to the inevitability of India's role: "Given its size, population, strategic location, and historical past, India cannot but aspire to a great power role in international politics, however distant in the future."[81] The aspiration continued unabated in Indian policy circles. Their claim was boosted by India's capabilities, and by the late 1970s India was being accepted in both policy and academic circles as "a rising middle power," an independent center of power pre-eminent regionally.[82]

Indian strategic thinkers, especially during the governments of Indira Gandhi and Rajiv Gandhi, began to emphasize regionalism. This seemed to be the path that China was taking successfully. As mentioned, they took note of China's interventions in Southeast Asia and its successful split with the Soviet Union. They saw, as Nixon visited China, that it was the United States that took the initiative to thaw tensions over Taiwan. Looking closer toward home, they contended that containing Chinese (as well as US/Pakistani) influence in South Asia was the first logical step toward greater influence in a wider geographic area. With more attention to the regional power game, India began to move closer to the Soviet Union for political and strategic cooperation despite a professed non-alignment. The Soviet Union, in turn, supported India's bid for regional hegemony, especially since the Sino-Soviet split.[83] Pakistan's growing ties with the United States and China fueled the informal alliance between India and the Soviet Union. As shown in Table 3.1, China has historically provided most of the military hardware to Pakistan. Pakistan has been China's foremost ally in the subcontinent, even though its relations with the United States have irked China at times.

Table 3.1 Share of China in arms imports of Pakistan and Bangladesh, 1951–2006 (as percentage of total conventional arms imports for each given period)

Period	*Pakistan's arms imports*		*Bangladesh's arms imports*	
	From China (%)	*China's rank**	*From China (%)*	*China's rank**
1951–54	0	–	–	–
1955–59	0	–	–	–
1960–64	0	–	–	–
1965–69	42	1	–	–
1970–74	62	1	–	–
1975–79	40	1	31	1
1980–84	40	1	67	1
1985–89	36	2 (USA)	96	1
1990–94	53	1	58	1
1995–99	20	2 (Ukraine)	13	2 (Russia)
2000–06	47	1	27	2 (Russia)
Total**	37	1	53	1

Source: Percentages are calculated from the Trend Indicator Value database of Stockholm International Peace Research Institute (SIPRI): http://armstrade.sipri.org/.

Notes

* Among all suppliers of arms for that period for the given country. When China is ranked below the top spot, the leading supplier for that period is given in parentheses.

** China's share in total arms imports of Pakistan, 1951–2006, and of Bangladesh 1975–2006.

China's arms exports to Pakistan began almost immediately after its war with India in 1962. The ties developed quickly into what some observers have called "an all-weather friendship." The following year, Zulfikar Ali Bhutto, then Foreign Minister and later Prime Minister of Pakistan, stated the nature of the alliance: "In event of war with India, Pakistan would not be alone. Pakistan would be helped by the most powerful nation in Asia."[84] After 1965, China broke from its past policy and began to support the Pakistan position on Kashmir. To the chagrin of Indian policymakers, it then announced the right of self-determination for the Kashmiri.[85] Since 1951, China has provided 37 percent of all conventional arms imports of Pakistan, a share larger than any other supplier country. Chinese support for Pakistan included nuclear and missile technology, aircraft, warships, submarines, tanks, ammunition, integrated weapons systems, and communication equipment. Because of the close ties between Pakistan and China, Indian military strategists have to plan for a two-front war. Similarly, more than half of military hardware imports in Bangladesh since 1975 has been of Chinese origin. China is the top supplier of weapons to every country that borders on India except Nepal (see Figure 3.2), thereby completing a full circle of vulnerability around India.[86] In Burma (Myanmar), located at the intersection of China, India, and Southeast Asia, China has been one of the main supporters and military suppliers of the military junta (see Figure 3.2). China has been trying to develop facilities and infrastructure there that could give it direct commercial as well as military access to the Bay of

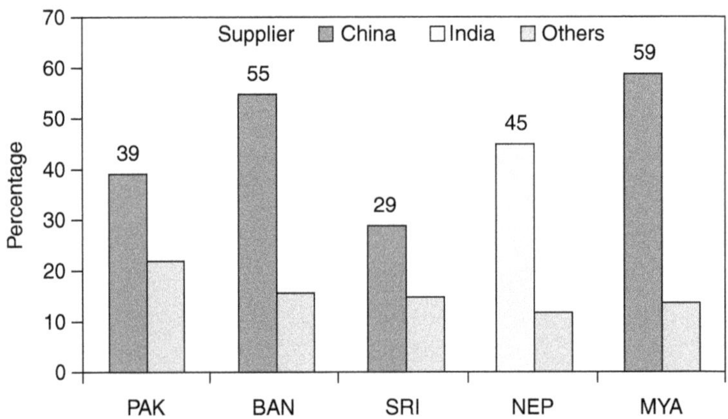

Figure 3.2 Top suppliers of conventional weapons to India's neighbors, 1980–2006 (as percentage of total conventional arms imported) (source of data: percentages are calculated from the Trend Indicator Value database of Stockholm International Peace Research Institute (SIPRI), online at: http://armstrade.sipri.org/).

Note
The percentage share of the top two suppliers of each country over 1980–2006 is shown in the figure.

Bengal, the Andaman Sea, and the Indian Ocean.[87] This type of influence on India's perimeter has focused India on strengthening its regional defense and influence, and seeing all its neighbors with a degree of suspicion. More importantly, as India's policy-thinking has become more institutionalized, technocratic, and rational, it has sought a multidimensional strategy through which it could address its multiple emerging insecurities and competitive arenas with China.

Securing "India's due": prestige and power

As realpolitik became dominant among the China analysts within Indian government, India's strategy evolved to include two key elements: to provide a strong deterrent to direct conflict while countering China's military influence in the countries that encircle India. As it were, the strategic choices seen by the analysts were influenced simultaneously by a third imperative – its globalist aspirations, which led toward promoting "big science," prestige weaponry, and power projection capabilities, mediated through a persuasive and increasingly powerful narrative about India's self-perception. In other words, India's China strategy became a perfect conduit to delineate its globalism in concrete terms.

India's due

India's bid for global prominence had been based historically on an assertion of rights, not capabilities. Nehru and most other early strategists claimed great power status because in their view India *deserved* it as a large country, the world's largest democracy, and an ancient civilization. The rhetoric coming from some of India's allies added fuel to this claim. *Pravda*, for instance, commented back in 1955: "India is indeed a great power ... she should be given one of the first places among the great powers of the world."[88] The tone conveys idealist romanticism of a kind that Indian policymakers liked: India was to be "given" that status, rather than have to wrest it through manifesting its power and capabilities. It was India's due. Moral indignation, in addition to features of "giantism," was grounds for India's claim to stature: "The fact that the last several hundred years saw India under alien rule only makes aspirations to the restoration of greatness all the more deeply felt."[89] This is not to say that Nehru and his contemporaries naively thought that such right-based claims would be enough to attain the rank India deserved. They did not – but primarily because of India's economic weaknesses, they chose to pursue a normative, rather than realist, route to globalism.

Since the 1970s Indian thinkers have strengthened the pursuit of globalism by emphasizing a more visible, independent international role. From leadership in the Non-Aligned Movement, India moved into organizing developing countries in different international fora, such as UNCTAD, Group of 77, and the New International Economic Order. India has been trying to raise its capacity as a regional donor, creditor, and mediator. It has been keen to obtain permanent membership in the UN Security Council. India's promoters pointed out that its population was larger than all the permanent members combined, except China.

Moreover, as a member it would be a representative of the Third World in global decision-making. Indian diplomats also argued that China's inherent status was never questioned by the great powers; only the legitimacy of the regime representing China was periodically under doubt. If China were to have such status, so should India.[90]

Overall Indian diplomats have been disappointed by the lack of attention from traditional powers, including the United States. Through the mid-1970s, US policymakers as well as academia had negative and stereotypical views of India. One survey of 300 textbooks by the Asia Society in the mid-1970s found that India was presented more negatively than any other Asian country. In addition, the view that the US and India represented opposite values (material versus spiritual, for example) helped cultivate distance from India in US foreign policy circles, despite India's record of democracy.[91] The disappointment of Indian policymakers at such attitudes grew in the 1980s and the early 1990s, when US policies began to overlook China's political lapses in consideration of its growing military and economic power. C. Raja Mohan, a prominent strategic columnist, asked in 1995: "Why cannot we be like the Chinese? The effective combination of defiance and deal-making has been the hallmark of the Chinese approach to the United States." Raja Mohan at that time urged India to develop economic might, as well as declared nuclear capability, to achieve the kind of power China enjoyed.[92]

These influences conditioned the evolution of India's strategic capabilities. In the early part of this era, until the border war, economic policy and the notion of civilizational grandeur led Indian leaders to invest in "big" science in general. Between the 1960s and roughly the 1980s, investments into military technology were shaped by the need to deter China as a direct military threat to India's border with China, as well as other countries of South Asia. By the 1980s both of these influences became intertwined. What shaped the development of its capabilities since then is a sensitivity that India was being denied what it deserved on the global plane, combined with a realization that China is transitioning from a regional to a global player by virtue of sheer material strength.

Big science

The need to develop military technology and heavy industry has been felt since the heyday of India's anticolonial movement, evident as early as the 1938 deliberations of the National Planning Committee of Congress.[93] It was seen as part of a program to enhance national power and prestige. Nehru himself was a firm believer that high technology can catapult India into greater international visibility. He understood full well the potential rewards from injecting science into a military-industrial complex. Immediately after independence, he commented on World War II:

> Many things contributed to the winning of the last war, but I think the chief reasons were two, the amazing capacity of American industry and scientific research. It is this which won the war, not so much the soldiers and others.[94]

India's heavy industry strategy also reflected a leaning toward "big" science from an economic perspective. As mentioned in the previous chapter, India's economic program for almost forty years was geared toward import substitution and, to the extent possible, autarky. Even though importing capital goods would be necessary for some time, the vision was that economic independence could be achieved eventually with adequate investments in technology that could aid heavy industry. Nehru laid out his logic in *The Discovery of India*:

> [I]n the context of the modern world, no country can be politically and economically independent, even within the framework of international independence, unless it is highly industrialized and has developed its power resources to the utmost. Nor can it achieve or maintain high standards of living and liquidate poverty without the aid of modern technology in almost every sphere of life.[95]

From 1947–50, in addition to being the prime minister and foreign minister, Nehru was also the minister for scientific research. He went on to finance a large number of scientific laboratories around the country. He expanded government spending on scientific research almost tenfold in real terms and the total stock of scientific manpower almost fourfold, from 188,000 in 1950 to 732,000 in 1965.[96] Visanathan discusses the way in which state-led science created a fairly complex system of "bureaucratized grid of laboratories." He cites Homi Bhaba's observation that the creation of statist science had resulted in emptying the universities of talent, suppressing creative dissent, and promoting conformity. Another critic of the system was P. M. S. Blackett, a British Nobel laureate who served as a consultant to Nehru. Blackett warned that science was not a magic wand that could bring prosperity.[97] Nonetheless, Nehru and his followers persisted, and in the first two decades since independence, atomic energy and heavy industry research received the highest priorities in R&D allocation, claiming between them almost 50 percent of the government's R&D expenses in a country that was primarily rural and agricultural (see Table 3.2). The share of the Indian Council for Agricultural Research, the country's premier scientific agency in that field, dwindled from 16.2 percent in 1958–59 to 9.3 percent in 1965–66.[98] Such bias in budgeting led to some other interesting distortions. By the time of the Sino-Indian war of 1962, noted Sunil Sondhi, "India was fairly advanced in the field of nuclear technology but yet to produce its own semi-automatic rifle."[99]

In more recent times, the Indian government's emphasis on science has become less bureaucratized, but vestiges from big science remain strong. One example is that Indians have excelled in mathematics and physics, that is, areas that have direct relevance for security and prestige programs, but lagged behind in other areas, such as life sciences. Increased emphasis on academic science, combined with new investment by multinationals, may alter the trend of training over time. The other factor toward change may be familiar by now: "India is also looking over its north-eastern border, and the challenge coming from

Table 3.2 R&D expenditure by India's government, 1965–95 (in US$ million in constant 1995 prices and exchange rates)

Fiscal year	*Defense*[a]	*Atomic*[b]	*Space*[c]	*Share of total R&D*[d] *(%)*
1965–66	41	69	–	50
1970–71	55	73	–	55
1975–76	75	78	53	64
1980–81	110	86	66	51
1985–86	300	110	160	56
1990–91	410	140	200	63
1994–95	510	140	260	68

Source: Stockholm International Peace Research Institute, *SIPRI Yearbook 1999*, New York: Oxford University Press, 1999, table 9.1, p. 375.

Notes
a R&D by defense services.
b Department of Atomic Energy.
c Department of Space.
d Share of Defense, Atomic, and Space in total government R&D spending.

China." Indian policymakers have noted China's recent commitment to inject $125 million into its top ten universities, and a longer-term strategy to develop and promote 100 universities.[100]

Nuclear weapons

Mastering nuclear power within twenty-five years was the biggest part of India's big science program. The Department of Atomic Energy was established in 1954, and remained under the leadership of the charismatic Homi Bhaba, who not only led atomic research but became an ardent advocate for big science in general. In many instances he and the other scientists convinced Nehru to allocate greater funds for strategic technologies. As Bhaba justified it: "No country which wishes to play a leading part in world affairs can afford to neglect pure and long term research."[101] Bhaba's twenty-five-year plan was drawn up even before independence and then nurtured actively from the 1950s. Although developing weapons was not the main goal of the atomic program when it began, the goal was to acquire "complete technological capability," including competence to produce the bomb. By the mid-1970s, it had become the first country in the third world with the ability to indigenously construct complete commercial nuclear power plants.[102]

When big science by the 1960s became exposed to exigencies arising out of rivalry with China and its ally Pakistan, the atomic program only became more pressing. Bhaba claimed an ability to conduct a nuclear explosion within eighteen months of receiving a green light from the government, but the government was reluctant to give the go-ahead.[103] In 1964, just two years after the war, China conducted its first nuclear test at Lop Nor. This further raised the stakes for India to develop a deterrent. Minoo Masani expressed the fears of many of India's political leaders at that time: "The Chinese explosion cannot be ignored; it cannot be written off; it cannot be played down; it is of major significance. We are the country for which it has the most immediate importance."[104] In the wake of this explosion, Lal Bahadur Shastri, India's prime minister, tried to obtain security guarantees from other big powers. When that failed, as was admitted in the parliament in 1965, he authorized India's SNEP (subterranean nuclear explosion project) program, but with firm orders about its peaceful intent. The Indo-Pakistan-Bangladesh war of 1971, it is assumed, produced the final green light, especially after the United States tried to persuade China to intervene in the conflict. India's scientific establishment successfully produced a so-called "peaceful" explosion in 1974. Since then Indian strategic analysts have been repeatedly urging for the development of not just prototype but proven nuclear capability, especially since the 1980s when it became clearer that China had been transferring to Pakistan technologies related to nuclear weapons development. Prime Minister Rajiv Gandhi agreed in 1987, and provided secret authorization to rejuvenate India's nuclear weapons testing program. In June 1996, Pakistan deployed nuclear-capable M-11 missiles it had acquired from China. In April 1998, Pakistan tested an intermediate-range missile, named Ghauri, which was built with Chinese (or North Korean, according to some) technology. This, Sumit Ganguly argues, was the immediate trigger for India's second round of explosions in May.[105]

In view of the long-standing rivalry between India and China, Pratap Mehta remarked after the 1998 tests: "the surprise is not that these [nuclear] tests occurred but that it took so long for them to occur."[106] Following the nuclear tests in May 1998, India's government raised the defense budget by 14 percent. It increased spending on atomic research by 61 percent. In August 1999, Brajesh Mishra, the National Security Advisor, proposed a draft nuclear policy advocating the building of a credible land, air, and sea-based nuclear arsenal. By late 1999, the consensus on having a credible strategic arsenal was widespread, as was the threat perception from China. Some analysts suspected China of deploying nuclear-tipped missiles in Tibet. Further, while China has declared a "no-first-use" policy on nuclear weapons, it has also indicated that the doctrine does not apply to using nuclear weapons on their own territory, which some strategists interpret as including disputed border territories that China has claimed from India since 1962. China has also stated that its no-first-use policy does not apply to countries outside the Non-Proliferation Treaty (NPT), like India.[107] The consequent "security dilemma," in addition to China's alleged support of the weaponization of Pakistan, has provided a consistent pressure on India to build up its nuclear arsenal quickly. India is still in the process of developing an arsenal of reliable means of nuclear delivery against longer-range Chinese targets, and of developing second-strike capability to create credible deterrence. But nuclear weapons in the meantime have worked well for India as symbolic equalizers, a basis to claim a world-power status.[108] The utility of the explosions was apparent in their aftermath. The UN Security Council passed a resolution in

1998 demanding that India and Pakistan stop further nuclear development and enter existing international treaties restricting the use and spread of nuclear weapons. Separately, the United States imposed economic sanctions. But within a month US Deputy Secretary Strobe Talbott began meeting Indian special envoy Jaswant Singh (later foreign minister), and through a dozen such meetings initiated a "strategic engagement ... unparalleled in the relationship between the two countries."[109] Eventually the United States under the Bush administration began to treat India as a special case, as a responsible power that merited normalization of relationships. India's tests had been successful from almost any analytical angle.

Aside from strategic utility, globalism is the other reason that India has always wanted to "keep options open" on its international nuclear policy. If it is to be ranked as a great power, reasoned Indian strategists, then it must retain foreign policy independence and the option to develop and possess nuclear weapons. India's position on the Comprehensive Test Ban Treaty (CTBT) emphasizes two issues: a specific, time-bound disarmament plan to which all nuclear states would be committed, and a comprehensive ban including even laboratory tests. In the absence of such commitments it has rejected the CTBT. Indian strategists were similarly outraged when the NPT was extended indefinitely in 1995, perpetuating the legal possession of nuclear weapons by the five major powers, and denying it to others. Just four days after the extension, China conducted another nuclear test, which caused great uproar in the Indian press and solidified support for India's independent position on the CTBT and the NPT. The resolution of the BJP in 1995 summed up the position: "The BJP is in favour of a nuclear weapon free world, but not for a world in which a few countries possess nuclear weapons and the rest are subject to their hegemony."[110]

Power projection

The desire of India's nationalist policymakers to develop their country's capability to project its power far and wide evolved later, after its nuclear research was well established. This is due partly to lack of resources and need – rivalry with China was in its infancy – and partly to the strategic temperament India inherited from the British. British strategy for India during colonial rule in the twentieth century had been defensive, since Britain by that time had become a status quo power interested in preservation rather than expansion.[111] World War I had also significantly weakened Britain. That strategic stance, combined with the horrific experience of World War II right before independence and a pacifist globalism made India's strategy defensive, looking inward.

The need for power projection became acute especially after the humiliation of the 1962 war with China. The promise was now twofold: a large increase in power would act as a deterrent to China. In addition, prestige weapons with the capacity to project offensive power, Indian policymakers have reasoned, would concretely demonstrate India's capabilities to a global audience. The initial priority was still defense, especially by raising trained infantry capable of holding the mountainous border. An early generation of anti-tank missile, based on Soviet technology, was developed as part of this phase. At the same time India would need to show that it was willing to use its powers, if needed. Its intervention in Bangladesh in 1971 was spurred mostly by a massive refugee problem but secured a quick victory against a Pakistan that was supported by China and the United States. This first major intervention emboldened India's power projection program further, but little need for further international intervention arose until the 1980s. As Prime Minister in the 1980s, Rajiv Gandhi authorized a military intervention in Sri Lanka and imposed economic sanctions against Nepal. In 2006, there was another demand for intervention in Sri Lanka, which the government rejected since a formal request had not come. There was also some pressure for India to intervene in Fiji against an authoritarian takeover there.

However, the main thrust of power projection has been less in intervention opportunities in smaller states, and more in modernizing the air force and navy to enable strikes farther from Indian territories in a wider circumference that includes all of Pakistan and key parts of China. The need for power projection heightened further after India's initial round of nuclear explosions. For its nuclear deterrent to work, India needed the right delivery technology. Accordingly, India's missile program, called the Integrated Guided Missile Development Programme (IGMDP), began in 1983. Under the program, five missile systems have been developed: Trishul and Akash, both surface-to-air missiles; Nag, an anti-tank missile; and Prithvi and Agni, which are surface-to-surface missiles. Prithvi was the first one to be developed. Targeted at Pakistan, its most recent version has a range of 250 km. Agni has a range of 2500 km, "capable of reaching the densely-populated centers and key scientific installations in China."[112] There are unconfirmed reports of the development of a nuclear-capable long-range intercontinental ballistic missile named Surya (Sun), which would be a step toward global power projection. Table 3.3 provides a summary of India's indigenous missile development program.

Indian strategists have also begun investing in a blue water navy, keeping in mind China's capability of projecting power. The Far Eastern Naval Command of Indian Navy is being strengthened in response to growing Chinese interest in the Indian Ocean. It acquired its first aircraft carrier as early as 1957. Plans are underway to build more in domestic shipyards. It leased a nuclear submarine from the Soviet Union during 1987–90; launched an indigenously-constructed diesel-electric submarine in 1989; acquired a Soviet Kilo-class attack submarine in 2000; and signed a deal in 2003 with Russia to lease two nuclear submarines. The navy is also continuing with a program dubbed ATV, the Advanced Technology Vessel, which is supposed to build a nuclear submarine by 2007–08 at a total development cost of nearly $1 billion. The navy has continued to equip its vessels with indigenous Dhanush and Soviet-made Klub cruise missiles "to acquire an assured capability to hit land targets from the sea."[113]

Table 3.3 Indigenously developed guided missiles of India

Name	*Type**	*Range*	*Initial test year*
Prithvi-I	Surface-to-surface	150 km	1988
Trishul	Truck-mounted surface-to-surface and surface-to-air	9 km	1988
Nag	Anti-tank surface-to-surface	4 km	1989
Agni-I	N-capable surface-to-surface	700 km	1989
Prithvi-II	Surface-to-surface	250 km	1996
Akash	Surface-to-air	25 km	1996
Agni-II	N-capable surface-to-surface	2000 km	1999
Dhanush	Ship-to-surface	350 km	2000
Agni-III	N-capable surface-to-surface	4000 km	2003
Sagarika	N-capable submarine-launched	250 km	2008 (planned)
Surya	N-capable intercontinental	12,000 km	Status unknown

Sources: Federation of American Scientists; Wisconsin Project on Nuclear Arms Control; Nuclear Threat Initiative; as well as multiple newspaper reports.

Note
* N-capable: Capable of carrying nuclear warheads.

The air force, similarly, is acquiring and developing its own strategic strike aircraft able to project Indian power far beyond its borders. It has already developed advanced light helicopters and unmanned aircrafts called Nishant and Lakshya, along with a supersonic Light Combat Aircraft (LCA). In 2003, it signed a lease agreement for four Russian Tu22 long-range bombers, capable of carrying nuclear warheads to China.[114] One prominent area of concern for the air force in future is power projection into space. This came to light in the wake of China's test in which it destroyed a low-orbit satellite with a ballistic missile in January 2007. Right after China's announcement, India's prime minister called for a "weapons free outer space." Within two weeks, Indian air force announced plans to build aerospace defense toward preventing possible attacks from space, a project that may replicate the North American Aerospace Defence Command (NORAD) run by the United States and Canada. Shashi Tyagi, the chief of Indian Air Force at that time, declared the next phase of India's power projection in a confident tone:

> As the reach of our air force is expanding it has become extremely important that we exploit space and for it you need space assets.... We are an aerospace power having trans-oceanic reach and we have started training a core group of people for the [planned] aerospace command.[115]

Space odysseys

While aerospace defense would be a new military undertaking, Indian policy-makers had been investing heavily in a civilian space program for decades, knowing that this might be the most prestigious capability to showcase globalist ambitions. India's space program, under the auspices of the Indian Space Research Organisation (ISRO), began in earnest in 1967 and gathered steam in the 1970s, advancing hand in hand with the development of missile rocketry. Within five years India had test-fired its first indigenous two-stage rocket and made significant advances in computer and guidance systems. Together the defense department, atomic program, and space program continued to command the bulk of total government funding for research and development, as shown earlier in Table 3.2.

India built its first satellite, the *Aryabhatta*, in 1975, which was launched by the Soviet Union. Five years later India launched a satellite from home base using indigenous technology. By 1994, Indian scientists had developed a fairly advanced rocket specifically for launching satellites frequently. Called Polar Satellite Launch Vehicle, it puts satellites into orbits over the earth's poles. By 1996 India had launched eleven satellites, and by 2000 the tally had reached nineteen. (Table 3.4 provides a comparative summary of satellites in space belonging to India and China.) In 2001, India developed the more complex ability to place satellites in geosynchronous orbit. This also ushered in opportunities for commercial space projects. India has been targeting to reach cost efficiencies in its space program. Some of India's satellites were allegedly launched at a cost twelve times less than what comparable satellites cost China. This has been the basis of commercial satellite launching services, from which ISRO has begun to earn an estimated $100 million annually, carrying satellites from countries like Germany, Italy, and Belgium.[116]

India's next frontier is manned space flight. In 2003, ISRO got a boost in its budget after announcing plans to build a reusable launch vehicle, spending 80 percent less than what such projects cost in the United States, Russia, and China. Since China's advances in sending astronauts and its announcement to send missions to the moon, ISRO announced its own unmanned mission to the moon scheduled for 2008. In January 2007, India successfully tested the technology (dubbed Space Capsule Recovery Experiment) by which astronauts would return from a space mission, noting that it was part of the plan to send an unmanned mission to the moon in 2008. This entered India into an exclusive club of five other countries that have developed this capability: the US, France, Russia, China and Japan. ISRO is now considered one of the leading space agencies in the world. It has joined hands with thirteen others, including NASA and China's

Table 3.4 Satellite programs of India and China (data current to June 2007)

	India	*China*
Year of first satellite launch from home soil	1980	1970
Active payloads in orbit	33	62
Decayed payloads	9	44
Total payloads	42	106

Source: Celestrak Satellite Catalog: http://celestrak.com/satcat/boxscore.asp.

national space agency, to jointly coordinate future explorations of the Moon and Mars.[117] India's leaders, in short, have used its space program successfully to elevate its visibility for a potential world role.

"Our voice is being heard"

The purpose of this chapter was to trace the interlaced evolution of India's pursuit of globalism and its perception of China as a rival, specifically in the security arena. Globalism began as part of the interpretation and construction of a historical and emancipatory project for the nation. India's leaders longed for what Nayar calls "a subject role in international politics."[118] There were cultural constraints against this role, most notably the lack of a strong strategic culture.[119] In addition, consistent with what was considered indigenous cultural tradition, a world role for India meant not only material power but also an ability to influence world politics according to values cherished in India's nationalist struggle: peace, democracy, self-determination, and non-alignment. Indian foreign policy, even through its vacillations between idealism and realism, never lost sight of the globalist project. But until the 1960s, globalism remained an abstract notion that resonated with a nationalist interpretation of India's past and generated images of a future when India would be given its due, but seemed at odds with the present. That has changed. To Indian statesmen now, a subject role is almost within reach.

Expressions of a subject role

In Indian policy thinking, one of the clearest expressions of this subject role has been in its claim for permanent membership of the Security Council. Nehru injected this desire into Indian foreign policy from the 1940s on the basis of India's future potential. He wrote in a government memorandum:

> It is absurd for India to be treated like any small power.... Whether we succeed in getting into the Security Council or not, I think we should take up this attitude at the beginning and throughout that India is the center of security in Asia and that, therefore, India must have a central place in any council considering these matters.... [T]he obvious course [is] that India, by virtue of her geographical and strategical [*sic*] position, resources and *latent power*, should be a member of the Security Council.[120]

While expressions of India's *potential* subject role abounded, what was obvious and fair in Nehru's mind more than fifty years ago has not materialized. India's criticism of the composition of the council continued, but with India's growing capabilities, the tone and justification have altered. The talk is no longer of latent power, but actual power, making India's case stronger than it has ever been in the eyes of Indians as well as most other powers. Consider what Foreign Minister M. Solanki said in 1991 with regard to India's bid for permanent membership: "[T]he composition of the Security Council has ceased to reflect a true cross-section of the international community. Nor can it be maintained that the Security Council and its Permanent Members any longer reflect the contemporary power configuration."[121] The other argument given for India's admission before was that it represented the non-aligned developing world. This also has given way to expressions that India has finally become too powerful to be neglected. Prime Minister Narasimha Rao echoed this sentiment in 1996: "Our voice is being heard internationally and we are being consulted on every major issue. Our defence might is well known."[122] At speeches at the UN and other international forums increasingly since the 1990s, Indian prime ministers have emphasized this approach based on material power capabilities and India's role as "an emerging global player."[123]

Through persistent diplomacy India has been able to garner significant support in favor of its permanent membership of a reformed and expanded UN Security Council. Among the other permanent members, Russia, France, and the United Kingdom have declared support for India's admission. The United States has stated that India had "a compelling case" but has not gone beyond that, a stance broadly similar to that of China. At the same time that other powers acknowledged India's capabilities, they also have become, from decades of interaction with India on this issue, cognizant of India's sensitiveness toward the notions of destiny and due in its globalist discourse. For instance, when France declared support for India's admission into the Security Council, the French President Jacques Chirac stated: "India is naturally destined to become a permanent member of the UN Security Council," adding that France wished to see "India occupy its rightful place" on the international scene.[124] Similarly Russian President Vladimir Putin endorsed India's candidacy for permanent membership by invoking India's globalism:

> I want to stress that, in our opinion, India plays one of the most important roles in world politics.... We are very interested in maintaining relations with such a great power as India, especially in the pursuit of creating a democratic multi-polar world and in bilateral cooperation ... as one of the biggest countries in Asia and the world, New Delhi is vital in establishing regional and international stability.[125]

Sensitivity to this issue at times can be embarrassing. In 2005, when China took steps to defuse the border impasse and issued a conciliatory joint statement with India during Prime Minister Wen Jiabao's visit to New Delhi, Indian officials and newspapers got carried away and reported that China had backed India's bid for permanent membership. In the statement China simply attached "great importance to the status of India in international affairs."[126] China has not yet endorsed India's bid, partly because of its close relations with Pakistan, but partly because its policymakers do not accord India the same attention as their Indian colleagues give China. Even though China expressed at that time what India wanted to hear, historically it has not considered India as one of the most important states in the world. Susan Shirk captures the situation in the following way:

> China's smug attitude toward India is not just a pose adopted in official statements for international effect; it is reflected domestically as well. India has many more experts on China than China has experts on India. Indian journalists, intellectuals, businesspeople, and the informed public are avid China-watchers, while their Chinese counterparts follow developments in Taiwan, Japan, and the United States with much greater interest than developments in India. Indian policies toward China are broadly debated and handled at the highest level of the political leadership, in contrast to Chinese policies toward India, which are ignored by the public and managed by the foreign affairs and military bureaucracies. China's indifference to India, and its disdainful, patronizing attitude toward India, infuriate the Indians.[127]

China's "subject role" in India

Indian reporters had become "carried away" because the sensitivity in Indian policy discourse is twofold. For all the effort that various Indian leaders had put into its bid for a world role, they are expectedly sensitive to international responses to that bid. Indian mainstream policy circles have also become sensitive to China, more than they are to any other country. This is partly due to Chinese reluctance to accept India as an equal, but mostly due to China's own subject role in the evolution of India's approach to international politics. What singularly turned an abstract and somewhat amorphous idea of globalism into a concrete set of policies was the emergence of a strong sense of rivalry with China. Globalism aims to project nationalism broadly; the target unit for globalism is the entire world. This results in confining globalism, at best, to a broad approach or a vision rather than a strategy. To give globalism focus and to generate well-defined, viable security and economic strategy out of it, Indian nationalist thinkers needed the emergence of multi-dimensional (or dense) rivalry with a single country. Moreover, China was a country that not only has globalist ambitions but was also seen to be "delivering" on them.

As this chapter showed, the roots of India's perception of rivalry went back to the balance of power politics practiced by the British. The 1962 war, subsequent border conflicts, China's growing strategic power, its material and diplomatic support to allies around India, and its higher status as a permanent nuclear state in international regimes – these have all come together in the Indian strategic mindset to elevate the image of China as India's most troublesome military and political rival and the strongest challenge to India's bid for a global role. Indian leaders began to invest in material capabilities, to emulate broadly the route by which they saw China become recognized as a world power. The subsequent shift from a normative to a material claim to globalism has not altered the sense of destiny and due in Indian strategic thinking. In the changing mindset of Indian policymakers, India's globalism was still deserved historically, but it was to be achieved through a demonstration of capabilities rather than an assertion of rights. It is the sense of India's inherent greatness and her historic due that has served as the moral justification for eventually building great-power capabilities. But it is the competition for China that has fueled continuous and increasing expenses to build those capabilities urgently, portraying atomic weapons, missile technology, aircraft carriers, and a comprehensive space program as necessities.[128] In fact, George Fernandes, India's controversial defense minister, affirmed that India's military modernization program is "running parallel" to that of China, and that India's defense budget would also be raised in the coming years to better match China's budget.[129]

Fernandes's much talked-about comment about China being "threat number one," thus, could not be discounted as shallow.[130] As an editorial in *The Business Standard* correctly observed, the comment brought back to public attention "an issue that has so far been raised discreetly only at seminars attended by foreign policy experts and security analysts and during closed door meetings within the government's security-foreign policy establishment."[131] Although contemporary mainstream strategic thought does not consider China to be an immediate military threat, it is uncertain about the longer term.[132] Some of these uncertainties are deep-seated, and cover a range of topics from the border war to containment strategy in a new cold war. Mohammed Ayoob, a veteran international relations expert, expresses some of these insecurities passionately in a newspaper essay:

> China's objectives toward India, despite the recently-witnessed bonhomie in bilateral relations, are clearly malevolent. Nothing else can explain the nexus between Beijing and Islamabad in terms of conventional arms supply and, more important, the transfer of nuclear weapon design and missile components and technology by China (and its surrogates) to Pakistan. There is a long-term Chinese design evident in this relationship. This is to tie down India so completely in the subcontinent as to prevent its emergence as a major power, and a competitor to China, in the wider Asian region.[133]

It is because of insecurity with regard to China's expanding sphere of influence that Indian policymakers have become "more relaxed" about increasing US influence in Asia, seeing it as a stabilizing force. Ayoob goes on to argue that India must cultivate close relations and possibly alliances with not only the US but also Japan. This is basically the moderate-realist view, according to Stephen Hoffmann's recent study of perceptions of China in India. This view consequently sees multipolarity or "polycentricism" (US–China–India–EU–Russia) as in Indian strategic interests and keeps open the option of friendly relations with China. In addition to the mainstream, Indian strategic circles contain ultra-realist as well as pacifist-idealist currents. The ultra-realist position urges a rapid increase in Indian military hardware, in pace with China's advances. India would need to keep up assertive diplomacy to forcefully wrest its deserved position in international relations. It also advocates active containment of China, by forging closer ties, even security arrangements, with countries like Vietnam and

Taiwan. The idealist position holds an essentially sanguine perspective about China, and prescribes continuity with India's non-alignment and traditional non-imperialist values. It views China as pragmatic and rational, and India's threat perception as overblown.[134] For our purposes, what is most significant is that in each of these three categories of perception, China features as the most important variable that shapes the parameters of India's grand strategy toward globalism.

This is not to deny the significance of India's military competition with Pakistan. Pakistan continues to play a major role in Indian strategic thought, but its role should be properly interpreted with two caveats in mind. First, Pakistan would hardly be a threat to India without China's continuous material, technological, and diplomatic support. Most Indian strategists concur with Ayoob's assessment above that the China-Pakistan arms transfer nexus is one of the most important security problems facing India in the international environment. Second, even with US and Chinese aid, Pakistan, all in all, is only a military competitor for India. China, on the other hand, presents India with a dense strategic context: by the end of the twentieth century it became India's foremost rival politically, militarily, technologically, and, as the next chapter will explore, economically. The evolution of Chinese policy toward Asia correlates with India's position and grand strategy, which evolved from idealist-pacifist in the 1950s to ultra-realist in the late 1990s. It may be settling now into a more moderate-realist position. As the next two chapters will attempt to make clear, Indian policymakers can now *afford* to settle into the moderate-realist position because of its earlier success with stronger realism, not just in security but also in the economic realm.

Domestic political benefits

The adoption of a realist route to power and prestige eventually strengthened the position of Indian policymakers and politicians with regard to their domestic constituencies. Indian policymakers began to experience a domestic political windfall in two areas. First, the state's capabilities increased with regard to strategic planning. In the 1950s and the 1960s, Nehru's vision essentially constituted foreign policy, Mahalanobis's closed-economy model confined economic policy, and as one analyst put it, "Bhaba's nuclear decisions were India's nuclear decisions."[135] A more rational and coordinated process of decision-making emerged out of a better understanding of India's strategic needs. This allowed greater capacity to absorb creative ideas within the strategic circles, impacted economic decisions in the 1990s, and made Indian policymakers more open about their strategies. Governments that have been in power especially since the late 1980s, when the four themes (science, nuclear weapons, power projection, and space program) gained considerable momentum, have become increasingly confident in their interaction with the domestic public about their intentions and rationale.

Second, and more importantly, all four of these themes heightened the sense and rhetoric of nationalism and thereby served to bridge political divides. Both "the China card" and the narrative of globalism became widely popular among pundits and the public alike, and most Indian policymakers at the helm of power became skilled at weaving the two together, in their perceptions and in their public politics. The initial phase of India's quest for power and prestige, from the mid-1960s to the 1980s, was focused on learning and internalizing lessons in realism and getting greater command of the regional power game. During this time Indian policymakers transitioned from prioritizing poverty alleviation and nation-building as the foremost focus to elevating globalism, hitherto influential but dormant, as an equally worthy objective. Globalism had the added convenience of being less politically charged; by contrast there were many more conflicting positions and domestic political challenges over issues like rural poverty.

Lack of international attention, especially compared to China, made many Indian politicians more assertive not just in diplomatic circles, but crucially, in domestic politics too. Nationalist leaders successfully courted public sympathy toward the state's strategic need to push for a concrete demonstration of power by developing prestige weapons and strategic forces. Since the 1980s, nearly every milestone in developing indigenous power projection capability, especially with regard to India's missile program, was celebrated across the political spectrum. The culmination of nationalist fervor, of course, was in the second round of nuclear explosions in 1998, and then with the announcement of building a credible nuclear arsenal, a position widely supported by the media. Emboldened, hawkish thinkers have gone further, urging India to increase its defense budget from 2.4 to at least 4 percent of GDP and produce "millions of tonnes of nuclear warheads" in order to compete effectively with China: "If China spends $80 billion for its defence budget, what's the logic of India spending just $15 billion or so?"[136] All governments in India have also enjoyed extensive domestic support on their stance toward international nuclear regimes, especially their refusal to join NPT and thereby legitimize the existing nuclear hierarchy in the international system.[137] Defense ministers and prime ministers have since then argued passionately that India deserved to build nuclear weapons, just as it deserved a seat in the table of great powers. The only meaningful opposition to India's stance came from international constituencies, including China and at times, the United States.

Each important event in India's space program, similarly, has brought glowing accolades from the public, which viewed it as another step in India's bid toward prominence. The way a national newspaper celebrated the news when ISRO launched the communication satellite Insat-3B in 2000 is a typical example:

> The very fact that there could be a live transmission of the launch from Kourou [the launch site in French Guyana] to the drawing rooms of millions of viewers around the world is itself a demonstration of the spectacular headway made in space science and technology … India has now kept pace with the progress which the developed countries have achieved in the launching of orbiting satellites.[138]

Although the pursuit of big science within a statist model brought with it bureaucratic problems, it also established a nationwide political esteem for science in general and for its instrumental value, from military technology to poverty reduction. The Nehruvian mantle was continued in some ways by Dr. Abdul Kalam, an aeronautical engineer and the father of the country's missile program, who became India's eleventh president in 2002. He continued to emphasize that investments in science can drive India's high economic growth, which by his calculation can lift 230 million people out of poverty by 2020. This would be helped by two trends absent in the previous era of state-led science. One is a reverse brain-drain (a brain gain). Between 2004 and 2007, more than 30,000 scientists and engineers are estimated to have returned to India.[139] The other is commercial investment in R&D. In fact, India's penchant for science is touted as one of its attractions as an investment destination. Yashwant Sinha, a finance minister (and later defense minister) during BJP's administration in 2000, captured this idea when he claimed to investors that India was moving towards the status of "a highly-developed nation based on strong social, cultural and economic foundations and [sitting] at the cutting edge in science and technology."[140] This is part of the strong globalist discourse that has developed in India. The argument that investments in science would empower India globally continues to have significant political power.

The domestic politics of causes and consequences, as reviewed in the previous chapter, obscured from public view, especially in the 1990s, India's perception of a continuous and inevitable competition with China. The purpose of this chapter was to establish the historical events and their interpretations that constituted the context in which China began to be viewed systematically as a rival. The context is intimately intertwined with Indian nationalist policymakers' understanding of the role and ambitions of India in the world order. The next chapter will analyze how perceptions at the intersection of globalist ideology and material rivalry influenced the context of India's pursuit of open-economy policies.

4 Evolution of economic globalism and economic rivalry

Defence forces are, of course, essential for protecting sovereignty and territorial integrity. But they are blunt and clumsy instruments for influencing the behaviour of other states or for power projection. The market place is the battlefield of the future.

Madhavsinh Solanki, Minister of External Affairs, 13 August 1991

I speak for generations of young Indians. We are not happy. We are not proud that smaller countries have outgrown India, but India can become a giant economy in ten years.

Palaniappan Chidambaram, Minister of Commerce, 6 April 1995

India's economic destiny is safe only when India knows how to stand on its own feet, to compete against everyone in the world on an equal footing. That is what we are trying to do.

Manmohan Singh, Minister of Finance, 6 October 1995

Like its security policy, Indian economic policy has been influenced strongly by globalism. Starting with Nehru, generations of Indian leaders have made clear the desire to play a strong role in world affairs and the belief that to do so is not just destiny but also good for India and the world. While this overarching philosophy of globalism has remained fairly constant in post-independence India, specific economic ideas contained within the larger vision have changed from time to time. One of these ideational shifts concerns the goal of external economic policy. Does globalism encompass the economy, such that India should devise policies specifically to influence the course of the world economy? Or does economic policy (or strength) serve a more instrumental role in a grander strategy of globalism that is expressed primarily in political and military terms? Ideational debates have also surrounded questions of rivalry with China. In what way should a rival's economic policy matter for Indian policy? Should it be a matter of separation, that is, something that distinguishes India's approach to economic issues from approaches pursued by a rival – say, China, Pakistan, or the United States – in the same way that Indian foreign policy sought to create a unique brand? Or should India adopt a perspective more realistic in nature, where success in China's policy signifies India's relative failure, and therefore deserves to be studied and perhaps emulated?

This chapter pays attention to how these questions were resolved as India's globalism evolved. In the late nineteenth century, the British were not as concerned with China as an economic threat as they were with its potential military threat. But Indian strategists in the 1960s began to note the military implications of China's rising industrial strength. It became a subject of study, and later object of envy, for Indian policymakers. As their perception of military and political rivalry with China became starker (reviewed in the previous chapter), some Indian policymakers concluded that the area in which China was the farthest ahead of India was the economy. Wider policy circles came on board as well. Academia, businesses, and thinktanks began displaying an automatic penchant to compare the economies of China and India, intensifying a sense of relative loss for India and relative gain for China along a variety of criteria. This eventually led toward modifications in India's traditional approach to globalism; the set of questions listed earlier would allow us to understand these modifications and their implications. The centrality of self-sufficiency, economic independence, and *swadeshi* had to be questioned, then altered, in the definition of a great power. Simultaneously globalist and nationalist, Indian leaders also began to take seriously the role of economic statecraft as an area that is close if not equal in stature to high politics. All these together formed the milieu of beliefs and understandings in which India's open-economy policy was initiated and continued.

In order to understand how events and trends became policy relevant, we shall adopt, in parts of this chapter, an Indian nationalist policymaker's perspective, attempting to reconstruct the probable interpretive route by which China began to be seen gradually as an economic rival. What has happened in essence, I hope to show, is the perception and construction of an economic reality, and then fitting it within the wider and more politically acceptable notion of globalism. A rivalry/globalism framework began to serve not just as a driver of policy but also as the criteria to interpret the success and failure of policies. The implication, as I will make clear in the next chapter, is that as long as nationalist leaders continue to use a rivalry/globalism framework to deduce that India's open-economy policy has been successful, they will continue their policy path regardless of domestic discontent or governmental changes.

Economic globalism in Indian thought

Postcolonial economic policy in India was strongly nationalist, and sought to strengthen India economically with state intervention toward the development of heavy industries, as noted in the previous chapters. This economic strategy, in which the state would be in control of the "commanding heights" of the economy, made sense not only in the context of India's nationalist struggle, but also as an effort to increase the legitimacy of the state during a period of economic and political fragility and uncertainty.[1] The exercise of state power in the fashion of "command politics" in turn was justified in the mind of India's nationalist elite because it was deemed necessary for economic empowerment.[2] It was needed to hold India together; large-scale state investment was a visible way to show that the state was in control of the nation's economic destiny. It was the height of modernist thinking: the state was the rational leader and organizer of economic and social life. Infrastructure development and giant factories would come to represent newer, more modern, aspects of national identity.[3] Parallel to the faith in India's potential for globalism, Nehru and his contemporaries had a strong faith in India's potential for economic empowerment through such modernization, even if they understood the country's current conditions as challenging. The economy, however, had an odd and somewhat contradictory role to play in their broader project of globalism. It was to be sheltered from the rest of the world, and it was to be secondary in importance to foreign policy.

Empowerment and independence

On the eve of independence India's economic direction was uncertain. But what seemed assured was that economic policy in India would be marked by its exclusion from rather than inclusion in the rest of the world. The philosophy and movement of *swadeshi* had become mainstream in anticolonial politics by then. In addition, Gandhi's fans advocated a return to agrarian cottage industries, shunning mass and factory-produced items in order to emancipate Indians "from the compulsion to imitate the imprisoning, destructive and iniquitous forms of industrial modernity dumbly cherished in the West."[4] Although Nehruvian economic policy took exception to this idea and opted for heavy industrialization, it situated India's economic program within the popular *swadeshi* logic and rhetoric. Economic empowerment was equated with economic independence. Economic independence meant, in particular, the avoidance of foreign capital and foreign imports. The Advisory Planning Board of the Interim Government, precursor to India's Planning Commission, made the case against both in clear terms in 1946:

> [T]he reasons for keeping the basic industries of the country free from foreign control are obvious.... Foreign capital should not be allowed to enter or where it already existed, to expand – even in non-basic industries such as consumer goods. If necessary, the country should rely on imports. In due course of time, it will be possible to restrict or discontinue foreign imports; but foreign vested interests once created would be difficult to dislodge.[5]

After the Planning Commission was formed, the model that guided economic policy in the 1950s through the 1970s was the Mahalanobis model, which assumed a closed economy, as noted in Chapter 2. Imports were to be allowed only to the extent that they were needed toward industrialization. In other words, imports were restricted to capital goods. Mahalanobis had no reason to be shy about his goal: "[A]lthough in the beginning India will, no doubt, have to depend on imports of capital goods, the policy would be to make India *independent* of such imports as soon as possible."[6] Exports were to be used only to the extent that export earnings could finance some of the external resources required for economic development.[7] Nehru and his followers were less enamored by humdrum rural development and more attracted to large industrial townships, in which "patriot-workers" would work, depicting images of modernity that could be reproduced on postcards or stamps. This was part of the national imagination, and big industrialization was the epitome of economic nationalism, the only reliable means to avoid "economic bondage" and "political subjection," to use Nehru's words.[8] While Gandhi's *swadeshi* looked to extol the traditional, the rural, and the craftsman, Nehru's *swadeshi* was modern, urban-industrial, centered on workers and scientists. But they were both *swadeshi,* focused inwards and intended to repel what was foreign.

To avoid bondage and subjection, Indian economic policy until the 1980s practiced essentially three levels of isolation. At one level, foreign trade as a sector was isolated from other domestic economic sectors. This was a common practice of macroeconomic models that informed Indian planning. Between the mid-1950s to the mid-1970s, foreign trade was even seen as a constraint on growth.[9] At another level, economic activities of the nation as a whole were isolated from the international economic system. This applied to foreign investment and foreign trade because of the risk that they might connect the demand structure of the economy to international capitalism. It also applied to foreign travel and foreign communication, especially with the West, which was seen with suspicious eyes. Finally, economic independence itself was viewed in isolation from globalism. Thus the inward-looking economic nationalism that characterized India until the 1990s and sought to shelter the economy from the world coexisted, oddly, with dreams of being "modern" and playing a strong role in the world affairs.

Economics at the margin

With sheltered self-reliance as its historical approach to economic empowerment, Indian policy-thinking made economics secondary to other components of globalism. Globalism represented high politics and high diplomacy. India's subject role in the world, in the mind of Nehru and generations of Indian political leaders, was very much a political role. This makes sense when one considers that the major accomplishments of the first two generations of India's leaders were considered political. India had been freed from colonial shackles by pursuing what was thought to be a unique and dignified political program. India's politicians were then able to unify the various regions of the country, including sovereign principalities, despite a bitter partition with Pakistan. They formed and held together the world's largest democracy, able to organize massive elections that were generally free and fair, despite resource constraints. In foreign policy, too, India's major accomplishments were political. Its leaders presided over three wars with Pakistan and one war with China. It has been able to withstand pressures from the West, and for most of its history, it was able to maintain a stance of non-alignment. The core values that India's globalism sought to promote were non-economic in nature: non-alignment, pacifism, self-determination, and democracy.

By contrast India's economic accomplishments were not worthy of attention. It tried to promote capital-intensive industrialization led by the state, creating significant distortions in the economy and a growing deficit. It was seen to languish at a so-called Hindu rate of growth, a historical average of 3.5 percent per year. During the low period of its international stature, from the mid-1960s to the mid-1970s, it had significant problems of hunger, and became dependent on foreign food aid. Its export, import, and investment links were marginal in both quantity and quality. Economically, the world's largest democracy mattered little.

Consequently, India's great power dreams were not based on economic logic. There was virtually no economic statecraft, nor was there any scope to economically influence any other country of significance. Unlike its foreign policy, its economic policy did not contain anything that was seen to be uniquely part of the national identity. The pursuit of state-led industrialization was not an Indian innovation; it was essentially acceptance of the type of modernization that was happening elsewhere, initiated by the West during the late mercantilist era, but perfected by interwar Germany and post-World-War-II Soviet Union. Moreover, competition and materialism, which were the hallmarks of the emerging international economic system, were not viewed as values for India to champion. Thus, although the economy was the "primary source of raw material for the nationalist imagination,"[10] and although nationalist imagination itself was the central part of India's globalism, the economy did not have any direct or appreciable role to play in India's bid for globalism through most of its history.

The only noteworthy link between India's economy and its globalism was indirect, and that concerned the strategic importance of industrialization. Nehru and most other Congress leaders concurred that it was impossible to become a great power without a large industrial base free of foreign control. A crucial benefit of industry was in the area of defense: India's leaders understood well the rationale behind a state-sponsored military industrial complex. As Nehru stated:

> [T]he only ultimate protection of our country is to advance on the economic and industrial front and make our country strong in that respect. War today is not merely a question of some gallant soldiers behaving gallantly. It is essentially a question of the industrial might of a nation, of the productive apparatus of a nation.[11]

The role of the economy in strengthening defense or offense became clearer through the experience of the war with China. India also needed to counter the effects of the increasing military aid that the United States was channeling to Pakistan. Both of these further enhanced the argument for rapid industrialization.

But in the end industrialization, and the economy in general, would serve an indirect role in how India interacted with the world. While globalism entailed political and moral interventions in the outside world, especially in the shape of an assertive and activist foreign policy, it did not entail economic intervention, let alone integration. Because it would make India susceptible to foreign influence, such intervention or integration were thought to actually weaken India's great-power potential.

Evolution of economic perception of China

The "traditional" approach toward the role of economic power in globalism was influenced over time by Indian leaders' perception of the Chinese economy. As stated, the idea that China is India's economic rival – indeed the principal economic rival – is a very recent development, as is the effect of such rivalry on Indian economic policy. But China, for a far longer period, has had an effect on India's understanding of globalism, as its image in Indian eyes evolved from friend to foe.

Solidarity in struggle

During India's anticolonial nationalist struggle, as the last chapter observed, China was held in high regard. When Nehru had likened the civilizational basis of India to that of China, he was one of the first political leaders to have done so. Essays on India by Tagore and Gandhi had also referred to conditions in China, compared to what they saw in India. Indian nationalists admired China's independence, even though it was at times only a paper tiger. They found a convergence of interests between India and China, and a parallel between India's effort to distance itself from colonialism-imperialism-capitalism and China's endeavor to forge an indigenous path toward rapid modernization.[12]

But these were impressionistic observations, all representing an underlying motive of narrating stories that might inspire India's nationalist movement. Slowly after independence, the need for impressionistic anti-imperial comparisons decreased, and as India and China began to undertake development plans, both influenced by Soviet-style industrialization, and to publish statistical records, windows for more systematic comparison emerged. In his review of their economic performance in the 1950s, Wilfred Malenbaum posited that the basis for comparing the two lay in their similarities – they had "similar enough economies so that analytical problems in making the comparisons are relatively small" – as well as their contrast as totalitarian and democratic regimes.[13] For their part, although Indian observers were uncomfortable with the authoritarianism and the human obliteration that accompanied modernization programs in the Soviet Union and China, they still considered the careful emulation of Soviet and Chinese policies to strengthen India's industrial sector superior to adopting capitalist means. They were especially interested to learn lessons on heavy industrialization, and on the role of the state in the economy.[14]

Enmity and rejection

The 1962 war and its aftermath left two simultaneous, yet somewhat contradictory, imprints on Nehruvian policymakers' perspectives. On one hand, China had convincingly proven its military might, which in turn reflected the strength of its heavy industries and indigenous technological development. Partly out of that experience, Indian plan allocations for industrialization increased substantially. Whereas the First Plan (1951–56) had allocated only 2.8 percent of development expenditures to industry and minerals, the Second and the Third plans, covering 1956–66, allocated over 20 percent. Indian R&D and military expenses also increased commensurately, as shown in the previous chapter.

On the other hand, the war had destroyed the bonds of solidarity that Indian leaders had felt toward China. Nehru admitted that he felt badly betrayed by Chinese aggression. China was now perceived to be an imperialist menace, a militaristic, expansionist, pseudo-communist dictatorship.[15] The Chinese model of economic, social, and political organization, therefore, was rejected as irrelevant to India. It was still imperative for India to develop its industrial base rapidly, but India was to pursue industrialization independently, according to its own development agenda. China, despite becoming a concrete military rival by now, did not fare in India's mindset as worthy to be emulated with regard to economic policy. This, in sum, turned the erstwhile Indian leaders even more inwards with regard to their overall economic approach, as China until this point had been one of the countries with which India was open to cultivating closer economic links.

In the 1960s it was also understood that the two countries were more or less advancing at a similar rate of progress, and that their differences were mainly in political rather than economic arenas. Outside India, Malenbaum published two economic studies in the 1950s, comparing China and India and noting China's relatively better economic performance.[16] But these results were mostly neglected in the policymaking circles. It was also too early to tell whether such performances were simply temporary or indicated longer-term sustainable trends. Chou En Lai's formidable propaganda machine, which India's government first confronted during the 1958–62 crisis, also damaged the credibility of China's claims about its economic achievements. To be sure, there were occasional references to China's economic and industrial potential. In 1966, for example, Indira Gandhi remarked in New York that the real threat from China was not as much military as it was political and economic.[17] But these were passing observations rather than policy recommendations. The government did not take up seriously the study of China's economy; nor did Indian analysts see or believe that there was much to learn or imitate from China at that time.

The cottage industry of comparison

The 1960s thus were a lost decade for India's economic examination of China. Interestingly, one of the observers who, for reasons related to the Cold War, began to notice with concern the possibility of a performance divergence between the two countries was John F. Kennedy. As a senator in 1960 he noted:

> I believe that India represents a great area for affirmative action by the Free World. India started from about the same place that China did. The Chinese Communists have been moving ahead the last 10 years. India ... has been making some progress, but if India does not succeed with her 450 million people, if she can't make freedom work, then people around the world are going to determine, particularly in the underdeveloped world, that the only way they can develop their resources is through the Communist system.[18]

By the 1970s, Indian analysts began to take China somewhat more seriously. One reason was the internalization of the war's lessons: now that rivalry was to continue, especially as China had been fostering a close alliance with Pakistan, comparison seemed more natural. Another reason was that Nehru's acknowledgment of China's superiority in economic power eventually percolated into India's policy circles. A third reason was noted in the previous chapter: The Indian government's approach to policymaking was beginning to become more analytical, with a greater level of interest in material power than shown before. Fourth, India seemed lost in the 1960s and needed direction, but China seemed firmly in control of its economic destiny. India's foreign policy was in disarray after 1962 and did not regain composure until its successful intervention in Bangladesh's liberation war in 1971. India narrowly averted a famine in the mid-1960s. Its experiment with devaluation of the rupee in 1966 had failed. By the end of the decade, the Congress Party's dominance of domestic politics was over. Though impressionistic, the contrast between their drift at sea and China's focused navigation became visible, perhaps making some Indian analysts more open to once again considering China's advances seriously. Finally, by the 1970s two full decades had already passed since independence, which made conclusions about long-term economic trends more credible.

There was increasing interest in China on the part of both the government and independent scholars. One of the early efforts at systematizing the study of China was the formation in 1969 of a "China Study Group," comprising an informal group of scholars from universities and think-tanks in Delhi. It brought together economists and social scientists with defense experts, and began to catch the attraction of government analysts who were interested in China. The group eventually headed India's first China journal, *China Report*, and has carried on its comparative research to date, expanding later into the Institute of Chinese Studies. Many of the comparative studies undertaken by scholars inside and outside India in the 1970s took such comparison to be only natural, along the reasoning that Malenbaum had given: both countries contained large populations, had undertaken modernization, were situated at "comparable" levels of development, and were political exemplars. The tone underneath some of the comparisons began to reveal an implicit recognition that China was a potential economic rival. The conclusions reached by most studies were not reassuring to

Indian policymakers: China seemed to have gained a lead. One area in which India usually had an advantage was in scientific and technical training and research. China was ahead in most other indicators of economic development, especially in industrial strength.[19] A notable exception to this view was an influential 1973 study by Subramanian Swamy, in which he found that the growth rates of India and China between 1952 and 1970 were about the same.[20] In an updated study in 1977, Swamy concluded that since 1969 China had been getting increasingly ahead of India, especially in industrial output. China had a greater output in fourteen of the sixteen key commodities that Swamy studied.[21] Swamy's studies generated interest in Indian government's planning circles, as did studies undertaken by several other economists: T. N. Srinivasan, Jagdish Bhagwati, and Amartya Sen.[22] One of the influential observers in the planning circle at that time was Manmohan Singh, who was Chief Economic Adviser of the Ministry of Finance during the first half of the 1970s, and had published a few years earlier his own extensive study of the progressive loss in India's share of world exports between 1951 and 1960.[23]

There was still doubt about the quality of China's economic data, and most analysts spent considerable effort to adjust the official statistics before proceeding with quantitative comparisons. Jean Drèze and Amartya Sen were among the doubters, noting: "There is much evidence that if the per capita growth rate of GNP in China was higher than that in India in the period up to the [Chinese] reforms of 1979, the gap was not especially large."[24] In addition to statistical problems, there were also difficulties in conducting primary research in China. Furthermore, Indian analysts could not assess the view from China's vantage, since comparisons between China and India undertaken by Chinese scholars were rare. But Indian observers had begun to accept that China was becoming economically more powerful than India, even though the extent was debatable.

A benchmark established

Deng Xiao Ping's economic reform of 1979 was a surprise, and increased India's policy curiosity about what was happening in "the Middle Kingdom." The results seemed starker than before. Comparisons of China and India by this time had become commonplace, reflecting, as Malenbaum wrote in the early 1980s, "a broad interest on the part of officials in rich and poor lands, of scholars, and indeed of citizens everywhere." Most studies by this time had accepted the assumption of an "equal starting point," that is, the two countries had similar levels of per capita income around 1950 (around US$50–60) and a life expectancy of about thirty-five years. By 1980, China had outpaced India on a number of criteria, from economic growth and per capita income, to industrial growth (which in China was double that of India), to life expectancy (sixty-four years in China versus fifty-two years in India), to adult literacy (66 percent in China versus 36 percent in India).[25] Malenbaum noted at that time a consistent tendency in comparative research that ventured to predict future trends:

> China could, indeed, achieve a tremendous increase in the living standards of its billion and more people by the year 2000. These outlooks for China are from expert literature. No comparable prospects over the next two decades are found in the expert literature on Indian development.[26]

This contrasting assessment of the future was crucial. Predictions such as these in the context of Deng's mysterious economic reforms in China, were the precursor to a new debate about the sustainability of economic growth in large countries. Another area that began to capture India's attention in the 1980s was China's increasing share of the world market. T. N. Srinivasan, an economist whose research was followed in India, observed in a study published a decade after the initiation of China's reforms:

> Because of their inward-oriented development strategies, both China and India failed to take advantage of opportunities offered by growing world trade. China's share of world exports fell from about 1.25 percent during 1952–55 to 0.75 percent in 1978 ... India's share fell from about 1.50 during 1952–55 to 0.57 percent in 1978.... After the reforms, China increased its share substantially to 1.70 percent in 1989, while India merely stabilized the share around 0.52 percent during 1980–88.[27]

The volume of comparative academic and policy works has increased tremendously since the 1980s. Achin Vanaik, representing a different end of the political spectrum, wrote in his Marxist analysis of India's political economy in the 1980s: "[T]he Chinese road to socialism, for all its detours, hiatuses, political drawbacks and indeed, its highly 'unsocialist' features, has nevertheless had a far more impressive record than the Indian road to capitalism."[28] The benchmark for India's performance was in the process of being set. In 1992 A. S. Bhalla contrasted the economic development policies and George Rosen compared the industrial policies of the two countries. Two years later T. N. Srinivasan published another study comparing agriculture and trade policies.[29] Even some important studies that focus exclusively on India have set aside space to compare India's economic experience to that of China.[30] "Indeed, it is natural to judge Indian successes and failures in comparative terms with China," observed Jean Drèze and Amartya Sen.[31] Natural though it may be, a comparison as such does not necessarily indicate rivalry. Yet the act of continually juxtaposing and comparing economic statistics is not entirely innocuous, for collectively it helps construct a sense of relative gains and losses. Once rivalry, because of political motive or historical experience, is perceived and injected into the calculus, the sense of gain and loss can become policy-relevant, even urgent.

"The dragon and the tiger": a brief comparison

While noting the evolution and mini-epistemology of India's perception of China, we may ourselves benefit from an overall comparison, in order to gauge the criteria and the magnitude and appreciate the perspective by which Indian policymakers concluded India's relative loss to China. Generations of such comparisons have begun with population. By number of inhabitants, China is the largest and India the second largest country in the world, together accounting for almost 40 percent of humanity. At current growth rate India's population is estimated to surpass China's by 2025. They are the two largest countries in Asia in land area, but China is almost three times the size of India. China's economy, at $2.2 trillion, is also almost three times the size of India's economy. China has 20 percent and India 17 percent of the world's population, but they respectively represent only 4.9 percent and 1.8 percent of the world's income. Accordingly, their ranks in per capita income are low, and they still contain significant pockets of poverty. According to 2004 data of the UNDP, 34.7 percent of India's population lived on $1 a day or less, compared to 16.6 percent of China's population. This corresponds to over 377 million people in India and about 217 million in China in absolute poverty. Tables 4.1, 4.2, and 4.3 summarize basic data about the two countries. As shown in Table 4.3, China on the whole fares better than India in human development (higher life expectancy, higher literacy, lower malnutrition and lower child mortality).

The comparison between the dragon and the tiger, so to speak, begins to give

Table 4.1 India and China, basic indicators

Indicator	*India*	*China*
Population (2006, millions)	1118	1314
Land area ('000 sq km)	2973	9326
GDP (2005, billions US$)	805.7	2225
GDP/Capita (2005, US$)	730	1702
GDP/Capita (2004, PPP$)	3139	5896
Share of world production (2005, %)	1.8	4.9
Share of world population (2006, %)	17.4	20.4

Sources: online databases of Asian Development Bank, World Bank, United Nations Statistics Division, and United Nations Development Programme.

Table 4.2 India and China, relative position in the world

Indicator	*India*	*China*
Land area (2006 rank)	7	3
Population (2006 rank)	2	1
Size of economy (2006 rank, by US$)	10	4
Size of economy (2006 rank, by PPP$)	4	2
Per capita income (2004 rank, by PPP$)	114	89
Human Development Index (2004 rank)	126	81

Sources: online databases of Asian Development Bank, World Bank, United Nations Statistics Division, and United Nations Development Programme.

Table 4.3 India and China, human and social development indicators

Indicator	*India*	*China*	*Difference* (%)*
GDP/Capita (2005, US$)	730	1702	+133
GDP/Capita (2004, PPP$)	3139	5896	+88
Adult literacy rate (2004, % ages 15 and older)	61.0	90.9	+49
Life expectancy (2004, years)	63.6	71.9	+13
People undernourished (2001–03, % of population)	20	12	+40
Under 5 mortality rate (2004, per 1000 live births)	85	31	+64
Access to safe water (2004, % of population)	86	77	−11
Physicians per 100,000 people (2004)	60	106	+77
Improvement in Human Development (%) 1975–2004**	+48	+46	–

Source: UNDP, *Human Development Report 2006* (online).

Notes

* This is a measure of the "distance" between China and India [(China–India)/India]. Positive number indicates the extent to which China fares better than India in a given indicator.

** Percentage change between Human Development Index of 1975 and Human Development Index of 2004 for given country.

a sense of relative loss and gain once we consider time-series data. These are the types of comparisons that began to come out frequently since the 1970s, eventually increasing pressures on policymakers who considered China to be a rival. Figure 4.1 plots the trajectory of real GDP of the two countries between 1960 and 2005, expressed in constant 2000 dollars. In 1960, at US$77 billion, India's GDP was higher than China's (US$70 billion). The two countries continued that trajectory till 1973, when China (US$120 billion) caught up to India's GDP (US$119 billion) in real terms. This in some ways justifies the disregard that Indian policymakers showed for China's economic trend in the 1960s. China's real GDP even dipped for a few years in the 1960s. (Underneath this trend, of course, is a forceful restructuring of Chinese economy and a much higher ratio of industrial value-added.) China's economy has taken off, literally, since the 1979 reforms. India's GDP grew as well, but its trajectory has not been as steep as China's. If looking at this picture of output from a per capita standpoint, India's real per capita GDP grew by 3.4 percent annually between 1975 and 2004, and by 4 percent between 1990 and 2004. By contrast, China's real per capita GDP grew by 8.4 percent between 1975 and 2004, and by 8.9 percent between 1990 and 2004 – at more than twice the rate of India. In the context of the evolution of India–China relations, no matter which way an Indian policymaker looks at comparative economic growth, (s)he would be sure to come away with a sense of relative loss. Moreover, judging from Figure 4.1, the gap, it seems, has been getting larger.

As their GDPs changed, so did the comparative structure of Chinese and Indian economies (Figure 4.2). Two changes stand out between 1960 and 2005. The importance of agriculture in each country's output has fallen. China's thrust at modernization had established it significantly as an industrial economy by

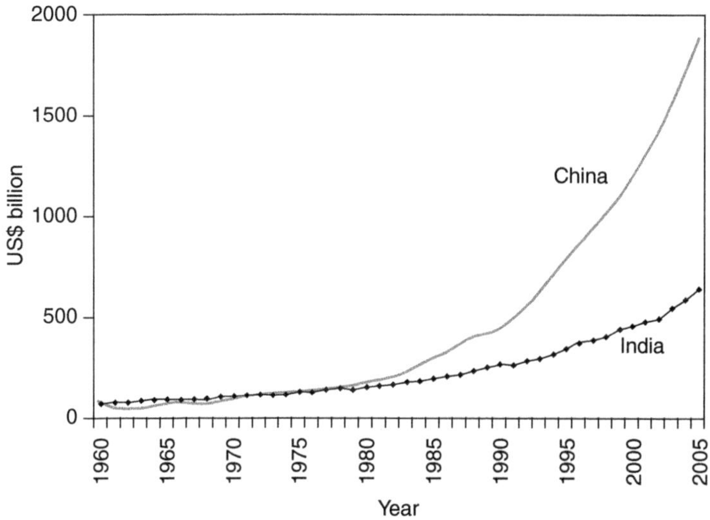

Figure 4.1 Comparative GDP of India and China, 1960–2005 (in constant 2000 US$ billions) (source of data: World Bank, *World Development Indicators* (online)).

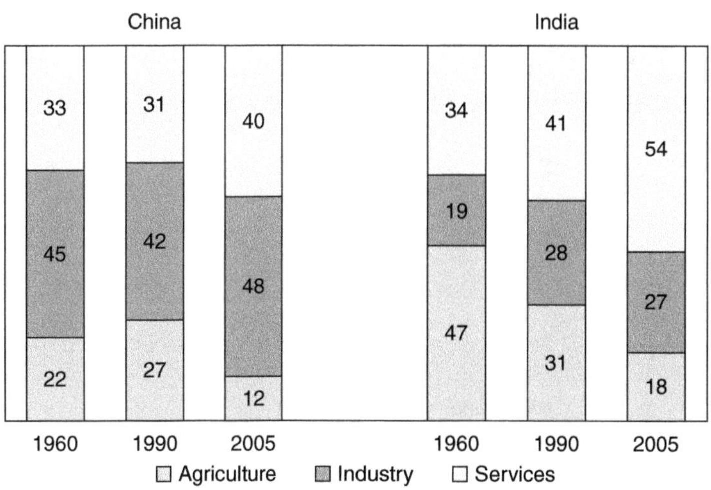

Figure 4.2 Changes in the structure of the economy (source of data: World Bank, *World Development Indicators* (online)).

Note

Depicted are percentage shares of agriculture, industry, and services value added in the GDP for each country and each period.

1960, and it remains so. India, however, has evolved to become a services-focused economy by 2005, the sector contributing more than half of the value of national output. Their respective focus on industry and services is a key differentiator between the two countries, and also defines to a large extent their comparative strengths in the world economy. (We will look at some implications on policy rivalry later in the chapter.) However, agriculture continues to be the single largest source of employment in both countries, contributing approximately 40 percent of China's employment and 60 percent of India's employment.

Progress in human development has been significant in both countries. Figure 4.3 plots life expectancy and infant mortality rates in five-year intervals. On both measures India began with a slight advantage around 1960 but has been trailing China for the last thirty years. China also has reduced malnutrition, absolute poverty, and disease prevalence, and increased literacy rates. As a comparison between Figure 4.1 and 4.3 will show, China made its leap over India in human development before it made a leap in GDP. As Drèze and Sen observe: "China's real achievement in this period [i.e., 1960s and 1970s] lies in what it managed to do *despite* poor economic growth, rather than what it could do *through* high economic growth."[32] Indian policymakers were oblivious to these changes taking place in China, especially in the 1960s, as they were to the possible implications of human development on economic growth, and later, economic competition.

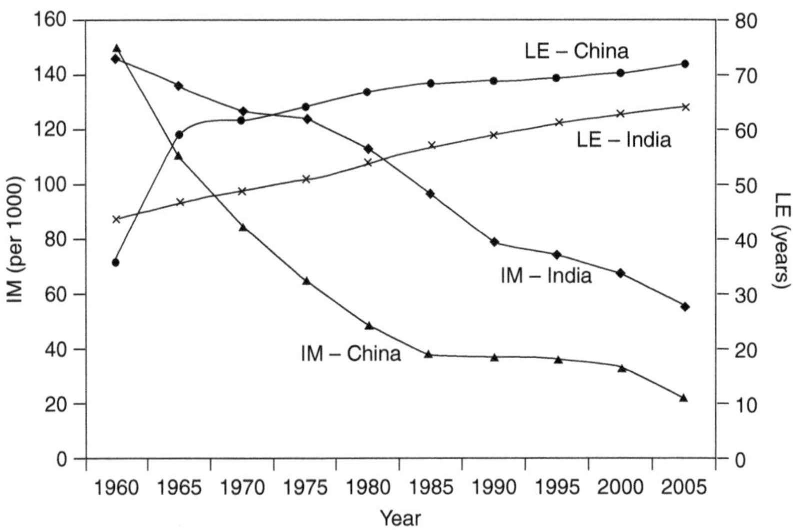

Figure 4.3 Trends in life expectancy and infant mortality rates (source of data: World Bank, *World Development Indicators* (online)).

Note
IM = infant mortality rate per 1000 live births, plotted against the left axis. LE = life expectancy in years, plotted against the right axis.

Drèze and Sen conclude from their study of comparative social change in the two countries: "the relative standings had been decisively established *before* the Chinese reforms [of 1979]."[33]

Taking stock of China in science and technology was also sobering. Although Indian policymakers had assumed a superior relative standing of their country on indicators of science and technology – India did have superiority in niches like software and pharmaceuticals – its overall scientific base was smaller upon closer inspection. In both India and China a significant proportion of the government's expenses go toward education (between 10 and 12 percent), and a considerable proportion is also channeled to support scientific and technical learning. Both countries enjoy a large number of skilled experts, scientists, engineers, and technicians, though China boasts a much higher density. In the mid-1990s, India had 151 scientists and engineers per million people; China had 537. Chinese residents filed more than six times the number of patent applications that Indian residents filed. Even though points are heard at times about the superior quality of science in India, China on average enjoys a higher level of technological and scientific penetration in society, partly due to the earlier investment and progress in human development. Over time even though both countries have made substantial gains on most key indicators of the prevalence of science and technology, India has fallen behind China in relative terms, as shown in Figure 4.4. In 1996, for instance, India published almost the same

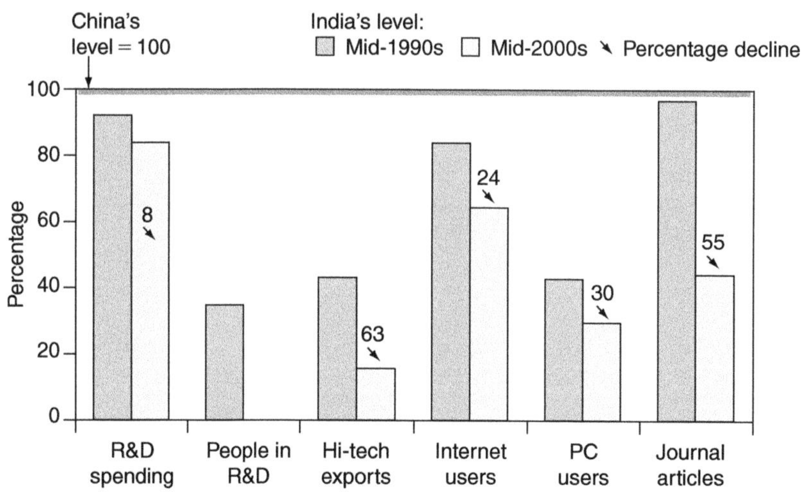

Figure 4.4 Comparative indicators of science and technology (India's relative proportion compared to China's, 1995–2005) (source of data: World Bank, *World Development Indicators* (online)).

Notes

The full descriptions of the indicators are: research and development (R&D) spending as a proportion of GDP; number of researchers in R&D per million people; high-tech exports as percentage of manufactured exports; number of internet users per thousand people; number of personal computers per thousand people; and number of articles published in scientific and technical journals.

number of articles (9700) in scientific journals as did China (10,036). Even though the absolute number for both countries increased, the relative proportion has declined steadily for India, such that in 2003 Indians published fewer than half as many scientific journal articles as the Chinese did.

Some of the starkest differences between the two countries were in foreign trade trends. In the pre-openness era for both, in 1975, India's foreign trade amounted to 14 percent of GDP. China's trade was less than 10 percent of GDP. China began its open-door policy in 1978, and continued liberalization through the 1980s, though there was periodic policy retrenchment. India's open-door policy started in 1991. By 1995, trade in India rose to represent 23 percent of GDP. But by that time China had increased its foreign trade to an impressive 40 percent of GDP (See Figure 4.5). In essence, between 1975 and 1995 China's trade/GDP ratio (often referred to as "openness ratio") grew at an average annual rate of 1.7 percent compared to India's 0.5 percent.[34] As a result of faster external trade, China had increased its share of world trade threefold between 1980 and 1996, while India raised its share from 0.5 to 0.6 percent.

China's rise as a recipient of foreign direct investment (FDI) is even steeper. Since India liberalized foreign investment regulations in 1991, it has attracted a respectable total of $46 billion as direct investment from abroad (1991–2005). However, China attracted more than $79 billion in FDI in 2005 alone. Table 4.4 depicts the current relative standings of China and India with regard to trade and FDI.

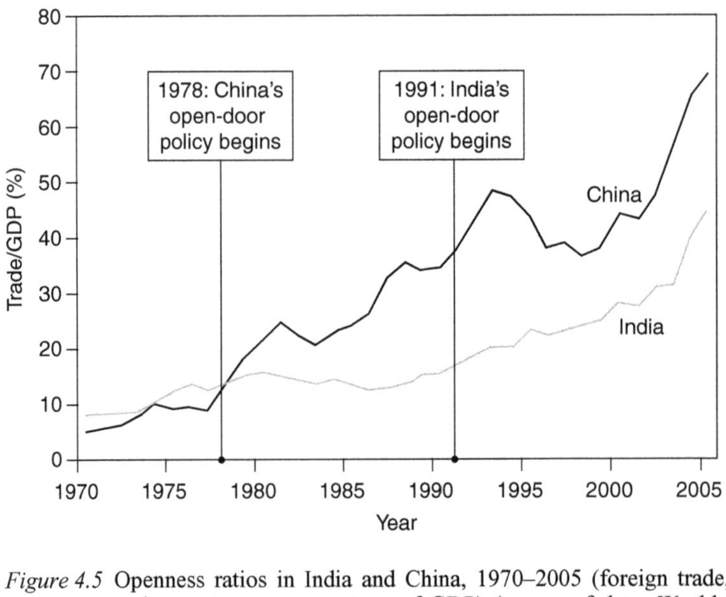

Figure 4.5 Openness ratios in India and China, 1970–2005 (foreign trade, i.e. imports and exports, as a percentage of GDP) (source of data: World Bank, *World Development Indicators* (online)).

Table 4.4 Current trade and investment statistics

Indicator	*India*	*China*
Average annual FDI inflow (US$ million)		
1985–95	458	11,690
1995–2005	4026	46,896
Trade as % of GDP		
1985–95, Average	17	37
1995–2005, Average	29	48
Exports (Annual % change)		
Merchandise Exports (1985–95)	13	18
Services Exports (1985–95)	n/a	15
Trade per capita (2005, US$)	235	962

Sources: World Bank, *World Development Indicators* (online); World Trade Organization, *Country Trade Profiles* (online).

"China has shown the way": rivalry, change, continuity

As mentioned before, the juxtaposition of comparative statistics had created pressures in Indian policy circles. There was academic acknowledgment of the trends, accompanied at times by policy concern and at times by a "so-what" attitude. Except on paper, any two countries hardly compete against each other on reductions in infant mortality or on growth that is focused on a sheltered domestic market. A trend of relative loss would have eventual implications for India's bid for global prominence, to the extent that China and India were competing for one spot. But they were not competing in that sense; China's role as a global power was assured and acknowledged, whereas India's bid was not. That is partly why India did not fare strongly in Chinese threat perceptions.[35] But by the mid-1980s what had been created is a sense of relative economic loss to China, which then became the policy-relevant context for interpreting China's economy. It should be underscored that this context was created *before* China emerged as a direct economic rival. Once China began to either displace Indian products in the world market or, later, appear as an established competitor in most new markets into which Indian firms wanted to expand, the earlier perception of relative loss helped to frame and invoke an acute sense of rivalry.

The ambience of policy options

As argued earlier, Indian analysts began to take notice of the consequences of China's new, if controlled, emphasis on foreign trade after China's economic growth rate increased, following the 1979 open-door policies. In 1986 the government-sponsored Indian Council for Research in International Economic Relations (ICRIER) published one of the first studies to detail the consequences of Chinese trade expansion for India. It noted that India during the 1960s and the 1970s had relied on the Soviet market, where its exports had privileged access but China's exports did not. China's trade expansion since 1979 took place in other markets that were growing substantially. Within a span of just five years China had not only gained a prominent position as a major exporter, but had displaced India's influence in a number of export areas. Table 4.5 summarizes some of the findings of that influential study.[36] The ICRIER study was one of the early efforts to bring back the prospect of rivalry with China. It also underscored the need for strategic response to the emerging Chinese challenge. It urged the government to undertake policies toward greater export competitiveness and to engage in aggressive economic diplomacy to open up larger markets. Importantly, it noted that China had been trying to increase its production from observing India's production methods in certain sectors, such as tea. The study recommended that the Indian government in a similar fashion should identify areas of competition and observe Chinese policies to emulate them.

In addition to China's export expansion, observers began to take notice of China's industrial capabilities and its possible contribution to its high growth rate. India pursued some domestic industrial reforms in the 1980s to open up more space for entrepreneurs. By this time it had been confirmed independently that China indeed was enjoying a higher rate of growth than it had in the 1960s and 1970s. This was the time that Indian analysts began to despair about India's chronic "Hindu rate of growth" between 3 and 3.5 percent per year. To look for other potential models, they turned greater attention to the high growth of East Asian NICs: South Korea, Taiwan, Hong Kong, and Singapore. But India's official plans – the Sixth Five Year Plan, 1981–85 and the Seventh Five Year Plan,

Table 4.5 Export competition between India and China, 1979–84

Product	*Country*	*Exports (US$ million)**		*Market share (%)**	
		1979	*1984*	*1979*	*1984*
Hand tools	India	46.4	27.7	1.3	0.7
	China	22.9	83.3	0.6	2.0
Industrial fasteners	India	16.4	4.1	0.6	0.1
	China	25.2	87.9	1.0	2.9
Cotton fabrics	India	187.7	188.3	3.4	3.2
	China	461.7	965.6	8.4	16.2
Leather footwear	India	25.8	38.4	0.3	0.4
	China	57.9	163.5	0.8	1.7
Cotton garments	India	467.5	563.3	6.5	5.4
	China	281.0	692.8	3.9	6.6
Hand-knotted carpets	India	202.4	208.7	13.4	18.0
	China	115.8	171.0	7.6	14.8

Source: Adapted from Sanjay Kathuria and Nisha Taneja, *India's Exports: The Challenge from China*, New Delhi: Indian Council for Research in International Economic Relations, 1986, table A.7, p. 68.

Note

* The export market here does not refer to the world market but to the combined market of twenty-two countries, most of them advanced industrial economies.

1986–90 – concluded that India's economy was too large and variegated to implement the type of export-oriented industrialization that the NICs pioneered.[37] Indian planners seemed caught between the recognition that China was outcompeting India, the suspicion that China's growth rate was not sustainable, and perhaps a lingering fixation that India still could innovate an economic path that had its own independent stamp.

Although this was the position of the official government plans, it no longer reflected a consensus. Unlike in the 1960s and 1970s, scholars and analysts outside the government were not ready to reject outright the Chinese or the East Asian model as inappropriate. They noted that the growth rates of China not only matched the earlier growth spurts of the NICs but also had proven sustainable for a giant country for a decade. As Drèze and Sen pointed out:

> China's choice of market-oriented reform and of a policy of integration with the world economy has given those policies a much wider hearing in India that they could have conceivably had on the basis of what had happened in countries that are much smaller and perceived to be quite dissimilar to India: Hong Kong, Taiwan, Singapore, even South Korea. From revolutionary inspiration to reformist passion, China has got India's ear again and again.[38]

In the late 1980s and the early 1990s many policymakers read with keen interest scholarly analyses of the NICs, trying to identify policy innovations or experiences that could be duplicated in India. Robert Wade's *Governing the Market*, for instance, was read by analytical policymakers, as they were particularly interested in promoting high growth while continuing an interventionist government.[39] Others, more adventurous, thought that India needed a decisive economic break from the past. As one policymaker stated in an interview:

> China's growth rates put Indian economists to shame. Here was a country that started at the same social and economic level.... We were boasting we could match [it] in greatness and capabilities. Well, that China just flew past us. We were bystanders.[40]

Immersed in this discourse, nationalist policy leaders, liberal and Western-trained, began to think that India needs not just to respond to China's progress but to consider emulating its economic path. But the political break had not yet appeared to initiate policy changes.

The context of the trigger

Although this study is focused primarily on explaining continuity rather than change, our review of the larger context requires considering the question of timing: if rivalry with China was so important, why did India's outward orientation begin coherently in 1991, thirteen years after China commenced its open-door policies? Aside from the simple answer that China is not the only influence on India's policymaking, I propose the following reasons. First, Indian policymakers took time to realize that India was falling far behind. They had to overcome the mentality of rejecting Chinese policies outright as inapplicable or unworthy; they also had to be certain that China's economic success was sustainable. Although China was already seeking foreign investment in the 1980s, especially in its export sector, the Indian state held on to its historically skeptical and restrictive stance on foreign capital. The Industrial Policy of 1985, enacted at the height of India's domestic economic liberalization program, stated for example a typical constraining clause on FDI: "foreign investment must be accompanied by transfer of technology."[41] As China's success in channeling foreign investment into export production became increasingly apparent, Indian policymakers began to take stock of the consequences of their restrictive policy stance. According to Jairam Ramesh, then Political Advisor to India's Finance Minister and later Minister of State for Commerce,

> 1990 has seen the rediscovery of East Asia by India. In the eighties, the East Asian model was rejected because it was seen as underwritten by the US and Japan. In the 90s it became evident just how wide the gap [between India and East Asia] has become.[42]

Along these lines a second reason can be proposed: the end of the Cold War quelled whatever ideological qualms India, the leader of non-aligned nations, might have had about adopting laissez faire and promoting the Western capitalist model of development and economic growth. C. Raja Mohan, a leading strategic analyst in India, put it in the following way:

> In 1978, when China changed policy, few people paid any attention. The success of East Asia became visible only in the mid to late eighties. We needed to catch up. It also helped that by the end of the eighties international capital became free from national identities. The Cold War was over. You no longer needed to depend on any particular country to get funds, you got it from the world market.[43]

The economic crisis of 1991 then provided a compelling circumstance to justify a switch in policy. After international reserves dwindled to just fourteen days' worth of imports, Indian policymakers felt extremely nervous. India was, in the words of Manmohan Singh at the parliament, "at the edge of a precipice … we have not experienced anything similar in the history of independent India."[44]

Envy and emulation, 1990s

It was in this policy ambience, both immediate and larger, that India began reforms toward opening up the economy, starting with a currency devaluation. In separate statements the Finance Minister, Manmohan Singh, and the Governor of the central bank, R. Venkitaramanan, explained the devaluation by pointing to competitive pressures from China in the export market.[45] It is important to note that this specific move was not triggered by dimensions of rivalry with China, but the policy objective was influenced strongly by the sense of *relative loss* for India that had been growing over the past decade. India needed to grow rapidly, and the prescription for growth was provided by China's experience, where exports and foreign investment were catalysts, the former to drive a rapid increase in the demand for output and the latter to inject the capital necessary to produce such output. The government's policy statements repeatedly made clear the importance of the connection among growth, exports, and investment. As justification of the opening up of India's economy, the government's annual *Economic Survey* pointed out in 1991 the success of East Asia: "Much more rapid growth is possible, as our neighbouring countries further east have demonstrated."[46] The *Economic Survey* the following year was also clear about the source of the main inspiration:

> The prosperity achieved by many developing countries in Asia, and also in other parts of the developing world, would have been unimaginable fifty years ago. The standard and quality of life of the citizens of these countries can be explained by neither their natural resources nor their domination of other countries. It is explained by sustained efforts at improving the quality of human resources, by policies that encourage investment and place a premium on efficiency, and a sustained thrust toward international competitiveness.[47]

Virtually every major policy survey in the 1990s came with envious references to China, with exhortations to emulate the path shown. The government's *Economic Survey 1993–94* stated:

> In some East Asian countries very high rates of FDI have been associated with high rates of growth of GDP and manufactured exports. China, a socialist market economy committed to self-reliance, attracted more than $15 billion of FDI in 1993 by allowing up to 100 per cent foreign equity and opening virtually every sector of the economy. India should not lag behind other Asian countries in reaping the benefits of foreign direct investment.[48]

In 1996, the *Economic Survey* again emphasized:

> India's economic development must harness the opportunities provided by international trade, modern technology, and world capital markets. China has shown how $30–$40 billion a year of foreign investment can be effectively harnessed for economic development.[49]

Interesting to observe is that China provided not just the prescription through its experience of sustainable growth but also possible targets or metrics. As the Finance Minister stated:

> For India to aspire to sustained growth at 7 to 9 percent over the next two decades, we have to be prepared to encourage a rapid increase in foreign direct investment to levels comparable to China's $30 billion or more per year.[50]

As noted in Chapter 2, given the political circumstances and the fragility of the government, neither policy continuity nor its political success was assured for the plan to raise growth through promoting economic openness. But the small pro-reformist policy circle, with the support of the prime minister, was convinced that sustained policies toward opening up India's economy, in the style of China, were the only way to close the gap with China and leverage the same opportunities that China was using to enrich itself rapidly. As Jairam Ramesh noted tersely, "One visit to east Asia is enough to show just where India is."[51] This was a purely outward-oriented assessment that was situated on a plane separate from domestic concerns, and thus it was unaffected by the boisterous "politics of causes and consequences," even though such politics resulted in electoral upheavals in India. The prevalent discourse on causes and consequences in fact failed to engage the government on the highly evolved motives for continuing with open-economy policies.

In the government's policy urgencies, the admiration of China blended simultaneously with a threat perception. Throughout this decade, the government, along with pro-reform interest groups and independent research organizations, continued to highlight the export threat posed by Chinese industry. While the government was implementing its open-economy agenda, research continued to emerge identifying a loss of India's competitive position to China and other Asian countries.[52] A study conducted by the Associated Chambers of Commerce and Industry (Assocham), one of India's major trade associations, identified new arenas of competition (such as seafood) in addition to the areas recognized previously, and urged for the development of "a strong export culture" like China's.[53] Another important analysis of exports was published in 1997.[54] It assessed India's competitive position in major export sectors and concluded that China had emerged as one of the three main competitors in virtually all of these areas, and was the strongest current competitor in textiles, tea, tapestry, and dyes, all of which were important exports for India. China was predicted in the future to become the strongest competitor also in textile yarn, jute, gems and precious stones, electrical machinery and non-electrical machine parts. The study, summarized in Table 4.6 below, however, treated China and Hong Kong as separate entities. Taken together, the two posed a competitive barrier in virtually every sector where India has a substantial market. There was only one major export category (iron ore, where Brazil is the main competitor) in which India did not face strong competition from China or Hong Kong at that time.

The situation has continued through 2000. As T. N. Srinivasan estimates, "In almost every commodity and market, China's share has grown rapidly since 1978, whereas India's share has grown much less, if at all." Srinivasan's findings on China's and India's shares of the world market in India's key commodi-

Table 4.6 India's export competition: Marjit/Raychaudhuri (1997) findings

Commodity group	*Strongest competitors*	*Emerging competitors*
Leather	Hong Kong	
Textiles: clothing	China, Hong Kong	
Textile products	China, Hong Kong	
Cotton fabrics	China, Hong Kong	
Textile yarn	Hong Kong	China
Non-cotton woven textiles	Hong Kong	
Jute and other fibres		China
Tea	China	Hong Kong
Floor cover, tapestry	China	Hong Kong
Pearl, precious stones	Hong Kong	China
Iron ore concentrates		
Synthetic dye	China, Hong Kong	
Electrical machinery	Hong Kong	China
Non-electrical machinery	Hong Kong	
Non-electrical machine parts	Hong Kong	China

Source: adapted from Sugata Marjit and Ajitava Raychaudhuri, *India's Exports: An Analytical Study*, Delhi: Oxford University Press, 1997, table 3.1, pp. 34–35.

Note
The chart marks whether Hong Kong and China are present among the top three competitors for each export commodity group under study.

Table 4.7 World market shares of China and India in select commodities

		1978–81 (%)	*1988–91 (%)*	*1998–2000 (%)*	*Change (%) (1978–98)*
China	Garments	3.9	14.9	20.4	423
	Fabrics	5.1	8.2	9.4	84
	Leathers*	0.4	2.6	4.8	1100
	Jewelry	1.1	2.7	9.4	754
India	Garments	3.9	3.8	5.3	36
	Fabrics	2.0	1.4	2.4	20
	Leathers*	8.9	5.5	3.4	–62
	Jewelry	0.6	2.2	4.6	666

Source: T. N. Srinivasan, "China and India: Economic Performance, Competition and Cooperation – an Update," Paper prepared at Economic Growth Center, Yale University, February 2004, Table 4.

Note
* Includes leather manufactures.

ties are reproduced in Table 4.7. Similarly, *The Economist* reported that "Chinese textile and garment firms have handily dominated their Indian competitors," raising their market share from 24 percent to 45 percent between 2001 and 2004 while the Indian share has been essentially stagnant.[55]

In order to spur trade and investment, both in foreign and domestic markets, one of the key measures taken by the government was to reduce import barriers, both tariff and non-tariff. Before liberalization, India's peak tariff rate was 300 percent, the highest in the world. In July 1991, India lowered peak tariffs to 150 percent, which brought it to the same level as China's. By the end of 1997 India had lowered its average tariffs to 20.3 percent, comparable to China's level (20.1 percent), in a series of steps, each of which seemed to match the level prevailing in China. A similar pattern existed with regard to promoting foreign investment, where a variety of Indian policies took cue from earlier Chinese policies.[56] One of the main Chinese initiatives that Indian policymakers studied closely was its Special Economic Zones (SEZs), which India tried to recreate first by modifying its existing (mostly underperforming) Export Processing Zones. In 2000 India decided to expand them, renaming them Special Economic Zones and stating that the aim was "to replicate the free trade zones in China which were contributing about 40 percent to Beijing's total exports."[57]

Understanding emulation

One part of ascertaining emulation is to look at the correspondence between two sets of policies, one promulgated earlier and another later – essentially what I did in the previous section. But by looking at patterns alone it is difficult to ascertain how the process takes place, and to reject the hypothesis that the pattern is merely coincidental rather than imitative of a rival's prior policies. I undertook a set of interviews of policymakers in India in 1997 in an effort to understand better the incentives and the process (the list of interviewees is given in Appendix 1). For the sake of brevity, I will restrict myself to one excerpt from one of the interviews that I found to be most representative. The interviewee was Dr. Arjun Sengupta, one of the major architects of India's Ninth Plan (1997–2002), which established "indicative planning" commensurate with a market economy and outward orientation.[58]

JA: Is India trying to match or imitate Chinese open-door policies?

AS: We respond to what we think will affect our export competitiveness. But we are not imitating the Chinese in that sense. We are adopting important aspects of their model, certainly, but we are always conscious about how those would serve our national interest.

JA: What do you see as the national interest?

AS: Well, of course, these are the ideals that go back to Gandhiji and other leaders, and they are specified clearly in our constitution: democracy, harmony, social justice, growth of opportunities, and a positive role in world affairs. These are the main pillars.

JA: Does Chinese competition affect those interests?

AS: It would affect particular interests in particular constituencies. Ultimately part of it must affect our competitive position and bargaining power in the world.

JA: In your policy discussions do you use concrete examples about China's lead on India?

AS: Yes, it comes up, but not always. We are interested to learn from them because we cannot deny that they have overtaken us economically. We've fallen behind, and everyone knows that we need to catch up with the rest of the world, with Asia, with China and the Southeast Asian countries. You'll hear about that in our meetings. So of course we want to emulate the success of East Asia. We are part of Asia and we cannot afford to stay behind.

JA: Why is China's lead important, from a planner's perspective?

AS: They have a successful model, first of all. And China is our main competitor. It's an economic powerhouse. If we don't catch up and protect our interests here and abroad, we will not be able to deliver what our people deserve.

Open-ended interviews can have problems of reliability and accuracy of interpretation. But based on several similar interviews, as well as secondary material reviewed above, it is possible to draw some inferences about the process or practice of policy emulation. First, Indian policymakers decided that the Chinese model should be studied closely and followed for four main reasons: China and India are similar in many respects; China has emerged as India's main economic rival, requiring a strategic response; China has proven that open-door policies are sustainable for a large developing country; and China's pursuit of such policies have accorded it a greater role and more advantageous bargaining position in world affairs.

It should be noted that although I have treated the state as a unified entity making national policies, the actual process of policymaking is more decentralized and haphazard. Policy deliberations seem to include discussions of China's policies, but they are not organized into a coherent, national strategy through a clear-cut process. Usually, various ministries and departments prepare internal analytical reports in different sectors, which are then discussed in the pertinent department, followed by policy response. Committees have been formed in specific areas to allow better coordination in forming strategies and policies. The Cabinet Committee on Economic Affairs was formed to advise on economic policy prior to promulgation. In 2000, a "Group of Ministers" panel was created to review foreign direct investment policy. Although the government, especially the finance ministry, has routine and fairly sophisticated ways of monitoring the economy, the push for policies to enhance competitiveness often comes from outside the government. One type of pressure is negative; it comes from the failure to emulate. One critic noted for instance:

> India remains a country inveterately hostile to FDI in practice even if not in theory. Between 1991 and 1998, only 21.7 per cent of the $55 billion of FDI approvals actually materialised as inflows.... The contrast with China ... could not be greater ... India failed to learn from China's experience that to

> mesh one's national economy into the global one it was necessary to attract investment not into "sophisticated" industries but into simple ones.[59]

Analysts in this vein have frequently recommended specific policies or policy modifications based on either competitive advantage or competitive loss to China. The three major peak industry organizations, Assocham, Federation of Indian Chambers of Commerce and Industry (FICCI), and Confederation of Indian Industry (CII) regularly meet with government executives, apprise them about needs to enhance India's competitive position, and obtain promises of policy response. After the government created SEZs, for example, Assocham and FICCI supported the move, but noted that Indian SEZs would not be able to compete with Chinese counterparts unless labor laws are made more flexible. In 2002–03 CII adopted a new theme: "Competitiveness for India Inc," with special attention to policies that can increase manufacturing competitiveness vis-à-vis China.[60] Since 2000, NASSCOM, the trade organization for information technology, has also been studying China and recommending policy to the government on a fairly regular basis. Advice also came frequently from investment firms who had established a foothold in India. In 2006, Goldman Sachs even asked India's government to "take a leaf out of the Chinese political system" and implement labor reforms, if it wanted to be the world's third largest economy by 2050.[61]

As a result of the myriad sources of observation, counseling, admonition, and pressure, emulation can be a haphazard process and not entirely a result of long-term strategy, even though informed by an underlying strategic and globalist frame of logic. In important parts, it is an outcome of numerous, and sometime unrelated, tactical policy decisions. Dispersed decision-making is partly a consequence of India's giantism, a function of "layers of official hierarchy," as John Lewis would put it.[62] Yet those disparate decisions, especially at the higher levels, are taken ultimately in a strong context of nationalism – and in India's case, globalism – influenced by years or decades of official training on the goals of the state. This has an effect of imparting a level of consistency even when policies may seem haphazard; in that environment, through efforts at tactical *micro*-policy responses, an effect of strategic *macro*-policy response is reached. Individual Indian states have also created their own investor-friendly policy regime. In particular, Maharashtra, Karnataka, and Tamil Nadu have been competing aggressively against each other to attract investment.[63] Investigating those, however, is outside the scope of this project, and so no conclusions can be reached about whether this effect of emulation is present at the level of India's states.

The logic of continuity

The specific way that envy and emulation combined in India offers us clues as to why policies were continued. To understand this logic of continuity we need to begin with ascertaining how India's post-1991 economic reforms were different from earlier episodes of liberalization in procedure and substance. Unlike earlier episodes, Indian policymakers concluded that this time the thrust of economic reforms must be on openness in the *external* economy. The external focus ensured that the policymakers from the start felt comparatively less accountable to the vagaries of domestic politics, and accordingly may have been less sensitive to the politics of causes and consequences that we reviewed in Chapter 2.

Second, policymakers' emphasis on raising openness of the external economy was due directly to their observed success of China and East Asia. China was treated publicly as the benchmark; Indian economy consequently would have to strive until the benchmark was reached. If China had shown "how $30–$40 billion a year of foreign investment can be effectively harnessed," India would need to sustain favorable policies until it too could attract and absorb a similar level of investment. Most of these newer definitions of success were loftier than what earlier domestic-focused reforms had aimed to accomplish, and they would thus require continuity over a fairly lengthy period. Subramanian Swamy, one of the pioneers of India–China comparisons, wrote in 2000 in a commentary titled, "Can India Catch Up With China?":

> India cannot close its per capita income gap [with China] by 2020, without a much faster GDP growth rate (for example, of 10 per cent a year), for which an even greater effort to raise the level of investment will have to be made. This is easier said than done.[64]

Three years later, Guruswamy, Kaul, and Handa estimated the required rate of growth upwards, assuming of course that the current policy trajectory would continue:

> The challenge ahead of us is not catching with China's growth rate, which inevitably must slow down. When nations compete, growth rates matter little if one is already well ahead.... To do that [i.e. catch up with China] in 2020 we need to grow at 11.6 per cent and to do that long after most of us are gone in 2050, India must grow at 8.9 per cent every year.[65]

Third, China had not only provided a future target, but once India had committed itself to striving toward the target, China's performance began to serve as a continuous gauge of India's performance and progress. This was a subtle yet significant shift in the evolution in India's rivalry with China, for rivalry was no longer expressed mainly through actual events but could be measured and perceived virtually at any point in time, by culling and comparing economic statistics. Every serious economic narrative – sections of this book included – now contained explicit or implicit markers, providing a verdict on comparative performance. By expanding into the economic arena, rivalry had become ubiquitous and continuous.

Fourth, as liberalization began to lead toward increases in exports and competitiveness, vigilance on and analysis of China increased rapidly in many different directions. Keeping a watch on China was no longer confined to research institutes supported by government grants or international universities. It became the concern of trade associations, unions, journalists, industrialists, investors and bankers, politicians of all hue, and policymakers from an increasing number of departments. At press conferences and briefings organized by the government's economic departments, it has become routine for reporters to ask questions about India's competitive position with China. From exchange rates to capital controls, foreign investment, imports and exports, subsidies, business regulation, banking, logistics, taxes, labor, infrastructure, technology, intellectual property, entertainment, retail, the environment, policing – virtually every possible area of comparative study opened up, as so much seemed to potentially have a bearing on India's competitiveness with China. One result was that policies were no longer promulgated primarily at sporadic milestones during the fiscal year. The regular annual budget process remains the major occasion of policy promulgation. Investment policies, which used to be promulgated usually once a year during "the budget season," have become more frequent. Changes in tariff rates or other import-related rules began to be announced several times a year. The reserve bank's exchange rate, of course, could be adjusted every morning. In between these, policy tweaks appear to have become more frequent throughout the year, propelled by new grievances, new analyses, and perhaps a political urge to outperform existing economic records. India has been transiting from a primarily episodic pattern of policymaking to a relatively more "real-time" and more continuous form of policymaking.

Fifth, the pursuit of openness itself exposed Indian businesses to Chinese competition in a way that they, previously sheltered, never had to face before. As noted by studies cited earlier, Indian exporters, prodded by the government's open-economy policies, confronted their Chinese counterparts in virtually every market to which they expanded. This created further pressure on the government to increase competitiveness of Indian industry, encouraging further external and domestic liberalization. Policy continuity and economic rivalry essentially fed into each other. A similar situation was faced with luring foreign investment, where, in the words of an Indian policymaker, "there's a common pool of investment resources we're all competing for."[66] Increased competition for scarce resources encouraged continual policy changes geared toward increasing the attractiveness of India's investment regime relative to those of its competitors, of which China was the most prominent.

Finally, China was showing little sign of slowing down. Thus, as Indian policymakers began to open up the economy with the goal of emulating or "catching up" to China, they were under pressure to increase the extent of openness rather than decrease it, even though important domestic constituencies had grievances against different aspects of liberalization. For example, even nine years into open-economy policies, C. Raja Mohan wrote in a passionate column after visiting China: "China thinks big; India thinks small. What a difference it has made in just one generation! By adopting a bold strategy, China has raced past the timid India on the economic front in just one generation."[67]

Similarly, Jeffrey Sachs was one of the economists urging faster policy change rather than a cautious approach:

> Why is it that India, which provides the largest market after China in the developing world is unable to attract substantial volume of FDI? Further, when it comes to comparing China and India, why can India not match or even outpace China in attracting FDI given India's superior conditions regarding the rule of law, democracy, and the widely-spoken English language?[68]

India's economic targets, accordingly, were always under intense pressure. Toward the beginning of the decade, the targets were expressed mostly as policy targets, such as "liberalization of import quotas." After the first two years of reform policies, for instance, the government noted that "the most striking evidence of progress has been in the external sector," urging that opening up the economy must be continued.[69] Increasingly since 2000, the targets have become specifically performance-related. The *Export–Import Policy 2000–2001* for example targeted 20–25 percent annual exports growth, citing China as an exemplar and urging for "a paradigm shift in the country's export policy."[70] The *Medium Term Export Strategy 2002–2007* targeted achieving a 1 percent share of the world's exports in 2007, for which it wanted exports to increase by 11.9 percent compound annual growth.[71] The first goal of the *Foreign Trade Strategy 2004–2007* was "[t]o double our percentage share of global merchandise trade within the next five years." In all major policy documents now, neither the conviction nor the underlying sense of competitiveness shows any sign of fading. Consider the following passage from the government's *Economic Survey 2006–7*, published fifteen years after reforms began:

> Among the priorities, first is rising to the challenge of maintaining and managing high growth.... It is necessary to make the required adjustments in mindsets, economic behaviour, and policy making. There is no scope for uneasiness or nervousness about high growth. In the latter half of the 20th century, the East Asian "miracle" has been followed by even more rapid growth in China in more recent times. Fostering the momentum of growth in India continues to be a top priority.[72]

"For India to become a major player": shifts in globalism

The very first line of India's *Foreign Trade Policy 2004–2009* begins: "For India to become a major player in world trade..."[73] The foremost inspiration is not for India "to develop," nor "to eradicate poverty," let alone "promote social justice"; it is to increase global influence and status. Without globalism framing the overall vision, the need to catch up to China would not have been so urgent. As the Chairman of India's Foreign Investment Promotion Board explained in an interview:

> There was a definite expressed need for catching up. India had to occupy its proper position in the global economy. Economic competition with China became more important after '91, when we also opened up and started to get investors to come here.[74]

While bilateral rivalry by itself would lead Indian policymakers to compare their country against China, globalism expanded the perspective and relativized India against the full international hierarchy. Thus a relative economic loss against China was simultaneously a deterioration in India's overall bid for globalism. In that vein, just as Baldev Nayar had previously observed in the security realm a mismatch between India's role-pretensions and capabilities, Jagdish Bhagwati comments on India's economic policymaking elite:

> [It] came to realize that there was a growing dissonance between India's traditional claim to respect and attention, and her shrinking ability to command them as her economic policies and failure became more widely known and a subject of derision ... a superiority complex and inferiority status."[75]

However, through its continuous presence and competitive pressure, the economic dimension of strategic rivalry brought about a reappraisal and important shifts in India's standard approach toward globalism. Successful globalism, Indian analysts recognized, required openness. Furthermore, self-reliance is better served by outward orientation. Finally, raising India's economic visibility required economic statecraft. We now turn to discussing these shifts.

Globalism and openness

In the calculus of Indian policymakers, the need to wrest export market share or to attract high foreign investment was not just for the sake of promoting Indian exports or feeding the investment-hungry economy. They saw it as the only way that India could hope to still reach its globalist aims after a decades-long decline to China. As one of my interviewees in the government in 1997 stated:

> If China continues in the fast-paced direction, India was sure to lose out more market share in exports and investment. We believed that it would hamper our technological progress and there might be no way left to match China's future domination of Asia.[76]

This view was propounded by outside analysts as well. In a review of foreign direct investment, Nirupam Bajpai and Jeffrey Sachs noted the connection between FDI and economic growth, one of the benefits of which, shown by India's neighbors, was an increase in "security and geopolitical influence."[77] Raising geopolitical influence required a high-performing economy, the fastest way to which was through attracting investment and promoting exports, as

China had shown. Seen another way, political influence was probably the most important by-product of economic power. A vivid example was in China's successful handling of the Asian crisis in a way that defied the prescriptions emanating from the IMF. Having been under a barrage of allegations about "surrendering" to IMF, Indian policymakers were impressed by the fact that China was not affected as deeply as Japan and Korea, which were thought to be strong Asian countries. This showed them China's confidence in its own abilities, and also increased India's confidence in emulating the Chinese model. China's successful coping with the Asian crisis, in addition, had increased its bargaining power vis-à-vis the United States. Some strategic thinkers, like Sanjaya Baru, urged Indian policymakers to study closely how China coped with the crisis and how others faltered, insisting that "India must adopt many of the key elements of the model."[78]

A power with globalist aspirations, as Indian strategists realized while watching China in the 1980s and 1990s, must be capable of projecting its economic power well beyond its borders. To do that, the economy would need to be opened up in order to create links with the outside world, even at the risk of allowing access to one's rival. An inward-looking China would not have had economic influence over the world; its influence was created through strong export and investment links. Ultimately, it is only through sustained openness, both inward and outward, that India can achieve its globalist aims. Baru makes this point clear:

> A more open Indian economy is a necessary condition for acquiring a higher profile in the region. Unless India's economic involvement with the region increases, it is unlikely to match the influence of the three Big Powers in the region, namely, the United States, China and Japan.[79]

Outward model of self-reliance

The more that Indian policymakers opened up their economy, the more they realized that their successful bid for globalism necessitated openness, thus creating additional incentives for policy continuity. But greater links with the outside world could threaten India's century-long project of achieving self-reliance. The *Economic Survey 1991–92*, which was the first major review of the economy after the 1991 policy break, argued that gaining strength and self-reliance have been objectives of economic policy in India since independence, but added a change in perspective:

> Self-reliance does not mean isolation. We live in a world of great variety – of people, resources, of knowledge and behaviour. It is there for us to cooperate with, trade with, learn from, and contribute to. It is there for us to measure ourselves against.[80]

A reappraisal of self-reliance is what the reformist government requested of citizens. The following year, the *Economic Survey 1992–93* emphasized change through introspection, proposing that "true self-reliance is to be found in the capacity for self-improvement."[81] Policy leaders continued to promote both openness and globalism as compatible with self-reliance. In a metaphor-laden budget speech to the parliament in 1996, the Finance Minister stated:

> In an interdependent world, Swadeshi [self-reliance] must not be interpreted to mean economic isolation but rather self-reliance in building a prosperous India which interacts as an equal with other countries in the world. We seek to build a new India which, in the words of Gandhiji, will be like a house with windows open on all sides; let ideas from all the cultures and civilisations of the world freely flow in; but we must refuse to be blown off our feet by any one of them.[82]

Openness was one aspect of this changed view. Another aspect related to empowerment. As reviewed earlier in the chapter, India's discourse of self-reliance was essentially synonymous with economic empowerment. With an inward orientation, India's means of empowerment was domestic industrialization, to gain the ability to produce goods that were needed in times of peace as well as war. With globalism now necessitating an outward orientation (following China's post-1979 trajectory), what was needed for empowerment, from the Indian strategic perspective, was strength in trade, perhaps more so than industrialization. Trade would promote faster growth, trade-dependence would provide a quicker ability to buy from the world market, if not produce, the necessary goods, even to wage war. In this neo-mercantilist equation, self-reliance essentially means having the wherewithal: access to international capital and large enough international reserves that increased a state's purchasing power. Back in 1971, when a much poorer and inward-looking India was preparing for its first nuclear explosion, a study by the US government predicted financial insolvency for India if it pursued the development of a nuclear force.[83] This type of possibility could not be allowed to happen. As one analyst wrote:

> At the core of any national security strategy towards Pakistan (and, even more important, in relation to China) must be a commitment to accelerate economic growth. Without a higher growth path, India will find itself incapable of handling security threats from Pakistan and will continue to fall behind China.[84]

Furthermore, economic security came less from independence from the world economy, and more from its polar opposite: cultivating strong economic ties with the world (including one's rival) such that the risk of disturbing those ties becomes too expensive a proposition. Security could be derived out of economic interdependence. As another strategic analyst wrote: "What India needs today is an outward-looking model of self-reliance that guarantees national security by giving the world a stake in India's stability and prosperity."[85]

The implication for the continuity of open-economy policy is clear. In fact, this logic of empowerment, of raising prominence internationally and deriving security from interdependence works only through the pursuit of economic openness.

Economic statecraft

The late-1990s and the early 2000s constituted a crucial transition in India's evolution of globalism. The nationalist party BJP had been elected to power. The Congress-led government in the early and mid-1990s had been successful in stabilizing the economy, changing its orientation outward, and expanding the legitimacy of the new economic platform. After ascending to power BJP utilized that platform and boosted India's bid for globalism with nuclear aggression and an economic assertiveness rooted in the new "outward" logic of self-reliance. For the first time in India's history, a concerted effort at economic statecraft had begun.

The term "economic statecraft" is often used to denote the use of economic instruments toward political aims, such as using economic sanctions to promote democratization or to punish human rights violations. In this study the term will convey the other side as well, that is, the usage of state resources to promote economic power internationally. India's practice could be described as a soft economic statecraft, geared toward securing new markets and investment, rather than a heavy-handed type that aims at colonial or punitive purposes. (There are exceptions: In 1989–90 India put economic sanctions on Nepal, and was considering it again in 2005. There were also some calls for India to impose economic sanctions on Fiji after a military takeover there in 2006.)

India's transition toward promoting and using economic power was an outgrowth of confidence arising out of success in open-economy policies. This confidence was perceptible in both policy makers and policy observers. From the late 1990s, major interests that supported efforts toward openness began to use language not only about competition but about global prominence. For example, when SEZs were announced in India, the influential newspaper *The Hindu* hailed the decision assertively: "It is a bold approach to the difficult imperative of placing India in the global mart as a player of no mean significance."[86] The cautious support of early 1990s had given way to confident optimism, and in turn, greater expectations. Some were exhorting the government toward becoming more aggressive at marketing India to international investors. Bajpai and Sachs wrote:

> China has achieved a lot more in manufactured export production than India and for no particular reason. India has the resource base, it has the entrepreneurship, has the access to the sea, a vast labour force, it has everything that coastal China has had except the interest of the Government.[87]

BJP was for some time the right marketing agent for India's new model of confidence and self-reliance. With an aim toward increasing international attention to

India, as well as India's own attention to the potential of economic change, the BJP government invested in two catch phrases. The first one was "Feel Good." This was adopted earlier in BJP's tenure, and was targeted mostly domestically, at Indian businesses as well as politically-conscious citizens, to highlight the progress that the government had made. It went into the 2004 election campaign banking on "the feel good factor."[88] The second one, "India Shining," was adopted later in the tenure, and directed both domestically and internationally. The expensive marketing campaign associated with "India Shining" showcased an increasingly consumerist Indian upper-middle class. Although successful internationally, the marketing backfired in BJP's election bid in 2004, in which rural and lower income constituencies expressed that they were not feeling that good about their own economic prospects.[89]

Nonetheless, the need for stronger economic diplomacy and marketing has been raised consistently by supporters of globalism. Writing from the United States, Bajpai and Sachs have urged India to take on greater economic leadership than before, using venues such as "the G-20, future international summits between developed and developing countries, the International Monetary Fund, World Bank, World Trade Organisation, and the World Health Organisation."[90] India has been more successful in international forums like these, where policy-makers were free from close scrutiny by their domestic constituencies. C. Raja Mohan, however, noted that the Indian approach in trade forums were still hostage to ideologies of the past which treated trade as "a necessary evil," instead of adopting a pragmatic form of economic statecraft. In a trenchant column he wrote:

> There is communist China engaging in difficult negotiations with the entire international community to find an entry into the World Trade Organisation. Here are the Indian ideologues – of the ruling party on the right as well as the left in the Opposition – suggesting India could walk out of the global trading system.... If China is pragmatic in its approach, India remains ideological ... China's experience shows trade can be a powerful instrument in promoting national prosperity, regional clout and international standing. If India is to emulate China, it needs to liberate its trade policy from the clutches of old ideological slogans and bureaucratic practices.[91]

Outside intergovernmental organizations, the BJP government went on a full marketing blitz to woo foreign investment and promote its capabilities, with an arsenal ranging from posters and tables at conferences, trade fairs, to gala shows at the World Economic Forum in Davos. Indo-US Summits were organized to market not only India as a whole, but specific areas or niches. The 1999 summit was titled "Dynamic South," which was held in Chennai to market the "Silicon Triangle" (Chennai, Bangalore, and Hyderabad were the vertices). In 2002, a "Destination India" conference for investors was held in Zurich, in which Commerce Minister Murasoli Maran marketed India as having a business environment better than China, and pledged to work toward matching China's rate in

FDI as a proportion of GDP.[92] The potential of the Silicon Triangle was highlighted by India's soft economic statecraft in many of these promotional events, taking IT and services as India's inherent strength and a key differentiator from China: India was the emerging knowledge center of the world, and therefore the fount of future innovations, while China was the world's manufacturing center. India spoke English widely and had already become a software power and a rapidly growing outsourcing hub for a variety of services, such as programming, data entry, medical transcripts, and call centers. Its engineers and project managers were said to be less expensive than China's.[93] In 2003, the Indian IT industry organized a novel event in which its blue-chip customers, like General Electric and Citibank, were to promote to other firms in Europe these advantages of doing business in India. This "hard sell" was done "against a backdrop of rising Western interest in China as the world's potential new workshop."[94] To promote its advantages further, India lobbied for removing restrictions on the supply of skilled workers in services during the Doha Round of world trade negotiations.

But China was working toward closing this gap. In 2001, India's software exports amounted to $3.9 billion, compared to China's $130 million. But China's domestic software sales were $2.1 billion, compared to $360 million in India.[954] This signaled the existence of significant software capability that was hampered mainly by language. When Bill Gates visited India in 2002, he counseled Indian policymakers to not become complacent about the country's IT lead, and asked them to watch China closely. A 2002 survey by NASSCOM, the trade association for IT and related services, stated that China already had a better infrastructure and had made considerable advances in the domestic IT market. A 2004 report by investment bankers Morgan Stanley predicted that China would likely catch up to India's dominance in IT services within five years. Indian media reacted with loud anxiety when they learned of the Chinese leadership's pledge to accelerate proficiency in English and further improve their technology infrastructure.[96]

What many considered to be India's inherent global strengths could not be taken for granted. Even though BJP's removal from power has removed some of the pure glitz in marketing India, Indian policymakers recognize the need to continue economic diplomacy aggressively in this area of rivalry. Interesting for us is the implication for openness. There is no doubt for either nationalists or critics that India's reputation as IT and services hub is a direct result of strong links with the international economy that have been created since 1991. Most now recognize that maintaining a global presence against China would require continuity with India's open-economy policy, and possibly, an intensification of economic statecraft.

Globalism and rivalry: emerging fronts

Newer sites have emerged as battlegrounds where the competing globalisms of India and China are beginning to collide. Some of them may even begin to provide incentives for *dis*continuities in policy. But what we will find in common across all these areas is an intensification of India–China rivalry across the world – and in that, the inception of a concrete manifestation of economic globalism. This chapter will conclude by briefly reviewing these emerging fronts, which may provide us with some basis to speculate, in the next chapter, on the future of India's open-economy policy.

Competing diasporas

As Indian strategists begin to encounter China's presence around the world, they have been eyeing potential sources of power abroad, the foremost of which is the large Indian diaspora, usually referred to as the NRIs (Non-Resident Indian). An even larger group has been designated beyond NRIs, referred to as the PIO (People of Indian Origin), who are able to trace some form of ties to India. NRIs number over twenty million, a fourfold increase over their number in 1960. They have been said to have generated about $160 billion in annual income in 2003, successful especially in high-technology industries. One study estimates that ethnic Indians run 7 percent of the 11,443 high-tech firms in Silicon Valley. Their presence is much greater once computer scientists, programmers, engineers, and other employees beyond the top management are counted. This high-tech diaspora is a source of knowledge and material resources, but they face fierce competition from the overseas Chinese, who total about fifty-five million. Even in the British space program, the vast majority of the scientists are from India and China.[97]

This worldwide arena of human resources is significant for both globalism and rivalry. NRIs and PIO give India a global presence and image, just as the overseas Chinese do. Recognizing this, India's Prime Minister Vajpayee called in 2001 for forging "a partnership among the Children of Mother India so that our country can emerge as a major global player." India's foremost strategy of engaging this population is to encourage them to invest in India, following China's success with its population abroad, which, by one Indian estimate, has been involved with 80 percent investment in China since liberalization began.[98] Past Indian policy was content with encouraging NRIs to open high-interest foreign exchange fund or bank accounts in India. More recently, as policymaking has become more strategic, the emphasis has been on trying to encourage closer investment and trading links between knowledge-based industries in India and the high-tech diaspora.[99] Needless to say, increasing the involvement of this global resource requires India to stay open economically.

Encounters in the extended neighborhood

In raising global influence, Indians firms are encountering China's presence virtually everywhere where it has a strategic economic interest. From within and outside the government, there has been increasing pressure for "rediscovering India's extended neighbourhood, regaining its strategic leverages in the region, and reclaiming its historic role in the areas abutting the subcontinent."[100] Indian policymakers have responded since the mid-1990s by pursuing a "Look East" policy, targeting greater interaction with what China considers its immediate neighborhood: the ASEAN countries. By 2003 India signed two agreements of broad cooperation with ASEAN. The erstwhile Prime Minister Vajpayee also offered a unilateral "open skies" policy between major Indian cities and all ten of the ASEAN capitals.[101] Within this region, Burma has emerged as a site of intense competition between Indian and Chinese strategies, interested in particular to exploit Burma's abundant energy reserves. Offered a pipeline by both China and India, Burma's ruling junta decided in May 2007 in favor of China. Both countries have agreements with Burma to share part of the trading gains from Shwe gas reserves, one of Asia's largest repositories of natural gas. In addition, China has been establishing military installations in the country, especially to obtain naval access to the Indian Ocean, a development that is not taken lightly by Indian strategists.[102]

India's economic statecraft in the Middle East, which provides almost three-quarters of its oil, is also on the rise. In exploring newer energy sources, state-backed Indian firms have been encountering China in regions as far flung as Sudan and Kazakhstan. Indian Prime Minister Manmohan Singh admitted that China has been in the lead in this competition: "I find China ahead of us in planning for the future in the field of energy security. We can no longer be complacent and must learn to think strategically, to think ahead, and to act swiftly and decisively."[103]

In 2005, both Chinese and Indian national oil companies scrambled to acquire PetroKazakhstan, which holds lucrative oilfields in central Asia. China National Petroleum Corporation (CNPC) has been planning to build a pipeline to channel oil from Kazakhstan directly to China. The auction was awarded to China even though India put in a higher bid. India's petroleum minister accused "lack of propriety and transparency" in the process, in an unusual outburst. India's Oil and Natural Gas Corporation (ONGC) lost bids to CNPC in Angola, Nigeria, and Ecuador as well. ONGC lost a $620 million bid to a Chinese company for an oilfield in Nigeria, even after offering $200 million to help develop railways in that region. A few months later, India changed tack, and joined hands with CNPC in a co-bid to purchase a 38 percent stake in Syria's largest oil producer, and signed an agreement to cooperate further. India's petroleum minister said that it would reduce "mindless rivalry" going on between the two countries over securing energy supplies.[104] It was a pragmatic tactical move for India, but it remains to be seen how long the cooperation lasts given the underlying competition between the two for resources. Meanwhile the Indian government has begun investing in Sudan, as has China, and has been in negotiations to construct a pipeline from Khartoum to the Red Sea to speed up oil exports.

In Africa, Chinese and Indian firms have also been investing in raw materials, supported by their respective governments. They have emerged as the largest investors in Sub-Saharan Africa, exceeding the FDI of OECD countries in that continent. Between 1999 and 2002, Indian FDI in the region ($415 million) exceeded that of China ($339 million). Between 2002 and mid-2005, Indian companies had twenty-nine investment projects underway in five Sub-Saharan countries (Kenya, Mauritius, Nigeria, Tanzania, South Africa), while Chinese companies had twelve (in Angola, Nigeria, Tanzania, South Africa, and Zambia).[1054] Evidently, economic openness and economic statecraft have been closely linked in service to India's bid for a global presence.

Growth of India Inc.

Large Indian companies, now often referred to as India Inc., have been expanding operations outside India since the 1960s, much before the Indian government began reaching out with economic statecraft. By the early 1980s India emerged as a major independent source of technology in the third world. By 1989 there were 193 Indian joint ventures abroad.[106] Indian businesses have been expanding even more rapidly since the 1990s. Their confidence is palpable, especially in the IT sector. In 2000, the chairman of Infosys, one of the largest Indian technology services firms, asserted: "We have to prove that an Indian company can be a market leader in G-7 [the seven largest industrial economies]." The company has been employing people from many countries, especially developing countries, and promoting multiculturalism.[107] By the mid-2000s, this type of confidence is seen in other sectors as well. A 2006 editorial in *Financial Express* put it appropriately:

> A zooming Sensex [Index of the Bombay Stock Exchange], a confident corporate sector and some global success stories.... What a difference from the insecure days of 1992 when the Bombay Club of industrialists got together to protest against economic liberalisation ... government policies may be indecisive, but corporate India is surging ahead with enviable confidence at all levels.[108]

The market value of listed companies in India was over $650 billion in mid-2006, representing an increase of $268 billion within just a year. With a large pool of resources available, Indian companies have made over 300 overseas acquisitions since 2000, worth over $10 billion. "India's role is no longer solely that of a global back-office," gushed one industry observer, paying a tribute to India Inc.[109]

With newfound confidence, many Indian companies have begun to target the Chinese market, which they used to avoid for fear of "China's brutal manufacturing power."[110] Figure 4.6 depicts the steep rise in mutual trade, which reached $33 billion in 2006 (including trade with Hong Kong). China is now India's second largest trading partner, after the United States. Since 2000, India's exports to Mainland China have been increasing by 55 percent a year on average. The potential for Indian companies to grow is estimated to be large. Bharat Forge, India's largest auto components firm, estimates the potential for exporting automobile parts to China as $30 billion, and has been making plans to be at the forefront of that expansion.[111] Indian firms have expanded from the automotive sector, industrial materials and fasteners, to even consumer goods. Although they are still a small presence in China, their rapid expansion there will open up a new, hitherto unknown, turf for rivalry. Fueled by India's liberalization, these global companies have now become the strongest supporter of the continuity of openness.

Bombay Club redux?

Corporate confidence notwithstanding, India's openness has boosted China's exports to India as well, creating both economic and political problems. Chinese exports to India have grown especially quickly since 2001, when the BJP government removed most remaining quantitative restrictions on imports. Between 1995 and 2000, Chinese exports increased by around 17 percent a year. Between 2001 and 2006, China's exports in India have been increasing by about 50 percent a year (see Figure 4.6).

Indian discourse about China shifted from export competitiveness and FDI to import competition within the Indian market, with imagery of a new Chinese invasion – this time by consumer products rather than soldiers, as one observer put it. In response to strong accusations from domestic producers, India began to lodge dumping complaints in WTO and impose its own anti-dumping duties. Of

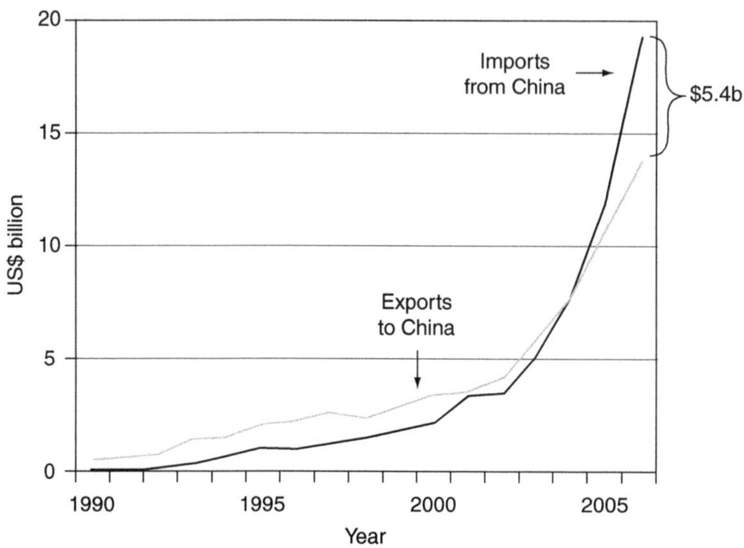

Figure 4.6 India's trade with China, 1990–2006 (source: International Monetary Fund, *Direction of Trade Statistics* (online).

Note
Figures include trade with both mainland China and Hong Kong.

the forty-one anti-dumping duties levied by India in 1999–2000, twenty were against Chinese companies. In the first half of 2002 India filed more dumping complaints at the WTO than any other country, with China as the main respondent. The President of FICCI warned of deleterious consequences of "smuggled, under-invoiced or low quality Chinese goods" in sectors ranging from batteries to bicycles, synthetic yarn, edible oil, and electronic parts, noting that Chinese batteries were selling at less than half the price of Indian batteries, but lasting also about half as long. FICCI began to conduct laboratory tests of Chinese products and persuade the government to investigate Chinese dumping. To discourage imports of cheap automobile parts from China, the Society for Indian Automobile Manufacturers asked the government to raise tariff barriers. To preempt political pressure, Yamaha of India announced publicly that it would not sell Chinese-made motorcycles. In the consumer durables industry, from air conditioners to televisions, "there seems to be just one growth yardstick," wrote one newspaper report: China.[112]

By this time, however, a stronger constituency had been created in favor of competition. There were many who argued that Chinese products were merely more competitive due to higher worker-productivity and other factors, and that Indian producers need to counter Chinese imports by increasing the competitiveness of their products. The government sided with the market-liberals, with the commerce minister stating that Indian companies have to raise their game rather than hope for the government to step in with protectionist measures.[113] At the same time, the government has been denying some Chinese applications for investment in ports and telecommunications, as "the China scare in the corridors of power," according to one report, "is for real."[114] Although protectionist politics in the vein of the Bombay Club of 1992 are unlikely to emerge soon, the threat of being surrounded by "Made-in-China" in national-cultural festivals is becoming politically contentious. Will this eventually provide a populist brake on India's open-economy policy? Or is the continuity of India's open-economy policy assured for the foreseeable future? The next chapter will take up these questions, in addition to offering an interpretive summary of the main arguments of this book.

5 Perception, policy, and persistence

> The ideas of economists and political philosophers, both when they are right and when they are wrong, are more powerful than is commonly understood. Indeed the world is ruled by little else. Practical men, who believe themselves to be quite exempt from any intellectual influences, are usually the slaves of some defunct economist. Madmen in authority, who hear voices in the air, are distilling their frenzy from some academic scribbler of a few years back.
>
> John Maynard Keynes, *The General Theory of Employment Interest and Money*, 1936

It is easy nowadays to take India's open-economy policies for granted. India is no longer seen as one of the poorest countries of the world, though it still contains almost half of the 700 million people worldwide in extreme poverty. One rarely encounters media analyses that categorize India as an LDC (Least Developed Country). The category in which it is placed every day by Wall Street, and increasingly by its own politicians, is BRIC (Brazil, Russia, India, China), an exclusive quartet of rising economic powerhouses.[1] The mainstream economic discourse in India does not dwell as much on agriculture, nutrition, or infrastructure; it employs the racy language of technology and foreign investment. In a culture where conspicuous consumption was reviled not long ago as crass materialism, the media now write in awestruck tones about an industrialist building a house costing $1 billion or giving his wife a private jet worth $60 million as a birthday gift.[2] Compared to most of its history, India seems certainly different in how it politically and culturally interprets the meaning of economy, economic policy, and success.

India's transformation, a result of pursuing high growth through economic openness since 1991, would have been impossible without a remarkable persistence in economic policy despite political disincentives. This book has sought to explain India's persistence with its open-economy policy, highlighting the role of ideas about globalism and rivalry. Globalism provided the broad lens through which India's reformist leaders saw and pushed their controversial program of opening up the economy. The perception of a long-term strategic rivalry with China, couched in expressions of relative loss and gain, provided economic reforms with a focus and a sense of urgency unlike any experienced by policymakers before. In the strategic calculus of India's leaders, ideas of globalism and rivalry combined to elevate the importance of the rest of the world, correspondingly reducing the significance of the fractious domestic politics of Indian democracy. The economic transformation to outward orientation was preceded by a political transformation to outward orientation, and constructing a belief that it was valuable to influence the world and that India was destined to do so. Policy continuity since then has hinged increasingly less on what domestic constituencies wanted – and as the most recent national elections showed, the greater part of India's electorate still harbors substantial qualms about the benefits of globalization. The continuity of unpopular policies in the world's largest democracy depended more on what reformist policymakers *believed* about India's past and future position in the world outside their electorate. On the surface this may imply that they lost political accountability.[3] But in their mind, their accountability was first and foremost ideational, wedded historically to a more fundamental project about Indian nationalism. The political expression of that was evident in their relentless efforts to win over skeptical citizens toward recognizing and supporting globalism.

The power of globalism

The realization that a change in India's economic approach was necessary could not have happened overnight at some point in 1991. This is why the book at hand has not placed emphasis on what is thought to be the "triggering event" for India's open-economy policy: a foreign exchange shortage in mid-1991. Crisis-driven policy changes can and have been reversed before. The post-1991 policy reforms toward openness are unique for their continuity. Since the 1991 crisis, Indian leaders have spoken out frequently about their commitment to weather political storms and persist with an open-economy policy, and they have also delivered on that commitment. A core group of leaders, first from the Congress Party and then from BJP, were convinced somehow that economic openness was a must, essentially non-negotiable, even though they felt uncertain about the extent to which they would be able to persist. Their commitment was ideational. It was not until the late 1990s that the economy began to shift in ways to confirm the potential material benefits and possible sustainability of India's open-economy policy; until those shifts were evident, the policy had to be initiated, justified, and continued on the basis of the *idea* of openness rather than its tangible effect. From where did this idea originate? Why was it powerful? How could it sustain politically risky commitments?

Nationalist policymakers believed that India's post-1991 economic direction was as much a decisive change in the state's economic goals as it was simultaneously a continuity of India's unrealized historic project of empowerment, rooted all the way back in India's anticolonial struggle that envisioned a globally strong and prosperous India. Globalism, the powerful desire to influence global affairs in line with one's local values, has been the dominant unbroken theme among India's policy elite since Nehru and his cohorts first established the foundations of India's strategic thought. Although analysts bemoaning India's economic performance prior to the 1990s tended to discredit Nehruvian policy, they could not undermine the strength of the globalist imperative that he had imagined and constructed. India was destined for a global role: that was the essence of the "tryst with destiny" that Nehru saw on the eve of India's independence, an idea that still drives the core beliefs and axioms in India's elite policy circles.

The idea of globalism, though romanticized, became established firmly because of three important reasons, discussed in Chapter 3. First of all, as Prime Minister, Nehru dominated the core areas of Indian strategic thought, from foreign policy, to "big-science" projects, to building economic strength. Second, the Congress Party dominated Indian politics. The party originated out of Indian National Congress, which led the independence movement, and was the fount of globalism, constructing India as an internationally influential civilization whose development was thwarted by the advent of the British. The themes that moved the Congress Party and provided its *raison d'être* are the ones that became eventually dominant in Indian politics, as for many years India was essentially a one-party rule within a formally multi-party democracy. Finally, globalism was an intensely nationalist idea. It was the widest frame of reference into which nationalism could be placed and relativized. Through the lens of nationalist globalism, India's empowerment was seen as not just an internal project of uplifting living standards, but a project that inherently looked outwards.

On a macro-historical scale, research by Angus Maddison quantifies the loss felt qualitatively by Indian nationalists. For the 1500 years since AD 1, India was the largest economy in the world, accounting for between one-quarter and one-third of the world's GDP. Around AD 1500, India still produced $34 billion (measured in 1990 international dollars) out of an estimated $117 billion world economy.[4] India's economic regress began around then. This "regress" was defined and sensed in two ways, both based on positioning India against the world. First, India's decline was relative to the gains made by Europe, for in absolute terms India's economy kept on expanding, at an annual average of 1.52 percent between 1500 and 1973, by Maddison's calculations. But Europe gained by leaps and bounds during that time. Second, India's relative decline was a direct result of the advent of European colonialism, whereby Europe siphoned off much of the investable surplus produced by India. Although these estimates appeared long after India's globalism began, they provide a useful visualization of the compeling sense of proportion and loss that has been inherent in Indian nationalist thought.

In promoting an imperative to regain lost power, globalism has remained the longest continuing ideational current in Indian policy circles. It shaped India's struggle for independence in the 1920s, and was used deftly to justify and market its economic policies in the 1990s. Most of all, globalism was a cultivated belief to which India's reformist policymakers as well as their critics subscribed. It was the least controversial frame that could be provided for the most controversial policy Indian leaders had undertaken: the effort to transform the economy from one controlled by the state and focused inwards to one dominated by private actors and integrated closely with the world. Reformist policymakers felt that the route to increase global presence taken by the first generation of Indian leaders had failed. Parallel to how regress during colonial times was interpreted, this post-independence failure was not interpreted by internal criteria: after all, India's domestic economy had been growing, living standards had been improving, and between 1975 and 1990 human development indicators showed a 25 percent improvement across the board.[5] Failure was interpreted mainly by external criteria, seen through a globalist lens. India was falling behind relative to referents in the world outside India. The policy imperative, from this perspective, is not as much to "develop," a concept that is focused internally, as it is to regain the share of power that has been lost. India's economic policy would be successful only if it enabled India "to stand on its own feet, to compete against everyone in the world on an equal footing," as Finance Minister Manmohan Singh noted in 1995.[6]

Though it may not have influenced day-to-day affairs and dealings across the multiple layers of Indian democracy, the broad objective of globalism enjoyed wide currency across the political spectrum, and provided the primary strand of continuity in the philosophy and disposition of policymakers. But the instruments to achieve this objective, in both foreign policy and economic policy, have been open to debate and modifications through the workings of democratic politics. As Chapter 4 argued, the notion of economic security has remained central to globalist empowerment. In the first-generation of policy thinking, influenced strongly by the anticolonial struggle, economic security was equated with economic independence, and as a consequence, Indian policy shunned close connections with Western economies. A newer generation modified the concept of *swadeshi*, realizing that economic security can be derived more effectively from economic *interdependence*. What was needed for empowerment was not strength in domestic industrialization but strength in international trade and access to global capital; self-reliance was redefined in an outward model. International trade and investment connections, fostered by open-economy policies, would enable India to attain faster and greater visibility in world affairs. This change in perspective came about because of a gradual evolution in Indian policymakers' conceptualization of rivalry and its implications.

The urgency of rivalry

Rivalry with China provided concrete focus to the broad project of globalism and eventually prompted India's nationalist leaders with specific policy urgencies, especially in the economic arena. But the current emergence of China as an economic competitor must be interpreted in an overall context of three phases of rivalry, all of which evolved under the broader rubric of globalism. After independence, as Chapter 3 detailed, the Indian policy elite, led by Nehru, foresaw the possibility of competition with China. But that perception was overshadowed by a view of China as a compatriot against the power-centered politics of the Cold War. This was the first phase of "seeing" China: India and China were advancing at the same slow and steady pace toward economic development and empowerment. In some areas China performed better than India, and in others India performed better than China. This perception was based on solidarity and admiration, not competition. Indian policymakers did not feel compelled to match China's advances; they were merely interested to learn from a partner in world politics.

The India–China war of 1962 destroyed that view altogether, and seriously questioned for the first time whether India was prepared to emerge as a world leader. The war firmly established China as a rival, a perception bolstered over the next two decades as China became the leading arms supplier to military regimes surrounding India – namely, Pakistan, Bangladesh, and Burma. It prompted India's investments in the requirements of material power. Big science benefited, as did the scientific education system, and India sounded the arrival of greater strength with its first nuclear test in 1974. But the enmity and bitterness that Indian leaders felt toward China after the war inclined them toward reflexive criticism of the Chinese model. This was the second phase of the perception of China. Indian leaders condemned China's authoritarianism, expansionism, economic centralism, and social and cultural rigidities, and identified India as distinctly different from China on those accounts. Even though China was now viewed as a rival, India's tendency was to reject, not to emulate, China's policies. This period corresponded to India's own experiments in inward-looking industrialization.

As the sense of rivalry became further entrenched in the mindset of Indian nationalist thinkers, China's advances, whether rejected or not, began to be interpreted as India's loss. Many studies, formal and informal, academic as well as industry-generated, that came out in the 1970s and 1980s began to compare India with China on almost every imaginable economic criteria, presuming and intensifying the image of rivalry. India could no longer take heart that China's leaps came at substantial human cost, while India trudged along with an admirably better record on democracy and human rights. India had to improve its economic record. China was not an economic competitor in any substantial way, but it was already *constructed* to be an economic rival. When observers began to report that China had sustained almost twice the annual growth rate of India through the 1980s, Indian nationalist leaders could no longer brush aside the Chinese economy as unsustainable, irrelevant, or statistically dubious. Despite increased military power, India's bid for global prominence seemed in peril, when compared to China's economic achievement and its geopolitical implications. This provided the compelling intellectual backdrop when a small group of leaders decided that India had no option but to emulate China's path of forging greater economic interdependence. In their view, repeated publicly throughout the 1990s, but obscured by the noisy narratives of causes and consequences (reviewed in Chapter 2), interdependence had become essential to the state's core project of empowerment, of India's tryst with destiny, which was a commitment that was not negotiable by the vagaries of the usual domestic politics.

As discussed in Chapter 4, economic rivalry induced continuity of open-economy policy in a number of ways. First of all, Indian policymakers' emphasis on openness of the external economy was due directly to their observed success of China and East Asia. In policy, business, as well as popular analyses, China provided, for better or worse, the economic benchmarks and targets for India. Indian policy needed to follow China's strategic lead and could not change until such targets were reached, projected in different cases for 2015, 2025, or 2050. Moreover, once India had embarked on reaching the various longer-term economic targets, China's ongoing performance served as a continuous gauge of India's own progress. By expanding into the economic arena, the chapter noted, rivalry had become continuous. It had also become ubiquitous. As India has opened up, the business of watching China has expanded. Not just strategic policy analysts, but Indian firms, trade associations, unions, investors, bankers, technology professionals, and of course, politicians now monitor, analyze, position, and forecast India's performance against China on a regular basis. Newer fronts of competition, from the diaspora to economic statecraft to the search for cheap energy are pitting the two countries against each other more frequently than ever before. All these have transformed economic policymaking from being primarily episodic to more real-time, or continuous. And because China itself is showing little signs of slowing down, the urgency of catch-up, spawned by rivalry, is unlikely to diminish soon in Indian policy thought.

Perception, construction, and relativity

The ideas of globalism and rivalry represent constructed realities. These constructions in Indian thought have evolved in an intellectual continuum inside which events such as the 1962 war and the 1991 crisis are interspersed. India's leaders in 1991 interpreted the significance of the economic crisis in the context of their accumulated ideational motivations relating to globalism and rivalry, even while tangible material conditions, such as a possible payments default, were clear and present in India's economy. The ideational bases, therefore, would have provided support for an open-economy policy even if the nature and timing of the triggering event were different.

The policy relevance of even something as material as war depends on the *interpretation* of war against a multifaceted backdrop of social, political, economic, and cultural contexts. Two countries that have fought frequently, such as France and Germany, can coexist as staunch allies in an ambitious project of European empowerment, but also as rivals for continental leadership. When interpreted as allies, what seem prominent are attributes such as their open borders, free movement of people and labor, single currency, or sharing of military intelligence. When constructed as rivals, their policy-relevance and priorities for each other seem altogether different. Amity and enmity, which are critical to national security, threat perception, and war, are cultural products. As Jepperson, Wendt, and Katzenstein put it:

> In terms of material power, Canada and Cuba stand in roughly comparable positions relative to the United States. But while one is a threat, the other is an ally, a result, we believe, of ideational factors operating at the international level.[7]

Constructed realities and imageries have featured prominently in India-China relations from the very beginning. The McMahon Line, dispute on which eventually led to the border war, was from the Chinese perspective a fiction, an illegitimate colonial artifact. To be sure, it was once a somewhat arbitrary line drawn on two pieces of paper.

Mainstream discourse, especially the material focus ubiquitous in the foreign policy and international business literatures, plainly assumes India and China to be solid rivals, almost as if it is ordained by nature. It is important to note that China was constructed to be India's economic competitor long before tangible economic competition began between the two countries. The *idea* of rivalry was constructed, in the context of cultural norms and national identity, from the cumulative interpretation of events and trends over time as instances of relative loss for India and relative gain for China. Even now, it is not entirely correct to think that India and China are rivals because they are both competing for the same limited pool of foreign investment. Most direct and portfolio investors would hardly expose all assets in either India or China; they would distribute assets between the two in order to diversify risk, take advantage of resources or conditions unique to each country, and maximize their potential market reach. In other words, despite short-term fluctuations, a foreign company's decision to invest in India would not necessarily come at the expense of investment in China. India and China are the two largest markets, and a presence in both is considered desirable and prudent in the long run. But in an environment where the two are constructed as rivals, increasing investment in China, regardless of the investor's strategies, will ring as a clarion call for Indian policymakers to further liberalize their investment regime.

Therefore, rivalry is influenced by what can be considered material reality – but it is largely a matter of perception; it is the *sense* of rivalry that becomes policy-urgent. Consider another example typical of the discourse common nowadays. A review of the 1990s in *India Today* noted: "If we were proud of the start of cellular services and flaunted the 1.3 million cell phones we purchased this decade [i.e. the 1990s], it was sobering to know that China buys that many in a month."[8] This one sentence captures the competitive approach toward China that had become dominant. In and of itself, the number of cellphones that the Chinese purchase would not concern India, just as the number of cellphones in Bangladesh or Pakistan would not be a concern. The French are hardly bothered by the number of cellphones that the Germans purchase. But if China is seen as a rival, this comparison immediately exudes a "sobering" experience, a sense of loss, in pride as well as in more material fronts – technology, communications, infrastructure, regulations. For some, it may even suggest broader economic and security implications. The sharp contrast in time-frame, a decade for India versus a month for China, injects in addition an intense urgency about the issue, especially if globalism is already inculcated into one's outlook. Now imagine a torrential outpouring of such comparisons and contrasts over two decades to get a sense of the milieu of urgencies that are constructed in the mass discourse in which policies are conceived, promulgated, and continued.

Within established policy-thinking in India, the defined sense of rivalry with China is framed within the broader imperative of globalism. In that frame of reference, globalism becomes in effect the "scarce resource" over which the two countries are competing, playing a zero-sum game, so to speak. Increased international influence of China corresponds to decreased influence of India. This is not to say that India's globalist thinkers harbor false pretensions or hopes of India's singular dominance of world affairs. To the contrary, as Stephen Hoffmann argues, the moderate-realism that has become mainstream in Indian strategic thought views multipolarity or "polycentricism" (US–China–India–EU–Russia) as the likely configuration of power in future, and considers such an outcome desirable.[9] The goal is to ensure that India emerges quickly as one of the great powers that constitutes such multi-polarity – and it is within that larger quest that China is constructed as a rival and becomes policy-relevant.

The "larger quest" has now become uncontested as a national goal. When rivalry was not defined well, progress for India meant improvement compared to the past, and global influence was seen as something India inherently deserved, and something that would occur naturally at some point during India's advancement. As rivalry with China became more defined and palpable, the meaning of progress expanded: India needed to become not only better than its own past but, simultaneously, better off compared to China. Globalist motivations project India's policymaking context even farther, using the world or the globe as the referent. In the perspective of strategic policymakers, all of these aspects coexist as criteria to devise policy and as benchmarks to judge performance. As the previous chapter showed, Indian policy documents simultaneously estimated whether India's share of world trade increased (using the world as a referent) over time (using the past as a referent), while monitoring continuously how much foreign investment China was attracting (using the rival as a referent).

In addition to emphasizing the power of ideas, a constructivism-influenced approach, which this book has promoted, underscores the role of identity. The state is a social actor. It lives in a community of states; it is "embedded in social rules and conventions that constitute its identity"; it is impacted by changes in historical contexts and cultural meanings.[10] India's open-economy policies were pursued to bolster a certain concept of national identity against a global context. This contextualization gives policy public appeal and provides policymakers with longer-term meaning for their strategic objectives, lowering the chances that policies would be haphazard and simply reactive. The nationalist project for independence, which generated India's globalism, was involved substantially in the construction of a national identity called "India." A significant part of the struggle was to unify and create, among many centrifugal cultural-institutional forces of religion, caste, class, political boundaries, race, and languages, something that could be termed Indian. As Chapter 3 recounted, unification efforts resulted in a blend of liberal-idealist identities that were hailed as elements of national culture, encompassing self-determination, non-violence, non-alignment, democracy, human rights, secularism, and multiculturalism. Globalism aimed to project these values and attributes externally, emitting an image of unified national identity that otherwise seemed impossible when viewed against India's fractious domestic polity. Some aspects of identity, such as non-violence, evolved out of the anticolonial project itself; others, such as democracy, were more tentative and became established as something "Indian" only in the course of India's political performance after independence.[11]

Being an extension of nationalism, globalism cannot be divorced ideologically from these values and priorities. In the context of India's rivalry with China, we can expect that policymakers will market aspects of national identity in order to claim competitive advantages. India's democratic performance, as Joseph Nye writes, "means it has passed a test that China still faces, and that makes India a source of attraction."[12] Even India's comparatively slower growth rate, though substantially higher than the "Hindu rate of growth" that came be associated with national identity two decades ago, could become an advantage. It may appeal to some investors by "offering a safer ride than China's roller-coaster." A slower growth rate may provide a better shield against inflationary losses. As a stock analyst's report put it: "India represents the better-safe-than-sorry emerging market, or perhaps the investment tortoise against China's hare."[13] China, in fact, offers a vivid example of how a particular economic growth rate can become established as part of national identity, to the extent that a 7 percent annual growth rate may be considered an economic failure. In India, the political battle over identity was importantly about the value of openness. As Chapter 2 showed, much of the resistance to India's open-economy policies related to interpretations of identity, whereby aggressive promotion of foreign trade and investment was perceived as a surrender of core values for which India had stood historically. Globalism and rivalry were powerful concepts precisely because they could bridge the divergent politics of identity and nationalism.

The future of India's open-economy policy

In their efforts to counter the bewildering onslaught of resistance, India's reformist policymakers – as Jenkins points out in his detailed study – resorted to manipulation, arm-twisting, lies, and betrayals across India's complex layers of democratic politics, from local to state to federal levels.[14] But they persisted, driven by powerful beliefs about India's international objectives and its position relative to its competitors. Moreover, they sought to market their ideas of globalism and rivalry actively in India's domestic polity. The future of India's open-economy policy will be determined by the political tenacity of these ideas, as well as the risk that the polity may reject costly internal changes attributed to external factors.

Pro-openness policymakers have been successful on the first count. Even left-leaning parties now provide broad support for the continuity of open-economy policies. Such broad-based support would not have been possible without the imagery of empowerment, loss, and global destiny employed consistently by the policymakers. All nationalist appeals are based on some concept of strengthening the nation. The idea of globalism encompasses that appeal and goes farther beyond, not only by showing congruence with the "Indian" identity derived through anticolonial struggles but also by bringing together politically diverse interests under its ideological and rhetorical orbit on economic matters. While various political platforms questioned specific policy measures, virtually none questioned the need for greater global visibility. As the broad idea to frame India's open-economy policies, globalism has proven to be an extremely useful vehicle to market open-door policies to the domestic constituency.

Relativizing India's position vis-à-vis China has also been politically useful. Pro-openness leaders were able to make globalism concrete by focusing specifically on a tangible competitor – and they did so to an extent never seen before in Indian economic policymaking. Unlike globalism, which was widely accepted, the image of China as a rival was at times controversial among the public. The debate surrounding Defense Minister George Fernandes's identification of China as India's top enemy is one example. Nevertheless, for both government and its critics, the threat of Chinese competition, framed within globalism, bridged domestic divides by directing attention to a common external rival. The transformation has been remarkable, such that policy leaders who a decade and a half ago justified their open-economy policy by expressing the need to catch up to China now find themselves periodically on the defensive, accused of going too slowly or not paying enough attention to shifts in China's strategy. Consider this passionate editorial in a national newspaper, *The Statesman*, in mid-2004, urging the government to pay closer attention to the advances China has been making in information technology and outsourcing:

> [T]he Chinese are fast catching up in the one area where India has some edge [i.e. information technology].... It is depressing to compare the performance of the Chinese with Indian politicians. The Chinese President has said that everyone in China will be speaking English in 20 years. National sentiment is not allowed to come in the way of national interest. In India, political interest obscures everything.[15]

Because it is now firmly rooted in a belief-system equated to the fundamental goals and the long-term existence of the state, India's open-economy policy is in no danger of being reversed in the foreseeable future. But what may determine the *pace* of continuity in the coming days is the perception of sufficient progress by India's majority rural voters. BJP realised this when it was defeated in the general elections in 2004. Although BJP did not lack conviction, its open-economy platform failed to show continuity with either "Indian-ness" or core strategic objectives in the way that Congress Party leaders preceding it were able to display to maintain support across political and social divides. Both of the major narrative campaigns of BJP – "Feel Good" and "India Rising" – showcased India's urban elite and marketed an idea of upward mobility that alienated the majority of rural Indians.[16]

This difficulty relates in part to crossing the foreign-domestic divide. Although in an open economy it is difficult to delineate clearly what is external and what is internal, there are policy arenas that are traditionally constructed and perceived to be primarily domestic, such as fiscal policy or labor laws. Making externally induced changes in those arenas can be politically charged and risky. In India, political difficulties have already arisen with labor market reforms, for strong constituencies have been created on both sides of the issue. Withdrawal of state subsidies is another controversial area. Domestic liberalization, furthermore, cannot be rationalized as easily under either a broad covering ideology such as globalism or a specific strategic need, such as competition with China.

The perception of relative inequality combined with an encroachment into more domestic policy arenas may provoke large parts of the Indian electorate. Their political action, especially the act of voting out aggressively pro-openness governments, can dampen the pace of open-economy policy. But it is unlikely that they would be able to reverse economic openness any time soon. One reason is that India's open-economy policy by now has created strong material interests in favor of its continuity. But the more primary reason goes back to constructed aims and beliefs. In the seventeen years since the current policy trajectory began, economic openness has become a "mission statement" for Indian leaders, perhaps on a par with other values that are thought to collectively form the pillars of the state, such democracy and territorial integrity. Most of the public has begun to accept openness as consistent with their historical imaginings of Indian identity, as an ancient civilization connected closely with and influencing the world outside. The ideational foundations of openness will remain strong as long as globalism and rivalry continue to provide the primary lenses for interpreting policy success in India. As long as policymakers can connect external exigencies persuasively to a project that empowers the nation and its identity, they will be able to reduce the fissiparous pressures on policy that may arise from domestic politics. But in there lies a longer-term contradiction. Continuity of economic openness will lead to greater integration between India and the world, and the domestic-foreign divide consequently will become blurred. And that may begin to dilute the power of nationalist-identity politics, which has so far provided India's open-economy policy an ideological sanctuary and fostered its growth.

Appendix

List of interviewees

The date of the interview is specified in parentheses.

1 Mr. Montek S. Ahluwalia, Secretary of Finance, Government of India (12 September 1997).
2 Dr. Sanjaya Baru, Senior Consultant, Research and Information System for the Non-Aligned and Other Economies. Formerly Business Editor, *Economic Times* (23 September 1997).
3 Mr. Dilip Bhattacharyya, Secretary of Planning and Development, Government of West Bengal, India (3 October 1997).
4 Ms. Krishna Bose, Member of the Parliament (Lok Sabha), India. Constituency: West Bengal. Party affiliation: Indian National Congress (3 October 1997).
5 Dr. Ashim Kumar Dasgupta, Finance Minister, Government of West Bengal, India. Party Affiliation: Communist Party of India Marxist (3 October 1997).
6 Dr. Ashok Lahiri, Economic Advisor, Ministry of Finance, Government of India (16 September 1997).
7 Mr. S. V. Mahapatra, Director General of Foreign Trade, Government of India (23 September 1997).
8 Dr. Amit Mitra, Secretary General, Federation of Indian Chambers of Commerce and Industry (Provided written answers to interview questionnaire (10 October 1997)).
9 Dr. C. Raja Mohan, Strategic Affairs Editor, *The Hindu* (11 October 1997).
10 Mr. S. Narendra, Principal Information Officer, Government of India (12 October 1997).
11 Mr. Jayram Ramesh, Political Advisor to the Finance Minister (Mr. P. Chidambaram), Government of India (11 October 1997).
12 Ms. Manashi Roy, Deputy Director General, Confederation of Indian Industry (11 September 1997).
13 Dr. Arjun Sengupta, Member, Planning Commission, Government of India. Previously Ambassador to the European Commission and Special Advisor

to Michel Camdessus, Managing Director of the International Monetary Fund (17 December 1997).

14 Mr. K. Subrahmanyam, Consulting Editor, *The Times of India*. Former Chairman, Joint Intelligence Bureau, former Secretary of Defense, Government of India and Director, Institute of Defense Studies and Analysis (10 October 1997).

15 Mr. A. N. Verma, Chairman, Foreign Investment Promotion Board, Government of India, 1991–96, and Principal Secretary to the Prime Minister (8 October 1997).

Notes

1 Explaining the continuity of openness

1 This reversal was the last-minute withdrawal of the Insurance Regulatory Authority Bill of 1997, which would have allowed foreign insurance companies to compete in the domestic market. It was only the second time in India's history that the government withdrew a bill poised for voting in the Parliament. See "Government Withdraws Bill on Insurance Authority," *The Hindu*, 7 August 1997, p. 1. Also, "Whither Unity on Economic Reforms?" *Financial Express*, 8 August 1997, p. 2.

2 See Jalal Alamgir, "Nationalist Globalism: The Narrative of Strategic Politics and Economic Openness in India," in Baldev Raj Nayar, ed., *The Politics of Globalization in India*, New Delhi: Oxford University Press, 2007.

3 There is no need to review the vast literature on social construction and its significance or insignificance. The pioneering work in the field of international relations is Alexander Wendt, *Social Theory of International Politics*, Cambridge: Cambridge University Press, 1999. For a critical approach toward social construction, see Ian Hacking, *The Social Construction of What?* Cambridge: Harvard University Press, 1999.

4 At the time that this book went to press, the latest to join in the fad was Shashi Tharoor, *The Elephant, the Tiger, and the Cell Phone*, New York: Arcade, 2007.

5 The literature on crisis-led reforms in both India and other developing countries is vast. See for instance Joan Nelson, ed., *Economic Crisis and Policy Choice: The Politics of Adjustment in the Third World*, Princeton: Princeton University Press, 1990; Ian Little, Richard Cooper, W. Max Corden, and Sarath Rajapatirana, *Boom, Crisis, and Adjustment: The Macroeconomic Experience of Developing Countries*, New York: Oxford University Press, 1993. On India, see Vijay Joshi and I. M. D. Little, *India: Crisis, Adjustment, Growth*, Oxford: Oxford University Press, 1993.

6 There has been a steady stream of articles corresponding to this view in *Economic and Political Weekly*.

7 Chapter 2 details some of this evidence.

8 Both Indira Gandhi and Rajiv Gandhi initiated efforts at liberalization. See Atul Kohli, *Democracy and Discontent: India's Growing Crisis of Governability*, Cambridge: Cambridge University Press, 1990, Chapter 11; Lloyd I. Rudolph and Susanne Hoeber Rudolph, *In Pursuit of Lakshmi: The Political Economy of the Indian State*, Chicago: University of Chicago Press, 1987, Chapters 7 and 8.

9 Rob Jenkins, *Democratic Politics and Economic Reform in India*, Cambridge: Cambridge University Press, 1999. I provide a more detailed evaluation of Jenkins's approach in Chapter 2.

10 Miles Kahler, "Orthodoxy and Its Alternatives: Explaining Approaches to Stabilization and Adjustment," in Nelson, ed., *Economic Crisis and Policy Choice*. See also Barbara Stallings, "International Influence on Economic Policy: Debt, Stabilization,

and Structural Reform," in Stephan Haggard and Robert R. Kaufman, eds., *The Politics of Economic Adjustment*, Princeton: Princeton University Press, 1992.

11 Stephan Haggard and Robert R. Kaufman, "Introduction: Institutions and Economic Adjustment," in Haggard and Kaufman, eds., *The Politics of Economic Adjustment*, p. 15. See also Peter Evans, "The State as Problem and Solution: Predation, Embedded Autonomy, and Structural Change," in Haggard and Kaufman, eds., *The Politics of Economic Adjustment*; Joseph Stiglitz, *Globalization and Its Discontents*, New York: Norton, 2002, Chapter 7.

12 Miles Kahler, "External Influence, Conditionality, and the Politics of Adjustment," in Haggard and Kaufman, eds., *The Politics of Economic Adjustment*, p. 100.

13 Paul Mosley, Jane Harrigan, and John Toye, *Aid and Power: The World Bank and Policy-Based Lending*, London: Routledge, 1991.

14 See Stiglitz, *Globalization and Its Discontents*.

15 Miles Kahler's conclusion is consistent with this view: "the influence of IFIs seemed to be most consistent in countries where the leadership was already committed to openness in the first place." See Miles Kahler, "International Financial Institutions and the Politics of Adjustment," in Joan M. Nelson *et al.*, *Fragile Coalitions: The Politics of Economic Adjustment*, New Brunswick: Transaction Books, 1989. For an empirical assessment in support of this statement, see Kahler, "External Influence, Conditionality, and the Politics of Adjustment," in Haggard and Kaufman, eds., *The Politics of Economic Adjustment*, p. 115, table 2.2.

16 Thomas J. Biersteker, "The 'Triumph' of Neoclassical Economics in the Developing World: Policy Convergence and the Bases of Governance in the International Economic Order," in James N. Rosenau and Ernst-Otto Czempiel, eds., *Governance without Government: Order and Change in World Politics*, Cambridge: Cambridge University Press, 1992, p. 110. For a summary of social learning and the merits of ideational explanations for policy reform, see also Biersteker, "The 'Triumph' of Liberal Economic Ideas in the Developing World," in Barbara Stallings, ed., *Global Change, Regional Response*, Cambridge: Cambridge University Press, 1995. Biersteker argues that this explanation is partial at best, and makes a case for a more integrative explanation.

17 Devesh Kapur, "Ideas and Economic Reforms in India: The Role of International Migration and the Indian Diaspora," *India Review* 3: 4, 2004, pp. 364–384.

18 Achin Vanaik, "Soldiers of Hindutva: The New Indian Right," *New Left Review* 9, 2001, pp. 43–67.

19 Haggard and Kaufman, "Institutions and Economic Adjustment," p. 23.

20 Ronald J. Herring, "Embedded Particularism: India's Failed Developmental State," in Meredith Woo-Cumings, ed., *The Developmental State*, Ithaca: Cornell University Press, 1999; Peter Evans, "The State as Problem and Solution: Predation, Embedded Autonomy, and Structural Change," in Stephan Haggard and Robert R. Kaufman, eds., *The Politics of Economic Adjustment*, Princeton: Princeton University Press, 1992; Robert Wade, "The Market for Public Office: Why the Indian State is Not Better at Development," *World Development* 13 (4), 1985, pp. 467–497; John P. Lewis, "Some Consequences of Giantism: The Case of India," *World Politics* 43 (3), 1991, pp. 367–389.

21 "What's Holding India Back," *The Economist*, 6 March 2008.

22 Haggard and Kaufman, "Institutions and Economic Adjustment," p. 23.

23 John Waterbury, "The Heart of the Matter? Public Enterprise and the Adjustment Process," in Haggard and Kaufman, eds., *The Politics of Economic Adjustment*. A similar argument can be made against the "epistemic community" theory that a global pro-reformist community of knowledge-based experts provided policy continuity by coordinating and disseminating convergent ideas. This argument also presupposes commitment and discounts ideological or political divisions within the community. It has been easier for epistemic communities to identify problems and high-level goals,

but much more difficult to agree on actual policy solutions to attain the goals. Examples are the 1992 Earth Summit in Rio de Janiero or the 2001 World Conference on Racism in Durban, South Africa.

24 Dani Rodrik, *The New Global Economy and Developing Countries: Making Openness Work*, Washington: Overseas Development Council, 1999, pp. 83–84, and figure 4.6.

25 The World Bank, *World Development Report 2003*, New York: Oxford University Press, 2003, pp. 51–54, 134–135.

26 See Dani Rodrik, "The Rush to Free Trade in the Developing World: Why So Late? Why Now? Will It Last?" in Stephan Haggard and Steven B. Webb, eds., *Voting For Reform: Democracy, Political Liberalization, and Economic Adjustment*, New York: Oxford University Press, 1994; Jagdish Bhagwati, *India in Transition: Freeing the Economy*, Oxford: Clarendon, 1993, p. 92; James Manor, "India's Reform Strengths," in Edward Friedman and Bruce Gilley, eds., *Asia's Giants: Comparing China and India*, New York: Palgrave Macmillan, 2005, pp. 102.

27 Jeffry Frieden and Ronald Rogowski's works, for example, explore the effects of economic openness on domestic material groups and, in different ways, corroborate this claim. Jeffry Frieden, "Invested Interests: The Politics of National Economic Policies in a World of Global Finance," *International Organization* 45 (4), 1991, pp. 425–451. See also his *Debt, Development, and Democracy: Modern Political Economy and Latin America, 1965–1985*, Princeton: Princeton University Press, 1991. Ronald Rogowski, *Commerce and Coalitions: How Trade Affects Domestic Political Alignments*, Princeton: Princeton University Press, 1989.

28 Robert H. Bates and Anne O. Krueger, "Generalizations Arising from the Country Studies," in Bates and Krueger, eds., *Political and Economic Interactions in Economic Policy Reform*, Oxford: Blackwell, p. 461.

29 Angus Deaton and Jean Drèze, "Poverty And Inequality In India: A Reexamination," Woodrow Wilson School, Princeton University and Delhi School of Economics, July 2002, p. 20. The economists go on to point out: "It might be argued that a temporary increase in economic inequality is to be expected in a liberalizing economy, and that this trend is likely to be short-lived. Proponents of the "Kuznets curve" may even expect it to be reversed in due course. However, China's experience of sharp and sustained increase in economic inequality over a period of more than twenty years, after market-oriented economic reforms were initiated in the late 1970s, does not inspire much confidence in this prognosis. It is, in fact, an important pointer to the possibility of further accentuation of economic disparities in India in the near future" (p. 20).

30 Robert W. Cox, "A Perspective on Globalization," in James H. Mittelman, ed. *Globalization: Critical Reflections*, Boulder: Lynne Rienner, 1996, p. 21. See also the works of Andre Gunder Frank, Samir Amin, Immanuel Wallerstein, Terence Hopkins, Roland Robertson, Paul Sweezy, Harry Magdoff, and Leo Huberman.

31 Richard O'Brien, *Global Financial Integration: The End of Geography*, New York: Council on Foreign Relations Press, 1992; Walter Wriston, *The Twilight of Sovereignty*, New York: Scribners, 1992; Philip Cerny, *Finance and World Politics: Markets, Regimes, and States in the Post-Hegemonic Era*, London: Edward Elgar, 1993; John B. Goodman and Louis W. Pauly, "The Obsolescence of Capital Controls? Economic Management in an Age of Global Markets," *World Politics* 46 (1), 1993, pp. 50–82; Katherine Verdery, "Whither 'Nation' and 'Nationalism'?" *Daedalus* 122 (3), 1993, pp. 37–46; Erik R. Peterson, "Surrendering to Markets," *The Washington Quarterly* 18 (4), 1995, pp. 103–115; William D. Coleman, *Financial Services, Globalization, and Domestic Policy Change*, New York: St. Martin's, 1996; Don Tapscott, *The Digital Economy*, New York: McGraw-Hill, 1996; Benjamin J. Cohen, "Phoenix Risen: The Resurrection of Global Finance," *World Politics* 48 (2), 1996, pp. 268–296; Stephen J. Kobrin, "Electronic Cash and the End of National Markets," *Foreign Policy* 107, 1997, pp. 65–77. Vincent Cable, "The Diminished

Nation-State: A Study in the Loss of Economic Power," *Daedalus* 124 (2), 1995; Susan Strange, "The Defective State," *Daedalus* 124 (2), 1995, pp. 55–74. See also Masao Miyoshi, "A Borderless World? From Colonialism to Transnationalism and the Decline of the Nation-State," in Wilson and Dissanayake, eds., *Global/Local*, Durham: Duke Uni Press, 1996, pp. 78–106. Pronouncements about the powerlessness of the nation-state have a long intellectual pedigree going back to the 1960s. In 1968, Richard Cooper cautioned about the perils that economic interdependence spelled for the autonomy and effectiveness of national policymaking. See Richard Cooper, *The Economics of Interdependence: Economic Policy in the Atlantic Community*, New York: McGraw-Hill, 1968. The next year Charles Kindleberger predicted, "the nation-state is just about through as an economic unit." Kindleberger, *American Business Abroad*, New Haven: Yale University Press, 1969, p. 207. Raymond Vernon, in his 1971 study of multinationals, claimed that state power to control corporations is waning: "[s]uddenly, it seems, the sovereign states are feeling naked." Raymond Vernon, *Sovereignty At Bay*, New York: Basic Books, 1971, p. 3.

32 This view of globalism is proposed by Roger D. Spegele, "Is Robust Globalism a Mistake?" *Review of International Studies* 23 (2), 1997, pp. 211–239.

33 In this vein, Joseph Nye argues, if America can continue to adapt to the changing nature of power due mostly to new technologies, it is "bound to lead." See Joseph S. Nye, Jr., *Bound to Lead: The Changing Nature of American Power*, New York: Basic Books, 1990.

34 Walter LaFeber, *The New Empire: An Interpretation of American Expansion 1860–1898*, 35th anniversary ed., Ithaca: Cornell University Press, 1998.

35 Stephen E. Ambrose, *Rise To Globalism: American Foreign Policy Since 1938*, seventh edition, New York: Penguin, 1993. See also Fareed Zakaria, *From Wealth to Power: The Unusual Origins of America's World Role*, Princeton: Princeton University Press, 1998, p. 182.

36 Paul Kennedy, *The Rise and Fall of the Great Powers*, New York: Random House, 1987, p. 158.

37 I borrow from the writing of Malcolm Waters, "[it] does not imply that every corner of the planet must become Westernized and capitalist but rather that every set of social arrangements must establish its position in relation to the capitalist West ... it must relativize itself." Malcolm Waters, *Globalization*, London: Routledge, 1995, p. 3.

38 Paul Krugman, *The Accidental Theorist*, New York: W. W. Norton, 1998, p. 77.

39 See the essays in Dean Baker, Gerald Epstein, and Robert Pollin, eds., *Globalization and Progressive Economic Policy*, Cambridge: Cambridge University Press, 1998. Note a similar line of acceptance in Peter Evans's argument: "The only explanation for the belief that globalization is associated with decreased 'stateness,'" claims Evans, must be an "ideological climate that proscribes using territorial sovereignty to limit the discretion of private economic actors." See Evans, "The Eclipse of the State? Reflections on Stateness in an Era of Globalization," *World Politics* 50 (1), 1997, p. 71.

40 William R. Thompson, "Why Rivalries Matter and What Great Power Rivalries Can Tell Us About World Politics," in William R. Thompson, ed., *Great Power Rivalries*, Columbia: University of South Carolina Press, 1999, p. 4.

41 Jack S. Levy and Salvatore Ali, "From Commercial Competition to Strategic Rivalry to War: The Evolution of the Anglo-Dutch Rivalry, 1609–52," in Paul F. Diehl, ed., *The Dynamics of Enduring Rivalries*, Champaign: University of Illinois Press, 1998.

42 On the evolution of the Japan–America rivalry, see David P. Rapkin, "The Emergence and Intensification of US–Japan Rivalry in the Early Twentieth Century," in Thompson, ed., *Great Power Rivalries*, pp. 337–370.

43 This is related to the idea proffered by the literature on "fungibility" of power assets. Some believe economic wealth is the most fungible, as it can be used easily to buy

other power assets, such as "a good press, top-flight international negotiators, smart lawyers, cutting-edge technology, bargaining power in international organizations, and so on." See Robert J. Art, "The Fungibility of Force," in Robert J. Art and Kenneth N. Waltz, eds., *The Use of Force: Military Power and International Politics*, Lanham: Rowman and Littlefield, 2004, p. 7.

44 The basic concept of strategy as a series of moves comes from game theory. See, inter alia, Anatol Rapoport, *Fights, Games, and Debates*, Ann Arbor: University of Michigan Press, 1974; Thomas C. Schelling, *The Strategy of Conflict*, Cambridge: Harvard University Press, 1980; Robert Axelrod, *The Evolution of Cooperation*, New York: Basic Books, 1984.

45 For a basic, non-technical overview, see Jeffrey A. Hart, *Rival Capitalists: International Competitiveness in the United States, Japan, and Western Europe*, Ithaca: Cornell University Press, 1992. For more theoretical treatments, see Paul Krugman, ed., *Strategic Trade Policy and the New International Economics*, Cambridge: MIT Press, 1986; John Conybeare, *Trade Wars: The Theory and Practice of International Commercial Rivalry*, New York: Columbia University Press, 1987.

46 A real-world analogue to this example is China's decision in 2001 to enter the international organic green tea market, which caused wide apprehension in India, which had hitherto dominated the niche sector. See Kunal Bose, "Chinese issue challenge to India on 'green' tea," *Financial Times*, 4 May 2001, p. 34.

47 Giuseppe Di Palma, *To Craft Democracies: An Essay on Democratic Transitions*, Berkeley: University of California Press, 1990, pp. 141–143.

2 The politics of causes and consequences

1 A succinct review of the frameworks and experience of development in post-independence India is in Jagdish Bhagwati, "The Design of Indian Development," in Isher Judge Ahluwalia and I. M. D. Little, eds., *India's Economic Reforms and Development: Essays for Manmohan Singh*, Delhi: Oxford University Press, 1998. Another excellent review of the evolution of Indian political economy is Baldev Raj Nayar, *Globalization and Nationalism: The Changing Balance in India's Economic Policy*, New Delhi: Sage, 2001.

2 The major work on Indian planning is Sukhamoy Chakravarty, ed., *Development Planning: The Indian Experience*, Delhi: Oxford University Press, 1987. See also Jagdish Bhagwati and Padma Desai, *India: Planning for Industrialization*, Oxford: Oxford University Press, 1970; and Anil Kumar Jain, *Economic Planning in India*, New Delhi: Ashish Publishing House, 1986.

3 Nayar, *Globalization and Nationalism*, p. 57.

4 Deepak Nayyar, "The Foreign Trade Sector, Planning and Industrialisation in India," in Terence J. Byres, ed., *The State, Development Planning and Liberalisation in India*, New York: Oxford University Press, 1997, pp. 340–368.

5 Quoted in Nayar, *Globalization and Nationalism*, p. 69.

6 Nayyar, "The Foreign Trade Sector," p. 344.

7 During that "lost decade," OECD countries grew by only 2.9 percent and the low and middle income countries grew by only 2.7 percent annually. India's growth rate in the 1980s is also striking in contrast to its overall annual growth rate between 1950 and 1980: 3.52 percent, which was dubbed by some as the "Hindu" growth rate. See Kirit S. Parikh, ed., *India Development Report 1997*, Delhi: Oxford University Press, 1997, p. 28, table 1.

8 World Bank, *India: Sustaining Rapid Economic Growth*, Washington: World Bank, 1997, p. 39, table 3.

9 Nirupam Bajpai and Jeffrey D. Sachs, "Fiscal Policy in India's Economic Reforms," in Jeffrey D. Sachs, Ashutosh Varshney, and Nirupam Bajpai, eds., *India in the Era of Economic Reforms*, New Delhi: Oxford University Press, 1999, p. 81. See also

Amit Bhaduri and Deepak Nayyar, *The Intelligent Person's Guide to Liberalization*, New Delhi: Penguin, 1996, Chapter 2.

10 See Isher J. Ahluwalia, *Industrial Growth in India*, Delhi: Oxford University Press, 1985; Arun Ghosh *et al.*, *Indian Industrialization: Structure and Policy Issues*, Delhi: Oxford University Press, 1992; George Rosen, *Contrasting Styles of Industrial Reform*, Chicago: University of Chicago Press, 1992. On the political effects of the reforms in the 1980s, see Achin Vanaik, *The Painful Transition*, London: Verso, 1990.

11 See Miria Pigato *et al.*, *South Asia's Integration into the World Economy*, Washington: World Bank, 1997, p. 40, table 4.2.

12 Montek S. Ahluwalia, "India's Economic Reforms: An Appraisal," in Sachs, Varshney, and Bajpai, eds., *India in the Era of Economic Reforms*, p. 28.

13 Government of India, Ministry of Finance, *Economic Survey 1991–1992*, Part I: General Review, New Delhi: Ministry of Finance, 1992, p. 10.

14 Achin Vanaik, "Soldiers of Hindutva: The New Indian Right," *New Left Review*, No. 9, May–June 2001, pp. 43–67.

15 Government of India, Ministry of Finance, *Speech of Shri Manmohan Singh Presenting Central Government's Budget for 1991–92*, New Delhi: Ministry of Finance, 1991, p. 4 (emphasis added).

16 "India's Two Years," *Financial Times*, 6 July 1993, p. 19.

17 Swaminathan S. Aiyar, "Paradise Lost," *Economic Times*, 15 August 1997, p. 5.

18 "Rupee Again Devalued by 11.83 p.c. Against the Pound," *The Hindu*, 4 July 1991, p. 1; "Further Steep Devaluation to Make Exports Competitive," *The Hindu*, 4 July 1991, p. 7.

19 Government of India, Ministry of Finance, *Economic Survey 1991–92*, New Delhi: Government of India, 1992, p. 23.

20 "'Reforms Will Take a Decade': Manmohan Singh," interview with *India Today*, 31 March 1993, p. 104.

21 The review in the following two sections draws significantly from Jalal Alamgir, "Narratives of Open-Economy Policies in India, 1991–2000," *Asian Studies Review* 31 (2), 2007, pp. 155–170. Excerpts are reprinted with permission.

22 Prabirjit Sarkar, "IMF/World Bank Stabilisation Programmes: A Critical Assessment," *Economic and Political Weekly* 26 (40), 5 October 1991, pp. 2307–2310; Michel Chossudovsky, "India Under IMF Rule," *Economic and Political Weekly* 28 (10), 6 March 1993, pp. 385–387; Arun Ghosh, "1994–95 Budget: A Total Surrender," *Economic and Political Weekly* 29 (16–17), 16–23 April 1994, pp. 889–892; Prabhat Patnaik, *Whatever Happened to Imperialism?*, New Delhi: Tulika, 1995; Bhaduri and Nayyar, *The Intelligent Person's Guide to Liberalization*, Chapter 3.

23 Nayar, *Globalization and Nationalism*, p. 101.

24 "Devaluation: A Signal to IMF," *The Hindu*, 2 July 1991, p. 9.

25 "Appropriate Step, Says IMF," *The Hindu*, 4 July 1991, p. 1.

26 "IMF Concludes Article IV Consultations with India," IMF Press Information Notice No. 97/11, 16 July 1997.

27 Government of India, Ministry of Finance, *Economic Survey 1991–92, Part I: General Review*, Delhi: Ministry of Finance, 1992, p. 27.

28 Government of India, Ministry of Finance, "Speech of Shri Manmohan Singh, Minister of Finance, Introducing the Budget for the Year 1992–93," *Budget Speeches of Union Finance Ministers*, Vol. II, New Delhi: Ministry of Finance, 1997, p. 30.

29 Agence France Presse, "India Steps Up Security Ahead of Anti-Reform Strike," 8 September 1993, newswire.

30 C. T. Kurien, "Structural Adjustments," *Frontline*, 15 December 1995, p. 93. See also Agence France Presse, "Indian Loan Talks With IMF Run Into Political Uncertainty," newswire, 28 July 1993.

31 "Harvesting India's Reforms," *The Economist*, 6 March 1993, p. 33.

32 "India: Look Out, Asia," *The Economist*, 26 June 1993, p. 34.
33 "An Indian Tiger," *The Economist*, 9 April 1994, p. 15.
34 Batuk Ghatani, "Where the Rich Lecture the Poor," *The Hindu*, 6 February 2000.
35 N. Vasuki Rao, "India: Ripe For Foreign Products As Curbs Lifted," *Journal of Commerce* (New Delhi), 9 February 2000, p. 9.
36 C. Rammanohar Reddy, "National Interest Will Be the Touchstone at Seattle: Maran," *The Hindu*, 28 November 1999.
37 "CPI Expects Budget to Toe Dictates of IMF/World Bank," *Economic Times*, 27 January 2000.
38 See, for instance, "On the Warpath," *The Indian Express*, 9 October 1997, p. 7. Also, Govind R. Agarwal, *South–South Economic Cooperation: Problems and Prospects*, New Delhi: Radiant Publishers, 1987.
39 On India's role in these organizations, see Richard L. Jackson, *The Non-Aligned, the UN, and the Superpowers*, New York: Praeger, 1983; Thomas G. Weiss and Hans W. Singer, *Multilateral Development Diplomacy in UNCTAD: The Lessons of Group Negotiations 1964–84*, New York: St. Martin's Press, 1986; Bibek Debroy, *Beyond the Uruguay Round: The Indian Perspective on GATT*, New Delhi: Response Books, 1996; Anthony Rowley, "G-9 Takes On G-7," *Business Times*, 6 October 1994; Agence France Presse, "Indian Finance Minister Slams Trade Hypocrisy Among Rich Nations," newswire, 29 September 1994; Marc Williams, *Third World Cooperation: The Group of 77 in UNCTAD*, London: Pinter, 1991. An excellent theoretical treatment of the organized interest articulation of developing countries in multilateral settings is Stephen Krasner, *Structural Conflict: The Third World Against Global Liberalism*, Berkeley: University of California Press, 1985.
40 David Gardner, "Indian Minister Takes on the Mantle of Trade Round Saviour," *Financial Times*, 2 February 2000.
41 Rohit Saran, "WTO Conference: Sleepless over Seattle," *India Today*, 8 November 1999; "A WTO For Everyone," *Business Week*, 14 February 2000.
42 Rohit Saran, "Interview of the Week: Mike Moore," *India Today*, 24 January 2000.
43 Some of these interviews are recounted in Chapter 4. See Appendix A for list of interviewees.
44 Martin Wolf, "India resists IMF pressure over currency," *Financial Times*, 26 May 1994; Agence France Presse, "Indian Finance Minister Slams Trade Hypocrisy Among Rich Nations," newswire, 29 September 1994.
45 See Arturo Escobar, *Encountering Development: The Making and the Unmaking of the Third World*, Princeton: Princeton University Press, 1995.
46 Jagdish Bhagwati, "The Design of Indian Development," p. 35.
47 There was also diversity of ingredients in the Washington Consensus. See Moises Naim, "Fads and Fashion in Economic Reforms: Washington Consensus or Washington Confusion?" *Third World Quarterly*, 21 (3), 2000, pp. 505–528.
48 For a review of the Bank's early relationship with India, see Mahendra Pal, *World Bank and the Third World Countries of Asia, With Special Reference to India*, New Delhi: National Publishing House, 1985. See also John P. Lewis, *India's Political Economy: Governance and Reform*, Delhi: Oxford University Press, 1995, Chapter 3.
49 The World Bank, *India: Recent Economic Developments and Prospects*, Washington: World Bank, 1994.
50 The World Bank, *India – Country Economic Memorandum: Recent Economic Developments, Achievements, and Challenges*, Washington: World Bank, 1995.
51 The World Bank, *India: Sustaining Rapid Economic Growth.*
52 The World Bank, *India 1998 Macroeconomic Update: Reforming for Growth and Poverty Reduction*, Washington: The World Bank, 1998.
53 P. Devarajan, "Talking to the World Bank," *The Hindu Business Line*, 6 November 1998.

54 Stefan Wagstyl, "India Asks IMF for Three-Year Support," *Financial Times*, 14 May 1993.
55 Shiraz Sidhva, "IMF Urges New Delhi to Speed Up Reform Pace," *Financial Times*, 28 July 1994.
56 "Camdessus Sees Scope for India to Achieve Asian 'Tiger' Status," *IMF Survey*, 10 March 1997.
57 S. D. Naik, "IMF's Assessment," *The Hindu Business Line*, 28 September 1998. See also Rukmini Parthasarthy, "Economy 2000: The Damning Deficit," *Business Today*, 22 October 1999.
58 "India's Fiscal Deficit Worrisome – IMF board member," *The Hindu*, 13 May 1999.
59 Arjun Sengupta, "Planning for Policies: A Note on the Approach to the Ninth Indian Five Year Plan," paper presented at the National Economic Council, Dhaka, Bangladesh, 15 December 1997.
60 Government of India, Planning Commission, *Eighth Five Year Plan 1992–1997*, New Delhi: Planning Commission, 1997.
61 Ibid.
62 For example, see Agence France Presse, "Indian Industry Urged to Shape Up for Competition," newswire, 27 November 1993; "Ministry to Rally Support on IRA Bill," *Business India*, 11 August 1997.
63 Pankaj Chandra and P. R. Shukla, "Manufacturing Excellence and Global Competitiveness," *Economic and Political Weekly*, 26 February 1994; "FM Has Double Standards," *Economic Times*, 12 August 1997. A good review of the efforts of Indian companies to expand abroad is S. Shiva Ramu, *Globalization: The Indian Scenario*, New Delhi: Wheeler Publishing, 1996. For an early review, see Dennis J. Encarnation, "The Political Economy of Indian Joint Industrial Ventures Abroad," *International Organization* 36 (1), 1982, pp. 31–59.
64 Montek S. Ahluwalia, "India's Economic Reforms," in Robert Cassen and Vijay Joshi, eds., *India: The Future of Economic Reform*, Delhi: Oxford University Press, 1995, pp. 13–29.
65 For Assocham's recommendations, see Assocham, *Globalisation – Emerging Role of Business in India*, New Delhi: Assocham, 1994.
66 When asked about Bajaj's foreign expansion plans, the company chairman, Rahul Bajaj, exclaimed: "Globalisation? Ha! Let's first talk about how Indian industry can survive in India! We are being wiped out." Quoted in "Dreams of Going Global?" *Sunday Observer*, 7 September 1997.
67 A number of informative interviews can be found in T. N. Sindhwani, *India's Role in Globalisation*, New Delhi: Capital Foundation Society, 1992.
68 Nayar, *Globalization and Nationalism*, p. 159.
69 "Dreams of Going Global?" p. 1.
70 Ibid.
71 "Dull and Brittle," *Business India*, 14–27 July 1997.
72 "IRA Bill Runs Into Rough Weather," *Indian Express*, 7 August 1997; "Industry Backs BJP," *Indian Express*, 7 August 1997.
73 Nayar, *Globalization and Nationalism*, pp. 159–160.
74 Quoted in Nayar, *Globalization and Nationalism*, pp. 179–180. See Chapter 5 of this volume by Nayar for further details about the relations between Indian business and government in the 1990s.
75 Rob Jenkins, *Democratic Politics and Economic Reform in India*, Cambridge: Cambridge University Press, 1999.
76 United Press International, "Violence Mars Leftist General Strike in India," newswire, 9 September 1993.
77 "Coping with Changes," *Frontline*, 30 May 1997, pp. 101–102. See also Sarath Davala, "New Economic Policy and Trade Union Response," *Economic and Political Weekly*, 1994, pp. 406–408; and the essays in the special issue on

"Liberalisation Policy and Social Concerns," *Indian Journal of Public Administration* 42 (3), 1996.

78 Vijaya Katti, "India's Economic Reforms: An Assessment of the Impact on Industry and FDI," *Foreign Trade Review* 28 (1), 1993, pp. 77–90; B. Bhattacharya, "Foreign Direct Investment in India," *Foreign Trade Review* 28 (4), 1994, pp. 307–329; Isher Judge Ahluwalia, "Indian Industry and India's Economic Reforms," Sri Ram Memorial Lecture Part II, given to the Ludhiana Management Association, Punjab, India, 21 March 1997.

79 "A Disappointing Verdict," *Frontline*, 30 May 1997. CITU challenged the power purchase agreement between the government and Enron.

80 For a leftist critique of the Bank and the Fund's influence on developing countries, see the essays in Kevin Danaher, ed., *50 Years Is Enough: The Case Against the World Bank and the International Monetary Fund*, Boston: South End Press, 1994. For a rightist critique, see Doug Bandow and Ian Vasquez, eds., *Perpetuating Poverty: The World Bank, the IMF, and the Developing World*, Washington: Cato Institute, 1994. See also Catherine Caufield, *Masters of Illusion: The World Bank and the Poverty of Nations*, New York: Henry Holt, 1997.

81 James Manor, "The Political Sustainability of Economic Liberalization in India," in Robert Cassen and Vijay Joshi, eds., *India: The Future of Economic Reform*, Delhi: Oxford University Press, 1995, pp. 341–363.

82 Vanaik, "Soldiers of Hindutva," p. 50.

83 Cameron Barr, "India's Political Woes Shake Economic Plan," *The Christian Science Monitor*, 22 December 1992; Tim McGirk, "India's Poor Wait in Vain for Trickle-Down Miracle," *Independent* (London), 3 September 1994.

84 World Bank, *India: Five Years of Stabilization and Reform, and the Challenges Ahead*, Washington: World Bank, 1997, p. 28.

85 Vanaik, "Soldiers of Hindutva," p. 52.

86 "National Campaign Against Price Rise," *The Hindu*, 3 January 1992; Wishvas Rame, "Farmers Rally Against GATT Proposals," *Economic and Political Weekly*, 30 October 1993.

87 Amitava Krishna Dutt and J. Mohan Rao, "Globalization and its Social Discontents: The Case of India," CEPA Working Paper Series, New York: Center for Economic Policy Analysis, The New School University, 2000, p. 24.

88 Brajesh Jha and B. B. Mohapatra, "Liberalisation and Agricultural prices: Some Disconcerting Trends," *Indian Journal of Agricultural Economics*, 58 (3), 2003, pp. 375–386.

89 Vandana Shiva has written extensively on this issue, and also on the ecological damage to rural India accelerated by large-scale capital investment and trade. See for instance Shiva, *Stolen Harvest: The Hijacking of the Global Food Supply*, Boston: South End Press, 2000.

90 Shiva, *Stolen Harvest*, Chapter 2.

91 Vandana Shiva, Afsar H. Jafri, Ashok Emani and Manish Pande, *Seeds of Suicide: The Ecological and Human Costs of Globalization of Agriculture*, Delhi. Research Foundation for Science, Technology and Ecology, 2000.

92 "Indian Farmers Protest in Geneva," *BBC Online*, 10 June 1999, http://news.bbc.co.uk/2/hi/south_asia/365419.stm, accessed 4 February 2001; "India: Farmers Protest W.T.O.," the *New York Times*, 3 October 2001; "Over 50,000 Farmers Protest Against WTO in India," India Resource Center, http://www.indiaresource.org/news/2005/2017.html, accessed 23 May 2007.

93 "Turning Out the Lights: Opponents of India's Reforms Are Doing Its Rivals a Favor," *Asiaweek*, 25 August 1995; "A Port Project in Trouble," *Frontline*, 11 July 1997.

94 See C. Rammanohar Reddy, "Clouds Over the Summit," *The Hindu*, 6 February 2000.

95 Vanaik, "Soldiers of Hindutva," p. 54.

96 The study was done by the Centre for the Study of Developing Societies, based on a survey of 9111 respondents. A summary report is in Yogendra Yadav, "The BJP's New Social Bloc," *Frontline*, 6 November 1999.

97 See for example, "Swadeshi Army Planned to Take on MNCs," *Business Standard*, 5 September 1997.

98 "We Swadeshis Can Do With Videshi Ambanis," *Economic Times*, 4 September 1997.

99 The Dunkel Draft refers to the agreement drafted by GATT's Director General, Arthur Dunkel, as a final, compromise solution to the negotiating parties. It ushered the conclusion of the Uruguay Round in 1993 and paved the way to establish the WTO in 1995. In India, Dunkel was frequently posed and sometimes scapegoated as the nemesis of independent economic development in India and other developing countries.

100 See, for example, Inter Press Service, "India: Parliament Paralyzed by Anti-Dunkel Protest," *Newswire*, 17 December 1993.

101 "GATT Proposals Will Mean Economic Slavery: V. P. Singh," *The Hindu*, 12 January 1992.

102 "Government Withdraws Bill on Insurance Authority," *The Hindu*, 7 August 1997.

103 "Whither Unity on Economic Reforms?" *Financial Express*, 8 August 1997; "Congress Firm On Reform Path," *Business Standard*, 11 August 1997. At the Congress Party's plenary session, it was decided that reforms are supportable provided that the objective was "growth, self-reliance, and increased social justice."

104 "The State of Reform in India," *The Economist*, 6 August 1994. "Throes of a Textile Town," *Business India*, 16–29 June 1997.

105 "No Cause for Alarm, Says Chidambaram," *The Hindu*, 19 June 1996.

106 See the major Indian newspapers for the first week of August 1997.

107 Terence J. Byres, "From Ivory Tower to the Belly of the Beast: The Academy, the State, and Economic Debate in Post-Independence India," in Byres, ed., *The Indian Economy: Major Debates Since Independence*, Delhi: Oxford University Press, 1998, pp. 74–115.

108 Errol D'Souza, "How Did the Reforms Gain Acceptability?" *Economic and Political Weekly*, 26 July 1997; Mani Shankar Aiyar, "Globalising Swadeshi: Should All Mediocre Indians Give Way to Competent Foreigners?" *India Today*, 13 October 1997; Prabhat Patnaik and C. P. Chandrasekhar, "India: Dirigisme, Structural Adjustment, and the Radical Alternative," in Dean Baker, Gerald Epstein, and Robert Pollin, eds., *Globalization and Progressive Economic Policy*, Cambridge: Cambridge University Press, 1998.

109 See Prabhat Patnaik's essays: "International Capital and National Economic Policy: A Critique of India's Economic Reforms," *Economic and Political Weekly*, 19 March 1994; "Macro-Economic Policy in Times of 'Globalisation'," *Economic and Political Weekly*, 16–23 April 1994. See also R. G. Nambiar and Gopal Tadas, "Is Trade De-industrializing India?" *Economic and Political Weekly*, 15 October 1994.

110 Arun Ghosh, "Rent Seeking and Economic Reforms," *Economic and Political Weekly*, 1–8 January 1994.

111 BM, "Deepening Reliance on Foreign Capital," *Economic and Political Weekly*, 6 March 1993; Arun Ghosh, "GATT, MTO and the Indian Constitution," *Economic and Political Weekly*, 15 January 1994.

112 Arun Ghosh, "1994–95 Budget: A Total Surrender," *Economic and Political Weekly* 29, 16–23 April 1994.

113 Ajit Kumar Singh, "Social Consequences of New Economic Policies," *Economic and Political Weekly*, 13 February 1993.

114 BM, "An Irresponsible Budget," *Economic and Political Weekly*, 12 March 1994. See also, Ashok Rudra, "Privatization and Deregulation," *Economic and Political*

Weekly, 21 December 1991; Prayag Mehta, "New Economic Policy, Workplace and Human Development," *Economic and Political Weekly*, 28 May 1994; Arun Ghosh, "Ideologues and Ideology: Privatisation of Public Enterprises," *Economic and Political Weekly*, 23 July 1994. Countering these popular claims, some argued that the supposed threat by posed the multinationals was hyperbole. See for example, Mehta, "Globalisation of the Indian Economy"; S. Ganesh, "Who Is Afraid of the Foreign Firms? Current Trends in FDI in India," *Economic and Political Weekly*, 3 May 1997.

115 Chitra Subramaniam, *India is For Sale*, New Delhi: VBS Publishers, 1997; S. P. Shukla, "Resisting the World Trade Organization: Agenda for Marrakesh," *Economic and Political Weekly*, 12 March 1994.

116 JM, "GATT, the Dunkel Draft, and India," *Economic and Political Weekly*, 25 January 1992; S. P. Shukla, "Sovereignty vs Small Pickings," *Frontline*, 14–20 October 1997.

117 Deepak Nayyar, "Intellectual Property Rights and LDCs: Some Strategic Issues," *Economic and Political Weekly*, 8 February 1992; Biswajit Dhar and C. Niranjan Rao, "Dunkel Draft on TRIPs: Complete Denial of Developing Country Interests," *Economic and Political Weekly*, 8 February 1992; Suman Sahai, "Dunkel Draft is Bad for Agriculture," *Economic and Political Weekly*, 19 June 1993; Suman Sahai: "Intellectual Property Rights for Life Forms: What Should Guide India's Position?" *Economic and Political Weekly*, 15 January 1994; Suman Sahai, "GATT and the Patenting of Micro Organisms," *Economic and Political Weekly*, 9 April 1994; "Transparency in the Patents Regime," *The Hindu*, 23 August 1996; S Venkitaramanan, "Patent injustice," *The Hindu Business Line*, 29 December 1997.

118 Vijay Joshi and I. M. D. Little, *India's Economic Reforms, 1991–2001*, Oxford: Clarendon, 1996, pp. 257–258.

119 James Manor, "India's Reform Strengths," in Edward Friedman and Bruce Gilley, eds., *Asia's Giants: Comparing China and India*, New York: Palgrave Macmillan, 2005, pp. 100–101.

120 Jenkins, *Democratic Politics*.

121 Joshi and Little, *India's Economic Reforms*, p. 258.

122 Dutt and Rao, "Globalization and its Social Discontents," p. 17.

123 Chris Lefkow, "Rough Seas Ahead for India's Economic Reforms," Agence France Presse newswire, December 16, 1994; John Thor-Dahlburg, "India's Prime Minister Faces Familiar Political Problems," *Los Angeles Times*, 22 December 1994.

124 Mala Lalvani, "Sounding the Alarm: Impact of Political Instability on Growth and Fiscal Health of the Indian Economy," *Economics of Governance* 4 (2), 2003, pp. 103–114.

125 Manor, "India's Reform Strengths," p. 101. Manor argues that India's democratic structure and federalism have been advantageous, because without them much greater social dislocation may have occurred, as happened in China. While I agree with Manor, the point is that there was, nonetheless, significant social turmoil against economic openness, which failed to get the government to reverse its policies even at the risk of being forced out of power.

126 Jenkins, *Democratic Politics*, p. 5. See also Chapter 5.

127 Ramani Kumar and Pranab K Banerjee, "Role of States in Export Promotion Efforts: A Case Study of Rajasthan," *Foreign Trade Review* 31 (3), 1996, pp. 53–65.

128 S. Guhan, "Centre and States in the Reform Process," in Robert Cassen and Vijay Joshi, eds., *India: The Future of Economic Reform*, New Delhi: Oxford University Press, 1995, p. 73. See also V. A. Pai Panandiker, "The Political Economy of Centre-State Relations in India," in Ahluwalia and Little, eds., *India's Economic Reforms and Development*, pp. 375–394.

129 Quoted in Bruce Gilley, "Two Passages to Modernity," in Edward Friedman and Bruce Gilley, eds., *Asia's Giants: Comparing China and India*, New York: Palgrave Macmillan, 2005, p. 32.

130 Eswaran Sridharan, "Coalition Politics in India: Lessons from Theory, Comparisons, and Recent History," Centre for Policy Research, Monograph, New Delhi: CPR, May 1997, p. 18. On reforms and the electoral cycle in India, see Sridharan, "Political Institutions and Economic Reform: Lessons from the Indian Experience 1991–96," Centre for Policy Research, Monograph, New Delhi: CPR, May 1997.

131 Martin Wolf, "Survey of India," *Financial Times*, 30 September 1993. In another interview with Stefan Wagstyl of the *Financial Times*, Manmohan Singh remarked again: "Given the democratic nature of our political system, it's a miracle we have got this far." *Financial Times*, 30 September 1993.

132 "Economic Reforms and Elections," *The Hindu*, 25 April 1996.

133 "Globalising India," *The Hindu*, 8 May 1996.

134 "The Economic Reality," *The Hindu*, 20 May 1996.

135 Lally Weymouth, "India is Open Globally," Interview with Prime Minister Deve Gowda, *Newsweek*, 16 December 1996.

136 "Economic Reforms to Provide Comfort," *The Statesman*, 1 February 1999.

137 "BJP Alliance Will Continue Reforms, Says Advani," *The Hindustan Times*, 29 April 1999.

138 For academic analyses of the various sources of political conflict in India, see Lloyd I. Rudolph and Susanne Hoeber Rudolph, *In Pursuit of Lakshmi: The Political Economy of the Indian State*, Chicago: University of Chicago Press, 1987; Paul R. Brass, *The Politics of India Since Independence*, Cambridge: Cambridge University Press, 1994; Ashutosh Varshney, *Democracy, Development, and the Countryside: Rural–Urban Struggles in India*, Cambridge: Cambridge University Press, 1995; T. V. Sathyamurthy, ed., *Region, Religion, Caste, Gender and Culture in Contemporary India*, Delhi: Oxford University Press, 1996.

139 Jenkins, *Democratic Politics*. The quotation is from p. 85.

140 Vincent Cable, "Indian Liberalization and the Private Sector," in Cassen and Joshi, eds., *India: The Future of Economic Reform*, p. 224.

141 Jenkins, *Democratic Politics*, p. 178.

142 Vijay Joshi and I. M. D. Little, *India: Macroeconomics and Political Economy, 1964–1991*, New Delhi: Oxford University Press, 1994.

143 Nayar, *Globalization and Nationalism*, p. 106.

3 Roots of globalism and rivalry

1 See the *New York Times*, 5 May 1998, 12 May 1998, 15 May 1998. See also Richard Weixing Hu, "India's Nuclear Bomb and Future Sino-Indian Relations," *East Asia: An International Quarterly* 17 (1), 1999, pp. 40–69.

2 George Perkovich holds this view in *India's Nuclear Bomb: The Impact on Global Proliferation*, Berkeley: University of California Press, 1999. Perkovich contends that Fernandes was "out of the loop" because the government had no integrated strategy about nuclear testing. But it seems unlikely that the defense minister would be out of loop, especially within a unified nationalist party like the BJP. Moreover, it would have been difficult to hide the testing under such tight secrecy in the absence of an integrated strategy.

3 Dorothy Woodman, *Himalayan Frontiers: A Political Review of British, Chinese, Indian and Russian Rivalries*, London: Barrie and Rockliff, 1969, Chapter 1.

4 Neville Maxwell, *India's China War*, New York: Pantheon, 1970, p. 21.

5 Imagination of boundaries is common to both imperialist and nationalist movements, as shown by Benedict Anderson in *Imagined Communities*, London: Verso, 1991.

6 Sunil Khilnani, *The Idea of India*, London: Hamish Hamilton, 1997, p. 155.

7 See John Rowland, *A History of Sino-Indian Relations: Hostile Co-Existence*, Princeton: D. Van Nostrand, 1967, pp. 25–40; Sneh Mahajan, *British Foreign Policy, 1874–1914: The Role of India*, London: Routledge, 2002.

8 Incidentally, Mackinder was made Britain's ambassador to Russia when Lord Curzon, who was Her Majesty's viceroy to India, became the Secretary of State. Curzon was one of the most committed voices of the "forward school."
9 Maxwell, *India's China War*, pp. 40–43.
10 Rowland, *A History of Sino-Indian Relations*, p. 41.
11 This section draws from the definitive, and fascinating, history of the boundary: Alastair Lamb, *The McMahon Line: A Study in the Relations between India, China and Tibet, 1904 to 1914*, London: Routledge and Kegan Paul, 1966, esp. pp. 459–567.
12 Maxwell, *India's China War*, pp. 54–55.
13 David Strang, "Contested Sovereignty: The Social Construction of Colonial Imperialism," in Thomas J. Biersteker and Cynthia Weber, eds., *State Sovereignty as Social Construct*, Cambridge: Cambridge University Press, 1996.
14 Quoted in Maxwell, *India's China War*, p. 65.
15 Sumit Ganguly, "India and China: Border Issues, Domestic Integration, and International Security," in Francine R. Frankel and Harry Harding, eds, *The India–China Relationship: What the United States Needs to Know*, New York: Columbia University Press, 2004, p. 106.
16 See Nehru's famous speech given to the Indian Constituent Assembly on the eve of independence, 14 August 1947. It begins, "Long years ago we made a tryst with destiny, and now the time comes when we shall redeem our pledge.... At the stroke of the midnight hour, while the world sleeps, India will awake to life and freedom."
17 Churchill, speaking to the House of Commons, February 1931; cited in the opening of Larry Collins and Dominique Lapierre, *Freedom at Midnight*, New York: Simon and Schuster, 1975.
18 Khilnani, *The Idea of India*, p. 157.
19 Nationalist historiography started from repopularizing the *Vedic* and *puranic* myths, and then recasting many of them with a pan-Indian appeal. See Partha Chatterjee, *The Nation and Its Fragments: Colonial and Postcolonial Histories*, Princeton: Princeton University Press, 1993, esp. Chapters 4 and 5.
20 Bimla Prasad, *The Origins of Indian Foreign Policy: Indian National Congress and World Affairs, 1885–1947*, Calcutta: Bookland, 1962, pp. 3–4.
21 Ibid.
22 Ibid., pp. 37–39.
23 Ibid., pp. 42–47.
24 Ibid., pp. 68–69.
25 Ibid., p. 70.
26 Chatterjee, *The Nation and Its Fragments*, p. 7.
27 Prasad, *The Origins of Indian Foreign Policy*, p. 73.
28 Nayar and Paul, *India in the World Order: Searching for Major-Power Status*, Cambridge: Cambridge University Press, 2003, p. 141.
29 J. Bandopadhyaya, *The Making of India's Foreign Policy*, Bombay: Allied Publishers 1970, pp. 71–72.
30 Ibid., p. 85.
31 Stanley Wolpert, *Nehru: A Tryst with Destiny*, New York: Oxford University Press, 1996, p. 77.
32 Michael Brecher, *Nehru: A Political Biography*, London: Oxford University Press, 1959, pp. 564–565. See also Bandopadhyaya, *The Making of India's Foreign Policy*, Chapter 5.
33 Khilnani, *The Idea of India*, p. 178.
34 Quoted in Baldev Raj Nayar, "A World Role: The Dialectics of Purpose and Power," in John W. Mellor, ed., *India: A Rising Middle Power*, Boulder: Westview Press, 1979, p. 123.
35 Debating foreign affairs, January 22, 1947; Jawaharlal Nehru, *India's Foreign*

Policy: Selected Speeches, September 1946–April 1961, New Delhi: Publicity Division, Ministry of Information and Broadcasting, Government of India, 1961, p. 13.

36 Nehru, speech in Constituent Assembly, 8 March 1948; in Nehru, *India's Foreign Policy*, p. 36.

37 Jawaharlal Nehru, *Independence and After: A Collection of Speeches, 1946–1949*, New York: John Day, 1950, p. 248.

38 Chatterjee, *The Nation and Its Fragments*, p. 6.

39 Sunil Khilnani also points to this in *The Idea of India* (p. 153): "a sense of region and nation emerged together, through parallel self-definitions."

40 Prasad, *The Origins of Indian Foreign Policy*, p. 11.

41 Prime Minister's speech in the Parliament, 7 December 1950, in A. Appadorai, *Select Documents on India's Foreign Policy and Relations 1947–1972*, vol. 1, Delhi: Oxford University Press, 1982, doc. 19, p. 26.

42 Baldev Raj Nayar and T. V. Paul, *India in the World Order: Searching for Major-Power Status*, Cambridge: Cambridge University Press, 2003, pp. 124–127.

43 Nayar, "A World Role," p. 122.

44 See ibid., p. 122.

45 Rowland, *A History of Sino-Indian Relations*, p. 81; Prasad, *The Origins of Indian Foreign Policy*, p. 116.

46 For a useful summary, see A. K. Damodaran, "India's China Policy: A Retrospective Survey," in Surjit Mansingh, ed., *Indian and Chinese Foreign Policies in Comparative Perspective*, New Delhi: Radiant, 1998, pp. 35–50.

47 Ganguly, "Border Issues," p. 108.

48 Michael Brecher, *India and World Politics: Krishna Menon's View of the World*, New York: Praeger, 1968, p. 310.

49 Rowland, *A History of Sino-Indian Relations*, p. 76.

50 Ibid., pp. 78–90.

51 Steven A. Hoffmann, "Perception and China Policy in India," in Francine R. Frankel and Harry Harding, eds., *The India-China Relationship: What the United States Needs to Know*, New York: Columbia University Press, 2004, p. 37.

52 Wolpert, *Nehru*, p. 471. See also Ganguly, "Border Issues," pp. 110–111.

53 See Rowland, *A History of Sino-Indian Relations*; Maxwell, *India's China War*; and T. S. Murty, *India–China Boundary: India's Options*, New Delhi: ABC Publishing, 1987.

54 For details about the war, consult Steven A. Hoffmann, *India and the China Crisis*, Berkeley: University of California Press, 1990.

55 Ibid.

56 Quoted in Gopalji Malviya, "The Sino-Indian Security Environment: Inadequate Responses from New Delhi," in Mansingh, ed., *Indian and Chinese Foreign Policies*, p. 130.

57 Nayar and Paul, *India in the World Order*, pp. 131–132; Hoffmann, *India and the China Crisis*, p. 214; Baljit Singh, *Indian Foreign Policy: An Analysis*, New York: Asia Publishing, 1975; V. Longer, *The Defense and Foreign Policies of India*, New Delhi: Sterling, 1988, Chapters 3 and 4; and Damodoran, "India's China Policy."

58 This is not to say that he was closed to outside consultations, but as Wolpert noted in *Nehru*: "Throughout the 1950s Nehru enjoyed unlimited, indeed, virtually unchallenged power" (p. 457). The war was the beginning of his political decline, and it took a heavy emotional toll on him.

59 Hoffmann, *India and the China Crisis*, p. 215. See also Yaacov Y. I. Vertzberger, *Misperceptions in Foreign Policymaking: The Sino-Indian Conflict, 1959–1962*, Boulder: Westview, 1984.

60 Maxwell, *India's China War*; Achin Vanaik, *The Painful Transition: Bourgeois Democracy in India*, London: Verso, 1990, p. 236.

61 Nayar, "A World Role," pp. 140–141.

62 J. N. Dixit, *Across Borders: Fifty Years of India's Foreign Policy*, New Delhi: Picus, 1998, esp., Chapter 4.
63 Ibid., p. 219.
64 Naheed Murtaza, *Parliament and Foreign Policy: Reflections on India-China Relations*, New Delhi: Cadplan, 1998.
65 Hoffman, *India and the China Crisis*, pp. 229–230.
66 Ibid.
67 See "Peace on the Border," *The Economist*, 26 August 1995, p. 30; "All Quiet on the Eastern Front," *The Economist*, 7 December 1996, p. 34.
68 See Shashi Tharoor, *Reasons of State: Political Development and India's Foreign Policy Under Indira Gandhi 1966–1977*, Delhi: Vikas, 1982.
69 K. Subrahmanyam, "Indira Gandhi's Quest for Security," in Damodaran and Bajpai, eds., *Indian Foreign Policy*, New Delhi: Radiant, 1990, p. 70.
70 Gargi Dutt, "India–China Relations," in Damodaran and Bajpai, eds., *Indian Foreign Policy*, p. 96.
71 See Sumit Ganguly, *The Origins of War in South Asia: The Indo-Pakistani Conflicts Since 1947*, Boulder: Westview, 1994.
72 U. S. Bajpai, "Indira Gandhi and India's Neighbours," in A. K. Damodaran and U. S. Bajpai, eds., *Indian Foreign Policy: The Indira Gandhi Years*, New Delhi: Radiant, 1990, p. 129.
73 Nayar, "A World Role," p. 145.
74 Tharoor, *Reasons of State*, Table IV.5, pp. 228–229.
75 Timothy George, "Sino-Indian Relations: Opportunities and Limitations," in Timothy George, Shahram Chubin, and Robert Litwak, eds., *India and the Great Powers*, Aldershot: Gower/IISS, 1984, p. 13.
76 Bhim Sandhu, *Unresolved Conflict: China and India*, New Delhi: Radiant, 1988; A. Appadorai, *National Interest and India's Foreign Policy*, Delhi: Kalinga, 1992.
77 The events during this time escalated quickly. But India's actions and reactions were confident. The escalation is narrated succinctly in this excerpt from an essay by V. R. Raghavan:

> In 1986, a police patrol came upon clear signs of the Chinese having camped in Indian territory in Arunachal Pradesh. The Indian reaction was swift and unambiguous when the Army occupied the heights on the Hathongla–Lungrola ridge north of monastery town of Tawang. The Chinese response was hostile and violent. The People's Liberation Army came up and occupied posts within shouting distance of Indian positions and demanded that the Indian army withdraw. The PLA went on to build tracks, barracks, helicopter landing sites etc., as demonstration of its strength. Indian political resolve and military positions were strong, and before long the Chinese agreed to negotiate on reducing the risks of a military conflict in the area by a mutual pullback.

See V. R. Raghavan, "Defining India's China Border," *The Hindu*, 9 November 2000.
78 Mira Sinha Bhattacharjea and C. V. Ranganathan, "India and China – I," *The Hindu*, 8 May 2000.
79 "Sino-Indian Ties Look Up," *The Hindu*, 25 November 2000.
80 Peter Lyon, "The Foreign Policy of India," in F. S. Northledge, ed., *The Foreign Policies of the Powers*, New York: Praeger, 1968, cited in Baldev Raj Nayar, "A World Role," p. 121.
81 Nayar, "A World Role," p. 121.
82 See the essays in Mellor, ed., *India: A Rising Middle Power*.
83 Hemen Ray, *Sino-Soviet Conflict Over India*, New Delhi: Abhinav Publications, 1986.
84 Quoted in Rowland, *A History of Sino-Indian Relations*, p. 188.

85 Bhattacharjea and Ranganathan, "India and China – I."
86 See Suchita Ghosh, *China–Bangladesh–India Tangle Today: Towards a Solution?* New Delhi: Sterling, 1995; Lal Babu Yadav, *Indo-Bhutan Relations and China Interventions*, New Delhi: Anmol, 1996; S. C. Bhatt, *The Triangle India–Nepal–China: A Study of Treaty Relations*, New Delhi: Gyan Publishing, 1996.
87 Ashley J. Tellis, "China and India in Asia," in Francine R. Frankel and Harry Harding, eds., *The India–China Relationship: What the United States Needs to Know*, New York: Columbia University Press, 2004, pp. 134–177. Tellis, however, believes that direct military bases in Burma would be a strategic liability for both China and Burma. See also Andrew Selth, "Burma And The Strategic Competition Between China And India," *Journal of Strategic Studies*, 19 (2), 1996, pp. 213–230.
88 *Pravda*, 14 December 1955, quoted in Hemen Ray, *Sino-Soviet Conflict Over India*, p. 39.
89 Nayar, "A World Role," p. 122.
90 Ibid., p. 125.
91 Paul and Nayar, *India in the World Order*, pp. 95–98.
92 Cited in Perkovich, *India's Nuclear Bomb*, p. 363.
93 For more on early history see Sunil Sondhi, *Science, Technology and India's Foreign Policy*, Delhi: Anamika Prakashan, 1994, Chapter 4.
94 Cited in ibid., p. 56.
95 Jawaharlal Nehru, *The Discovery of India*, New York: John Day, 1946, p. 411. Cited in Baldev Raj Nayar, *Globalization and Nationalism: The Changing Balance in India's Economic Policy 1950–2000*, New Delhi: Sage, 2001, p. 71.
96 Nayar and Paul, *India in the World Order*, p. 154.
97 Shiv Visvanathan, "A Celebration of Difference: Science and Democracy in India," *Science*, 3 April 1998, p. 42.
98 Ibid., pp. 62–67. See also Perkovich, *India's Nuclear Bomb*, Chapter 1.
99 Sondhi, *Science, Technology and India's Foreign Policy*, p. 59.
100 "Science 'can lift India's poor'," *BBC News Online*, 9 February 2007, news.bbc.co.uk/go/pr/fr/-/2/hi/south_asia/6340201.stm.
101 Cited in ibid., p. 61.
102 Onkar Marwah, "India's Nuclear and Space Programs: Intent and Policy," *International Security* 2 (2), 1977, p. 99.
103 Ibid.
104 Quoted in Sumit Ganguly, "India's Pathway to Pokhran II," *International Security* 23 (4), 1999, pp. 152–153.
105 Nayar and Paul, *India in the World Order*, p. 199; Ganguly, "India's Pathway to Pokhran II." See also Perkovich, *India's Nuclear Bomb*; Muchkund Dubey, "Nuclear Options: The Choice Cannot Wait," *Frontline*, 26 January 1996, pp. 4–11. In *India's Nuclear Bomb*, George Perkovich holds a dissenting view. He argues that strategic competition does not fully explain India's nuclear program. Domestic and moral considerations also played a strong part in determining the course of India's nuclear policy.
106 Pratap Bhanu Mehta, "Exploding Myths," *The New Republic* 218 (23), 8 June 1998, p. 17. See also by Mehta, "India: The Nuclear Politics of Self-Esteem," *Current History* 97 (623), 1998, pp. 403–406.
107 Hoffmann, "Perception and China Policy in India," pp. 41–43.
108 In *India's Nuclear Bomb*, George Perkovich maintained the position that the use of India's nuclear power is largely symbolic.
109 Nayar and Paul, *India in the World Order*, pp. 232–233.
110 Cited in Perkovich, *India's Nuclear Bomb*, p. 360. Additional information in this section comes from G. Balachandran, "Keeping the Option Open: India's Nuclear Dilemma," *Strategic Analysis* 18 (12), 1996, pp. 1579–1588; G. Balachandran, "CTBT and India," *Strategic Analysis* 19 (3), 1996, pp. 493–506.

111 George Tanham, *Indian Strategic Thought*, Santa Monica: Rand, 1992, Chapter 2.
112 John Cherian, "Indian Advances," *Frontline*, 11 August 1995, p. 45.
113 Jasjit Singh, "Securing Sea Power," *Frontline*, 20 October 1995, pp. 54–55; "The Nuclear Submarine," *The Hindu*, 12 July 1996; "Chinese Ocean: India Must Heed Moves in Indian Ocean," *The Statesman*, 18 May 1999; "Go In for Cruise Missiles," *The Hindu*, 20 April 2000; "Russia Leases Nuclear Bombers to India," *Guardian*, 20 January 2003.
114 "Making the IAF More Sophisticated," *The Hindu*, 2 January 1996; "A Significant Achievement," *The Hindu*, 27 January 1996; "Debut of the Nishant," *The Hindu*, 27 August 1996; "LCA Makes Maiden Public Flight," *The Hindu*, 10 February 2001; "Russia Leases Nuclear Bombers to India," *Guardian*, 20 January 2003.
115 "India in Aerospace Defence Plan," *BBC News Online*, 28 January 2007, news.bbc.co.uk/go/pr/fr/-/2/hi/south_asia/6307875.stm. See also Paul Reynolds, "China's Space Challenge to the US," *BBC News Online*, 23 January 2007, news.bbc.co.uk/go/pr/fr/-/2/hi/asia-pacific/6290525.stm.
116 "Satellite Put into Orbit," *The Hindu*, 22 March 1996; "Scaling New Heights," *Frontline* 19 April 1996, pp. 65–71; "India's Space Programme," *The Hindu*, 7 September 2000; "GSLV Launch Successful, Satellite in Orbit," *The Hindu*, 19 April 2001; "Three Satellites Placed in Orbit," *The Hindu*, 23 October 2001; "India Commercial Rocket Takes Off," *BBC News Online*, 23 April 2007, news.bbc.co.uk/go/pr/fr/-/2/hi/south_asia/6582773.stm.
117 "ISRO's Plans Get a Boost in Budget," *Economic Times*, 5 March 2003; "Indian Capsule Returns from Space," *BBC News Online*, 22 January 2007, news.bbc.co.uk/go/pr/fr/-/2/hi/south_asia/6286663.stm; "Space Agencies Will Coordinate," *BBC News Online*, 31 May 2007, news.bbc.co.uk/2/hi/science/nature/6708661.stm.
118 Nayar, "A World Role," pp. 132–133.
119 An excellent discussion of these constraints is in Nayar and Paul, *India in the World Order*, pp. 103–110.
120 Quoted in Nayar and Paul, *India in the World Order*, p. 133. Emphasis added.
121 M. Solanki, Speech on "India's Foreign Policy Perspectives in the 1990s," given at the India International Centre, New Delhi, 13 August 1991.
122 "We Will Not Close Our Defence Options: PM," *The Hindu*, 26 January 1996.
123 "Raising India's Profile," *The Hindu*, 11 September 2000.
124 "France backs India for Council seat," *The Hindu*, 19 April 2000.
125 "India 'Fitting Contender' for U.N. Seat: Putin," *The Hindu*, 2 October 2000.
126 "China and India: Too Early to Tell," *The Economist*, 14 April 2005.
127 Susan Shirk, "One-Sided Rivalry: China's Perceptions and Policies Toward India," in Frankel and Harding, eds., *The India–China Relationship*, pp. 75–76.
128 See for example, "Evolution of India's Nuclear Policy," Paper Laid on the Table of the House (Lower House of the Indian Parliament, Lok Sabha), meadev.gov.in/govt/evolution.htm, accessed 28 March 1999.
129 "Military Modernisation Programme 'Running Parallel' With China," *The Hindu*, 10 October 2000.
130 Later on, in 2003, George Fernandes withdrew his claim in some ways, once he was out of the government. He declared that he had been "erroneously" portrayed as a "China-baiter." See "George Says China Not a Threat to India," *Economic Times*, 30 January 2003.
131 "India's China Syndrome," *The Business Standard*, 5 May 1998.
132 Hoffman, "Perception and China Policy in India," pp. 39–40.
133 Mohammed Ayoob, "India and the Major Powers," *The Hindu*, 30 May 2000. See also Dutta, "India's Evolving Relations with China"; Malviya, "The Sino-Indian Security Environment."
134 Hoffmann, "Perception and China Policy in India."

135 Marwah, "India's Nuclear and Space Programs," p. 99.
136 Shantanu Nandan Sharma, "Does India Need More Nukes Now?" *Economic Times*, 31 March 2003.
137 N. Ram, "Nuclear Policy: What India Must Do," *Frontline*, 26 January 1996, pp. 17–21; Jasjit Singh, "India and the CTBT," *Strategic Analysis* 19 (6), 1996, pp. 835–850.
138 "Launching of Insat-3B," *The Hindu*, 24 March 2000.
139 "Science 'can lift India's poor'," *BBC News Online*, 9 February 2007, news.bbc.co.uk/go/pr/fr/-/2/hi/south_asia/6340201.stm.
140 "Sinha Showcases India's Potential," *The Hindu*, 7 May 2000.

4 Evolution of economic globalism and economic rivalry

1 Baldev Raj Nayar, *Globalization and Nationalism: The Changing Balance in India's Economic Policy 1950–2000*, New Delhi: Sage, 2001.
2 Lloyd I. Rudolph and Susanne Hoeber Rudolph, *In Pursuit of Lakshmi: The Political Economy of the Indian State*, Chicago: University of Chicago Press, 1987, p. 214.
3 For a fascinating discussion of this, see Andrew Wyatt, "Building the Temples of Postmodern India: Economic Constructions of National Identity," *Contemporary South Asia*, 14 (4), 2005.
4 Sunil Khilnani, *The Idea of India*, London: Hamish Hamilton, 1997, p. 73.
5 Cited in Nirmal Kumar Chandra, "Planning and Foreign Investment in Indian Manufacturing," in Terence J. Byres, ed., *The State, Development Planning and Liberalisation in India*, Delhi: Oxford University Press, 1997, pp. 370.
6 Quoted in Nayar, *Globalization and Nationalism*, p. 64.
7 Deepak Nayyar, "The Foreign Trade Sector, Planning and Industrialisation in India," in Terence J. Byres, ed., *The State, Development Planning and Liberalisation in India*, Delhi: Oxford University Press, 1997, pp. 342.
8 Quoted in Nayar, *Globalization and Nationalism*, p. 69. For these "imaginings," see Andrew Wyatt, "(Re)imagining the Indian (Inter)national Economy," *New Political Economy* 10 (2), 2005, pp. 163–179.
9 Nayyar, "The Foreign Trade Sector."
10 Satish Deshpande, "Imagined Economies: Styles of Nation-building in Twentieth Century India," *Journal of Arts and Ideas* 25–26, 1993, p. 7.
11 Quoted in Baldev Raj Nayar and T. V. Paul, *India in the World Order: Searching for Major-Power Status*, Cambridge: Cambridge University Press, 2003, p. 153.
12 See Nehru's *The Discovery of India*, New York: John Day, 1946.
13 Wilfred Malenbaum, "India and China: Contrasts in Development Performance," *American Economic Review* 49 (3), 1959, p. 291.
14 Baldev Raj Nayar, "A World Role: The Dialectics of Purpose and Power," in John W. Mellor, ed., *India: A Rising Middle Power*, Boulder: Westview, 1979, p. 121.
15 See for instance Nehru's speeches during the war years; also Stanley Wolpert, *Nehru: A Tryst with Destiny*, New York: Oxford University Press, 1996, pp. 485–487.
16 Wilfred Malenbaum, "India and China: Development Contrasts," *The Journal of Political Economy* 64 (1), 1956, pp. 1–24; Malenbaum, "India and China: Contrasts in Development Performance."
17 Gargi Dutt, "India China Relations," in A. K. Damodaran and U. S. Bajpai, eds., *Indian Foreign Policy: The Indira Gandhi Years*, New Delhi: Radiant, 1990, p. 102.
18 "Interview with Senator Kennedy," *Washington Post*, October 22, 1960, reproduced in www.mtholyoke.edu/acad/intrel/pentagon2/ps4.htm.
19 Barry Richman, "Economic Development in China and India: Some Conditioning

Factors," *Pacific Affairs* 45 (1), 1972, pp. 75–91; Thomas E. Weisskopf, "China and India: Contrasting Experiences in Economic Development," *American Economic Review* 65 (2), 1975, pp. 356–364.

20 Subramanian Swamy, *Economic Growth in China and India: A Comparative Appraisal*, Chicago: University of Chicago Press, 1973; Subramanian Swamy, "Economic Growth in China and India, 1952–1970: A Comparative Appraisal," *Economic Development and Cultural Change* 21 (4), Part 2, 1973, pp. 1–84. For dissent about the results of this study, see Wilfred Malenbaum, "A Review of Subramanian Swamy, Economic Growth in China and India 1952–1970," *Journal of Asian Studies* 34 (1), 1974, pp. 256–258.

21 Subramanian Swamy, "The Economic Distance between China and India, 1955–73," *The China Quarterly*, No. 70, 1977, pp. 371–382. See also Swamy's more historical study: "The Response to Economic Challenge: A Comparative Economic History of China and India, 1870–1952," *The Quarterly Journal of Economics* 93 (1), 1979, pp. 25–46.

22 As noted by senior officials of the Planning Commission with whom I spoke.

23 Manmohan Singh, *India's Export Trends and the Prospects for Self-Sustained Growth*, Oxford: Clarendon Press, 1964. In the second half of the 1970s Singh became Secretary of the Department of Economic Affairs in the Finance Ministry and by the early 1980s had become Planning Secretary.

24 Jean Drèze and Amartya Sen, *India: Economic Development and Social Opportunity*, Delhi: Oxford University Press, 1995, p. 67. As Gerald Segal put it, "Few economists trust modern Chinese economic data; even Chinese Prime Minister Zhu Rongji distrusts it." Segal, "Does China Matter?" *Foreign Affairs* 78 (5), 1999, pp. 24–36.

25 Wilfred Malenbaum, "Modern Economic Growth in India and China: The Comparison Revisited, 1950–1980," *Economic Development and Cultural Change* 31 (1), 1982, pp. 45–84.

26 Ibid., p. 48. Malenbaum, however, questions the validity of these predictions, particularly because of the inferior quality of China's official statistics.

27 T. N. Srinivasan, "External Sector in Development: China and India, 1950–89," *American Economic Review* 80 (2), 1990, pp. 113–117.

28 Achin Vanaik, *The Painful Transition: Bourgeois Democracy in India*, London: Verso, 1990, p. 50.

29 A. S. Bhalla, *Uneven Development in the Third World: A Study of China and India*, New York: St. Martin's, 1992; George Rosen, *Contrasting Styles of Industrial Reform: China and India in the 1980s*, Chicago: University of Chicago Press, 1992; T. N. Srinivasan, *Agriculture and Trade in China and India: Policies and Performance since 1950*, San Francisco: ICS Press, 1994.

30 See Vanaik, *The Painful Transition*, pp. 47–51; Drèze and Sen, *India*, Chapters 3 and 4.

31 Drèze and Sen, *India*, p. 57.

32 Ibid., p. 67; original emphasis.

33 Ibid., p. 68; original emphasis.

34 Miria Pigato *et al.*, *South Asia's Integration into the World Economy*, Washington: World Bank, 1997, Table 1.3.

35 On China's perception of India see Susan Shirk, "One-Sided Rivalry: China's Perceptions and Policies Toward India," in Francine R. Frankel and Harry Harding, eds., *The India–China Relationship: What the United States Needs to Know*, New York: Columbia University Press, 2004, pp. 75–102; John W. Garver, "Asymmetrical Indian and Chinese Threat Perceptions," in Sumit Ganguly, ed., *India as an Emerging Power*, London: Frank Cass, 2003, pp. 109–134.

36 Sanjay Kathuria and Nisha Taneja, *India's Exports: The Challenge from China*, New Delhi: Indian Council for Research in International Economic Relations, 1986.

37 Deepak Nayyar, "The Foreign Trade Sector, Planning and Industrialisation in India," in Terence J. Byres, ed., *The State, Development Planning and Liberalisation in India*, New York: Oxford University Press, 1997, p. 344.
38 Drèze and Sen, *India*, p. 58.
39 This was revealed to me in a number of interviews with policymakers at that time.
40 Dr. Ashok Lahiri, Economic Advisor, Ministry of Finance, Government of India, author's interview, New Delhi, 16 September 1997.
41 Government of India, Lok Sabha Secretariat, *National Industrial Policy*, New Delhi: Lok Sabha Secretariat, 1985, p. 17.
42 Mr. Jairam Ramesh, Political Advisor to the Finance Minister, Government of India, author's interview, New Delhi, 11 October 1997. Mr. Ramesh later also became a member of the upper house the Indian Parliament, and is currently the Minister of State for Commerce.
43 Mr. C. Raja Mohan, Strategic Affairs Editor, *The Hindu*, author's interview, New Delhi, 11 October 1997.
44 Government of India, Ministry of Finance, *Speech of Shri Manmohan Singh Presenting Central Government's Budget for 1991–92*, New Delhi: Ministry of Finance, 1991, pp. 1–2.
45 "Rupee Again Devalued by 11.83 p.c. Against the Pound," *The Hindu*, 4 July 1991; "Further Steep Devaluation to Make Exports Competitive," *The Hindu*, 4 July 1991.
46 Government of India, Ministry of Finance, *Economic Survey 1991–92*, New Delhi: Government of India, 1992, p. 23.
47 Government of India, *Economic Survey 1992–93*, New Delhi: Ministry of Finance, 1993, p. 17.
48 Government of India, *Economic Survey 1993–94*, New Delhi: Ministry of Finance, 1994, p. 12.
49 Government of India, *Economic Survey 1995–96*, New Delhi: Government of India, 1997, p. 21.
50 Quoted in Frank L. Bartels and Barry H. Pavier, "Enron in India," *Economic and Political Weekly* 32 (8), 22 February 1997, p. M–11.
51 Jairam Ramesh, "Let's Not Kid Ourselves," *India Today*, 24 May 1999.
52 See, for instance, Kamla Suri, *India's Economy and the World*, New Delhi: Vikas, 1992; S. Paul, *India's Exports: New Imperatives and Newer Vistas*, New Delhi: Commonwealth Publishers, 1992.
53 Associated Chambers of Commerce and Industry of India, *Export Perspective for 2000: Priorities and Competitive Advantages*, New Delhi: Assocham, 1995.
54 Sugata Marjit and Ajitava Raychaudhuri, *India's Exports: An Analytical Study*, Delhi: Oxford University Press, 1997.
55 "India and China: Clash of the Titans," *The Economist*, 4 November 2004.
56 For a fuller analysis, see Jalal Alamgir, "India's Trade and Investment Policy: The Influence of Strategic Rivalry with China," *Issues and Studies* 35 (3), 1999; Jalal Alamgir, "Strategic Rivalry and Tariff Liberalization in India," *Brown Economic Review* 7 (1), 1999.
57 "SEZs, A Humble Beginning: Maran," *The Hindu*, 2 April 2000.
58 Dr. Arjun Sengupta, Member, Planning Commission, Government of India, author's interview, Dhaka, 17 December 1997. Dr. Sengupta was previously India's ambassador to the European Commission and Special Advisor to Michel Camdessus, former Managing Director of the International Monetary Fund.
59 Prem Shankar Jha, "Why India's Globalisation Has Failed," *The Hindu*, 27 March 2002.
60 Ms. Manashi Roy, Deputy Director General, Confederation of Indian Industry, author's interview, New Delhi, 11 September, 1997; Dr. Amit Mitra, Secretary General, Federation of Indian Chambers of Commerce and Industry, author's interview; provided written answers to questionnaire, 10 October 1997. Also, "Steps

Must Be Followed Up: Assocham," *The Hindu*, 1 April 2002; "CII's Initiatives on Economic, Social Sectors," *The Hindu*, 4 May 2002.

61 "Follow Chinese Model – Goldman," *Financial Express*, 3 October 2006.

62 John P. Lewis, "Some Consequences of Giantism: The Case of India," *World Politics* 43 (3), 1991, pp. 367–389.

63 "The Competition Hots Up," *The Hindu*, 9 June 2000.

64 Subramanian Swamy, "Can India Catch Up with China?" *Frontline*, 22 July 2000.

65 Mohan Guruswamy, Abhishek Kaul, and Vishal Handa, "Is India Really Shining?" *The Hindu*, 3 December 2003.

66 Mr. Montek Singh Ahluwalia, Secretary of Finance, Government of India, author's interview, New Delhi, 12 September 1997.

67 C. Raja Mohan, "Thinking Big, Thinking Small," *The Hindu*, 3 June 2000.

68 Nirupam Bajpai and Jeffrey D. Sachs, "Foreign Direct Investment in India – I," *The Hindu*, 30 June 2000.

69 Government of India, *Economic Survey 1993–94*, p. 1.

70 "QRs on 714 Items Lifted to Allow Free Imports," *The Hindu*, 1 April 2000.

71 See Government of India, *Medium Term Export Strategy 2002–2007*, New Delhi: Ministry of Commerce and Industry, 2002.

72 Government of India, *Economic Survey 2006–7*, New Delhi: Ministry of Finance, 2007, p. 16.

73 Government of India, Foreign Trade Policy 2004–2009 (New Delhi: Ministry of Commerce of Industry, 2006), p. 7.

74 Mr. A. N. Verma, Chairman, Foreign Investment Promotion Board, Government of India, and Principal Secretary to the Prime Minister (Narasimha Rao), 1991–1996, author's interview, New Delhi, 8 October 1997.

75 Jagdish N. Bhagwati, *India in Transition: Freeing the Economy*, Oxford: Oxford University Press, 1993, p. 36.

76 Mr. S. Narendra, Principal Information Officer, Government of India, author's interview, New Delhi, 12 October 1997.

77 Nirupam Bajpai and Jeffrey D. Sachs, "Foreign Direct Investment in India – I," *The Hindu*, 30 June 2000.

78 Sanjaya Baru, "The Economics of National Security," *Business Standard*, 4 December 1998.

79 Ibid.

80 Government of India, *Economic Survey 1991–92*, New Delhi: Ministry of Finance, 1992, p. 27.

81 Government of India, *Economic Survey 1992–93*, p. 17.

82 Government of India, *Speech of Shri Manmohan Singh, Minister of Finance, Introducing the Budget for the Year 1996–97*, New Delhi: Ministry of Finance, 1996, p. 104.

83 Onkar Marwah, "India's Nuclear and Space Programs: Intent and Policy," *International Security* 2 (2), 1977, p. 110.

84 C. Raja Mohan, "Budget and Security Strategy, *The Hindu*, 28 February 2002.

85 Sanjaya Baru, "The Economics of National Security," *Business Standard*, 4 December 1998.

86 "A Bold Approach," *The Hindu*, 3 April 2000.

87 Nirupam Bajpai and Jeffrey D. Sachs, "Foreign Direct Investment in India – I," *The Hindu*, 30 June 2000.

88 "BJP to Focus on 'Feel-Good Factor,' *The Hindu*, 23 October 2003; "BJP Banking on 'Feel-Good' Factor," *The Hindu*, 23 January 2004.

89 Jalal Alamgir, "Nationalist Globalism: The Narrative of Strategic Politics and Economic Openness in India," in Baldev Raj Nayar, ed., *Globalization and Politics in India*, New Delhi: Oxford University Press, 2007. On BJP's rhetoric, see also Andrew Wyatt, "(Re)imagining the Indian (Inter)national Economy."

90 Nirupam Bajpai and Jeffrey D. Sachs, "Development and Goal-Setting – I," *The Hindu*, 10 May 2000.

91 C. Raja Mohan, "Trade as Strategy: Chinese Lessons," *The Hindu*, 16 August 2001.

92 "India Hopes to Do Better Than China in FDI," *The Hindu*, 21 June 2002.

93 "India Retains Edge in Offshore Outsourcing," *Economic Times*, 10 March 2003.

94 "Global Giants Set to Promote India in Europe," *Economic Times*, 28 January 2003.

95 R. Gopalakrishnan, "Chinese Miracle: Lessons for India," *The Hindu*, 4 October 2001. See also "China Leads in Domestic IT Market," *The Hindu*, 18 April 2002.

96 NASSCOM, National Association of Software and Service Companies, "Nasscom Reveals China IT Market Findings," www.nasscom.org/artdisplay.asp?Art_id=127, 2002 (accessed 20 August 2004); "India Has Edge in Becoming Major Global IT Outsourcing Centre," *The Hindu*, 22 November 2002; Andy Xie and Chetan Ahya, "China and India: New Tigers of Asia," *Morgan Stanley Global Economic Forum*, 26 July 2004, www.morganstanley.com/GEFdata/digests/20040726-mon.html#anchor6; "India Facing Challenge From China In Information Technology," *The Hindu*, 12 July 2004; "China Closing in on India in Software," *Financial Express*, 20 July 2004.

97 Jayram Ramesh, "US and We," *India Today*, 19 July 1999; Bajpai and Sachs, "Development and Goal-Setting – I"; Rajat Gupta, "The Brain Gain," *India Today*, 13 January 2003; Gurcharan Das, "Lessons from Greater India," *India Today*, 15 February 1993; "Foreigners 'power space industry,'" *BBC News Online*, 12 June 2006, news.bbc.co.uk/go/pr/fr/-/2/hi/uk_news/politics/6212830.stm.

98 V. Suryanarayan, "Indian Communities Abroad," *The Hindu*, 17 January 2001. See also "Calling All Patriots," *The Economist*, 25 July 1998, p. 71.

99 The 1999–2000 budget speech to the parliament by Finance Minister Yashwant Sinha is one example.

100 C. Raja Mohan, "India and Its Extended Neighbourhood," *The Hindu*, 8 June 2000.

101 Sultan Shahin, "India's 'Look East' Policy pays off," *Asia Times*, 11 October 2003; See also "Looking For New Friends," *The Hindu*, 27 May 2001.

102 "Myanmar's Pipeline Politics," *The Economist Intelligence Unit ViewsWire*, 23 May 2007; Matthew Smith and Naing Htoo, "Gas Politics: Shwe Gas Development in Myanmar," *Watershed* 11 (2), 2005–2006.

103 "Alert to Gains by China, India Is Making Energy Deals," *New York Times*, 17 January 2005.

104 "China and India Continue Battle for Energy Assets," *Times* (London), 17 August 2005; "Lesson for India From Energy Rivalry," *Financial Times*, 17 October 2005; "Chinese Link With Indians to Bid for Oil Field Stake," *Financial Times*, 14 December 2005; "China and India Forge Alliance on Oil With Aim of Ending 'Mindless Rivalry,'" *Financial Times*, 13 January 2006; Andrea Goldstein, Nicolas Pinaud, Helmut Reisen, and Xiaobao Chen, *The Rise of China and India: What's In It For Africa?*, Paris: OECD Development Centre, 2006.

105 Goldstein *et al.*, *The Rise of China and India*.

106 For more, see Dennis J. Encarnation, "The Political Economy of Indian Joint Industrial Ventures Abroad," *International Organization* 36 (1), 1982, pp. 31–59; S. Shiva Ramu, *Globalization: The Indian Scenario*, New Delhi: Wheeler, 1996, p. 50; Sadhana Srivastava, "Competing for Global FDI: Opportunities and Challenges for the Indian Economy," *South Asia Economic Journal* 5 (2), 2004, pp. 233–260.

107 "Hard options Can't Be Put Off: Sinha," *The Hindu*, 9 February 2000.

108 "India Inc Old Order Yields Place To The New," *Financial Express*, 2 October 2006.

109 "The Rise And Rise of India's Private Sector," *Financial Express*, 4 October 2006.

110 "Scaling The China Wall: A Tale of Two Companies," *Economic Times*, 8 March 2003.

111 "Forging Ahead," *Economic Times*, 24 January 2003; "The China Syndrome," *Economic Times*, 24 January 2003.

112 Prem Shankar Jha, "Making a Mess of Globalisation," *The Hindu*, 11 July 2000; "Chinese Dumping Retards Industrial Growth," *The Hindu*, 17 November 2000; "Raise Tariff Walls To Stop Chinese Dumping," *The Hindu*, 15 December 2000; "Anti-dumping Duty Imposed on China," *The Hindu*, 12 May 2001; "Yamaha Not to Sell Chinese Made Motorcycles," *The Hindu*, 16 May 2001; N. N. Sachitanand, "Indian Stones and the Chinese Dragon," *The Hindu*, 25 February 2002; "India Initiates Largest Number of Anti-Dumping Investigations," *The Hindu*, 25 October 2002; "Dragon Breathes Fire, Consumer Durable Makers Catch a Cold," *Economic Times*, 14 February 2003.

113 S. Arunajatesan and S. Balaji, "Chinese Phenomenon – A Case of Competition or Dumping?" *The Hindu*, 4 January 2001; "Take on the Challenge of Chinese Competition: Maran," *The Hindu*, 15 March 2001; N. C. Sridharan, "Chinese Goods: A Mission Impossible?" *The Hindu*, 7 June 2001; Arun Shourie, "Has India Really Missed The Bus?" *India Today*, 17 March 2003.

114 "Wanted Sinologists," *Financial Express*, 8 October 2006.

5 Perception, policy, and persistence

1 "The BRICs Are Coming – Fast," *Businessweek*, 27 October 2003. The investment bank Goldman Sachs is reputed to have come up with this acronym. See Goldman Sachs Global Economics Group, *BRICs and Beyond*, London: Goldman Sachs, 2007.

2 "Love your wife? Match this: In season of gifts, Mukesh unwraps birthday jet for Nita," *Telegraph* (Calcutta), 3 November 2007.

3 This is related to the allegation that globalization results in a loss of legitimacy, power, and authority of the state. See, *inter alia*, Walter Wriston, *The Twilight of Sovereignty*, New York: Scribners, 1992; Erik R. Peterson, "Surrendering to Markets," *The Washington Quarterly* 18 (4), 1995; Philip G. Cerny, "Globalization and the Changing Logic of Collective Action," *International Organization* 49 (4), 1995; Vincent Cable, "The Diminished Nation-State: A Study in the Loss of Economic Power," *Daedalus* 124 (2), 1995; Susan Strange, "The Defective State," *Daedalus* 124 (2), 1995. Jan Aart Scholte, "Global Capitalism and the State," *International Affairs*, 73 (3), 1997.

4 Angus Maddison, *The World Economy: A Millennial Perspective*, Paris: OECD Development Centre, 2001, Table B-18, p. 261.

5 Based on calculating the difference in Human Development Index between 1975 and 1990. Data from UNDP, "Human Development Statistics," online at http://hdrstats.undp.org/countries/, accessed 25 February 2008. The Human Development Index (HDI) combines measures of life expectancy, education (with adult literacy weighted more), and logarithm of income at purchasing power parity.

6 Interview with *The Financial Times*, 6 October 1995.

7 Ronald L. Jepperson, Alexander Wendt, and Peter J. Katzenstein, "Norms, Identity, and Culture in National Security," in Peter J. Katzenstein, ed., *The Culture of National Security: Norms and Identity in World Politics*, New York: Columbia University Press, 1996, p. 34.

8 Samar Halarnkar, "The Defining Decade," *India Today*, 3 January 2000.

9 Steven A. Hoffmann, "Perception and China Policy in India," in Francine R. Frankel and Harry Harding, eds., *The India–China Relationship: What the United States Needs to Know*, New York: Columbia University Press, 2004. See also Stephen P. Cohen, *India: Emerging Power*, Washington: Brookings Institution Press, 2001, Chapter 2.

10 Peter J. Katzenstein, "Introduction: Alternative Perspectives on National Security," in Peter J. Katzenstein, ed., *The Culture of National Security: Norms and Identity in World Politics*, New York: Columbia University Press, 1996, p. 25.

11 Some argue that democracy served a utilitarian value for the British, since it allowed

them to give Indians formal representation in lieu of full autonomy. From another angle it was the only model that could have been applied to prevent a "Balkanization" of India. See Sunil Khilnani, *The Idea of India*, London: Hamish Hamilton, 1997, Chapter 2.

12 Joseph S. Nye, Jr., "Springing Tiger," *India Today*, 2 October 2006.

13 Quoted in Alexander Nicoll, "Survey of India," *Financial Times*, 8 November 1994. See also Ray Heath, "Sound Growth and Established Markets Offer China Alternative: India to be New Investor Target," *South China Morning Post*, 9 August 1993.

14 Rob Jenkins, *Democratic Politics and Economic Reform in India*, Cambridge: Cambridge University Press, 1999.

15 "Editorial," *The Statesman*, 26 July 2004.

16 I have discussed this more in Jalal Alamgir, "Nationalist Globalism: The Narrative of Strategic Politics and Economic Openness in India," in Baldev Raj Nayar, *Globalization and Politics in India*, New Delhi: Oxford University Press, 2007.

Bibliography

Books, articles, reports, and documents

Agarwal, Govind R., *South–South Economic Cooperation: Problems and Prospects*, New Delhi: Radiant Publishers, 1987.

Ahluwalia, Isher J., *Industrial Growth in India*, Delhi: Oxford University Press, 1985.

——. "Indian Industry and India's Economic Reforms," Sri Ram Memorial Lecture Part II, given to the Ludhiana Management Association, Punjab, India, 21 March 1997.

Ahluwalia, Isher J. and I. M. D. Little, eds., *India's Economic Reforms and Development: Essays for Manmohan Singh*, New Delhi: Oxford University Press, 1998.

Ahluwalia, Montek S. "India's Economic Reforms," in Robert Cassen and Vijay Joshi, eds., *India: The Future of Economic Reform*, Delhi: Oxford University Press, 1995.

——. "India's Economic Reforms: An Appraisal," in Jeffrey D. Sachs, Ashutosh Varshney, and Nirupam Bajpai, eds., *India in the Era of Economic Reforms*, New Delhi: Oxford University Press, 1999.

Alamgir, Jalal, "Strategic Rivalry and Tariff Liberalization in India," *Brown Economic Review*, 7: 1, 1999.

——. "India's Trade and Investment Policy: The Influence of Strategic Rivalry with China," *Issues and Studies*, 35 (3), 1999.

——. "Managing Openness in India: The Social Construction of a Globalist Narrative," in Linda Weiss, ed., *States in the Global Economy: Bringing Domestic Institutions Back In*, Cambridge: Cambridge University Press, 2003.

——. "Narratives of Open-Economy Policies in India, 1991–2000," *Asian Studies Review*, 31 (2), 2007.

——. "Nationalist Globalism: The Narrative of Strategic Politics and Economic Openness in India," in Baldev Raj Nayar, ed., *Globalization and Politics in India*, New Delhi: Oxford University Press, 2007.

Ambrose, Stephen E., *Rise To Globalism: American Foreign Policy Since 1938*, Seventh Edition, New York: Penguin, 1993.

Anderson, Benedict, *Imagined Communities*, London: Verso, 1991.

Appadorai, A., *Select Documents on India's Foreign Policy and Relations 1947–1972*, vol. 1, Delhi: Oxford University Press, 1982.

——. *National Interest and India's Foreign Policy*, Delhi: Kalinga, 1992.

Art, Robert J., "The Fungibility of Force," in Robert J. Art and Kenneth N. Waltz, eds., *The Use of Force: Military Power and International Politics*, Lanham: Rowman and Littlefield, 2004.

Associated Chambers of Commerce and Industry of India (Assocham), *Globalisation – Emerging Role of Business in India*, New Delhi: Assocham, 1994.

——. *Export Perspective for 2000: Priorities and Competitive Advantages*, New Delhi: Assocham, 1995.

Axelrod, Robert, *The Evolution of Cooperation*, New York: Basic Books, 1984.

Bajpai, Nirupam and Jeffrey D. Sachs, "Fiscal Policy in India's Economic Reforms," in Jeffrey D. Sachs, Ashutosh Varshney, and Nirupam Bajpai, eds., *India in the Era of Economic Reforms*, New Delhi: Oxford University Press, 1999.

Bajpai, Nirupam, Tianlun Jian, and Jeffrey D. Sachs, "Economic Reforms in China and India: Selected Issues in Industrial Policy," Harvard Institute for International Development (HIID), Development Discussion Paper No. 580, Cambridge: HIID, 1997.

Bajpai, U. S., "Indira Gandhi and India's Neighbours," in A. K. Damodaran and U. S. Bajpai, eds., *Indian Foreign Policy: The Indira Gandhi Years*, New Delhi: Radiant, 1990.

Baker, Dean, Gerald Epstein, and Robert Pollin, eds., *Globalization and Progressive Economic Policy*, Cambridge: Cambridge University Press, 1998.

Balachandran, G., "Keeping the Option Open: India's Nuclear Dilemma," *Strategic Analysis* 18 (12), 1996.

——. "CTBT and India," *Strategic Analysis* 19 (3), 1996.

Bandopadhyaya, J., *The Making of India's Foreign Policy*, Bombay: Allied Publishers 1970.

Bandow, Doug and Ian Vasquez, eds., *Perpetuating Poverty: The World Bank, the IMF, and the Developing World*, Washington: Cato Institute, 1994.

Bates, Robert H. and Anne O. Krueger, "Generalizations Arising from the Country Studies," in Robert H. Bates and Anne O. Krueger, eds., *Political and Economic Interactions in Economic Policy Reform*, Oxford: Blackwell, 1993.

Bhaduri, Amit and Deepak Nayyar, *The Intelligent Person's Guide to Liberalization*, New Delhi: Penguin, 1996.

Bhagwati, Jagdish, *India in Transition: Freeing the Economy*, Oxford: Clarendon, 1993.

——. "The Design of Indian Development," in Isher Judge Ahluwalia and I. M. D. Little, eds., *India's Economic Reforms and Development: Essays for Manmohan Singh*, Delhi: Oxford University Press, 1998.

Bhagwati, Jagdish and Padma Desai, *India: Planning for Industrialization*, Oxford: Oxford University Press, 1970.

Bhalla, A. S., *Uneven Development in the Third World: A Study of China and India*, New York: St. Martin's, 1992.

Bhatt, S. C., *The Triangle India–Nepal–China: A Study of Treaty Relations*, New Delhi: Gyan Publishing, 1996.

Bhattacharya, B., "Foreign Direct Investment in India," *Foreign Trade Review* 28 (4), 1994.

Biersteker, Thomas J., "The 'Triumph' of Neoclassical Economics in the Developing World: Policy Convergence and the Bases of Governance in the International Economic Order," in James N. Rosenau and Ernst-Otto Czempiel, eds., *Governance without Government: Order and Change in World Politics*, Cambridge: Cambridge University Press, 1992.

——. "The 'Triumph' of Liberal Economic Ideas in the Developing World," in Barbara Stallings, ed., *Global Change, Regional Response*, Cambridge: Cambridge University Press, 1995.

Boyer, Robert, and Daniel Drache, *States against Markets: The Limits of Globalization*, London: Routledge, 1996.

Brass, Paul R., *The Politics of India Since Independence*, Cambridge: Cambridge University Press, 1994.

Brecher, Michael, *Nehru: A Political Biography*, London: Oxford University Press, 1959.

——. *India and World Politics: Krishna Menon's View of the World*, New York: Praeger, 1968.

Burch, Kurt, "The 'Properties' of the State System and Global Capitalism," in Stephen J. Rosow, Naeem Inayatullah, and Mark Rupert, eds. *The Global Economy as Political Space*. Boulder: Lynne Rienner, 1994.

Burton Jr., Daniel F., "Competitiveness: Here to Stay," *The Washington Quarterly* 17 (4), 1994.

Buzan, Barry, "The Interdependence of Security and Economic Issues in the 'New World Order'" in Richard Stubbs and Geoffrey R. D. Underhill, eds. *Political Economy and the Changing Global Order*, New York: St. Martin's Press, 1994.

Byres, Terence J., "From Ivory Tower to the Belly of the Beast: The Academy, the State, and Economic Debate in Post-Independence India," in Terence Byres, ed., *The Indian Economy: Major Debates Since Independence*, Delhi: Oxford University Press, 1998.

Cable, Vincent, "Indian Liberalization and the Private Sector," in Robert Cassen and Vijay Joshi, eds., *India: The Future of Economic Reform*, New Delhi: Oxford University Press, 1995.

——. "The Diminished Nation-State: A Study in the Loss of Economic Power," *Daedalus* 124 (2), 1995.

Caporaso, James A., "False Divisions: Security Studies and Global Political Economy," *Mershon International Studies Review* 39 (Supplement 1), 1995.

Cassen, Robert and Vijay Joshi, eds., *India: The Future of Economic Reform*, Delhi: Oxford University Press, 1995.

Caufield, Catherine, *Masters of Illusion: The World Bank and the Poverty of Nations*, New York: Henry Holt, 1997.

Cerny, Philip, *Finance and World Politics: Markets, Regimes, and States in the Post-Hegemonic Era*, London: Edward Elgar, 1993.

——. "Globalization and the Challenging Logic of Collective Action," *International Organisation* 49 (4), 1995.

Chai, Joseph C. H., *China's Transition to a Market Economy*, Oxford: Clarendon, 1997.

Chakravarty, Sukhamoy, ed., *Development Planning: The Indian Experience*, Delhi: Oxford University Press, 1987.

Chandra, Nirmal Kumar, "Planning and Foreign Investment in Indian Manufacturing," in Terence J. Byres, ed., *The State, Development Planning and Liberalisation in India*, Delhi: Oxford University Press, 1997.

Chatterjee, Partha, *The Nation and Its Fragments: Colonial and Postcolonial Histories*, Princeton: Princeton University Press, 1993.

Chatterjee, Partha, ed., *State and Politics in India*, New Delhi: Oxford University Press, 1997.

Cohen, Benjamin J., "Phoenix Risen: The Resurrection of Global Finance," *World Politics* 48 (2), 1996.

Cohen, Stephen P., *India: Emerging Power*, Washington: Brookings Institution Press, 2001.

Coleman, William D., *Financial Services, Globalization, and Domestic Policy Change*, New York: St. Martin's, 1996.

Collins, Larry and Dominique Lapierre, *Freedom at Midnight*, New York: Simon and Schuster, 1975.

Conybeare, John, *Trade Wars: The Theory and Practice of International Commercial Rivalry*, New York: Columbia University Press, 1987.

Cooper, Richard, *The Economics of Interdependence: Economic Policy in the Atlantic Community*, New York: McGraw-Hill, 1968.

Cox, Robert W., "A Perspective on Globalization," in James H. Mittelman, ed. *Globalization: Critical Reflections*, Boulder: Lynne Rienner, 1996.

——. *Approaches to World Order*, Cambridge: Cambridge University Press, 1996.

Crane, George T., "Special Things in Special Ways: National Economic Identity and China's Special Economic Zones," *Australian Journal of Chinese Affairs*, No. 32, 1994.

Damodaran, A. K., "India's China Policy: A Retrospective Survey," in Surjit Mansingh, ed., *Indian and Chinese Foreign Policies in Comparative Perspective*, New Delhi: Radiant, 1998.

Danaher, Kevin, ed., *50 Years Is Enough: The Case Against the World Bank and the International Monetary Fund*, Boston: South End Press, 1994.

Deaton, Angus, and Jean Drèze, "Poverty And Inequality In India: A Reexamination," Woodrow Wilson School, Princeton University and Delhi School of Economics, July 2002.

Debroy, Bibek, *Beyond the Uruguay Round: The Indian Perspective on GATT*, New Delhi: Response Books, 1996.

Deshpande, Satish, "Imagined Economies: Styles of Nation-building in Twentieth Century India," *Journal of Arts and Ideas*, 25–26, 1993.

Di Palma, Giuseppe, *To Craft Democracies: An Essay on Democratic Transitions*, Berkeley: University of California Press, 1990.

Dixit, J. N., *Across Borders: Fifty Years of India's Foreign Policy*, New Delhi: Picus, 1998.

Drèze, Jean, and Amartya Sen, *India: Economic Development and Social Opportunity*, Delhi: Oxford University Press, 1995.

Drucker, Peter F., "The Global Economy and the Nation-State," *Foreign Affairs* 76 (5), 1997.

Dutt, Amitava Krishna and J. Mohan Rao, "Globalization and its Social Discontents: The Case of India," CEPA Working Paper Series, New York: Center for Economic Policy Analysis, The New School University, 2000.

Dutt, Gargi, "India–China Relations," in A. K. Damodaran and U. S. Bajpai, eds., *Indian Foreign Policy: The Indira Gandhi Years*, New Delhi: Radiant, 1990.

Dutt, Sagarika, *India in a Globalized World*, Manchester: Manchester University Press, 2006.

Dutta, Sujit, "India's Evolving Relations with China," *Strategic Analysis* 18 (4), 1995.

Encarnation, Dennis J., "The Political Economy of Indian Joint Industrial Ventures Abroad," *International Organization*, 36 (1), 1982.

Escobar, Arturo, *Encountering Development: The Making and the Unmaking of the Third World*, Princeton: Princeton University Press, 1995.

Evans, Peter, "The State as Problem and Solution: Predation, Embedded Autonomy, and Structural Change," in Stephan Haggard and Robert R. Kaufman, eds., *The Politics of Economic Adjustment*, Princeton: Princeton University Press, 1992.

——. "The Eclipse of the State? Reflections on Stateness in an Era of Globalization," *World Politics* 50 (1), 1997.

Evans, Peter B., Dietrich Rueschemeyer, and Theda Skocpol, eds., *Bringing the State Back In*. Cambridge: Cambridge University Press, 1985.

Fair, C., "Learning to Think the Unthinkable: Lessons from India's Nuclear Tests," *India Review* 4 (1), 2005.

Frieden, Jeffry, "Invested Interests: The Politics of National Economic Policies in a World of Global Finance," *International Organization* 45 (4), 1991.

——. *Debt, Development, and Democracy: Modern Political Economy and Latin America, 1965–1985*, Princeton, Princeton University Press, 1991.

Ganguly, Sumit, *The Origins of War in South Asia: The Indo-Pakistani Conflicts Since 1947*, Boulder: Westview, 1994.

——. "India's Pathway to Pokhran II," *International Security* 23 (4), 1999.

——. "India and China: Border Issues, Domestic Integration, and International Security," in Francine R. Frankel and Harry Harding, eds, *The India-China Relationship: What the United States Needs to Know*, New York: Columbia University Press, 2004.

Garrett, Geoffrey, "Capital Mobility, Trade, and the Domestic Politics of Economic Policy," *International Organization* 49 (4), 1995.

Garver, John W., "Asymmetrical Indian and Chinese Threat Perceptions," in Sumit Ganguly, ed., *India as an Emerging Power*, London: Frank Cass, 2003.

George, Timothy, "Sino-Indian Relations: Opportunities and Limitations," in Timothy George, Shahram Chubin, and Robert Litwak, eds., *India and the Great Powers*, Aldershot: Gower/IISS, 1984.

Ghosh, Arun, K. K. Subrahmanian, Mridul Eapen, and Haseeb A. Drabu, *Indian Industrialization: Structure and Policy Issues*, Delhi: Oxford University Press, 1992.

Ghosh, Suchita, *China-Bangladesh-India Tangle Today: Towards a Solution?* New Delhi: Sterling, 1995.

Gilley, Bruce, "Two Passages to Modernity," in Edward Friedman and Bruce Gilley, eds., *Asia's Giants: Comparing China and India*, New York: Palgrave Macmillan, 2005.

Goertz, Gary, *Contexts of International Politics*, Cambridge: Cambridge University Press, 1994.

Goldman Sachs, Global Economics Group, *BRICs and Beyond*, London: Goldman Sachs, 2007.

Goldstein, Andrea, Nicolas Pinaud, Helmut Reisen, and Xiaobao Chen, *The Rise of China and India: What's In It For Africa?*, Paris: OECD Development Centre, 2006.

Goodman, John B. and Louis W. Pauly, "The Obsolescence of Capital Controls? Economic Management in an Age of Global Markets," *World Politics* 46 (1), 1993.

Gourevitch, Peter, *Politics in Hard Times: Comparative Responses to International Economic Crises*, Ithaca, New York: Cornell University Press, 1986.

Government of India, Lok Sabha Secretariat, *National Industrial Policy*, New Delhi: Lok Sabha Secretariat, 1985.

Government of India, Ministry of Finance, *Speech of Shri Manmohan Singh Presenting Central Government's Budget for 1991–92*, New Delhi: Ministry of Finance, 1991.

——. *Economic Survey 1991–1992*, New Delhi: Ministry of Finance, 1992.

——. *Economic Survey 1992–93*, New Delhi: Ministry of Finance, 1993.

——. *Economic Survey 1993–94*, New Delhi: Ministry of Finance, 1994.

——. *Speech of Shri Manmohan Singh, Minister of Finance, Introducing the Budget for the Year 1996–97*, New Delhi: Ministry of Finance, 1996.

——. *Economic Survey 1995–96*, New Delhi: Ministry of Finance, 1997.

——. "Speech of Shri Manmohan Singh, Minister of Finance, Introducing the Budget for the Year 1992–93," *Budget Speeches of Union Finance Ministers*, Vol. II, New Delhi: Ministry of Finance, 1997.

——. *Economic Survey 2006–7*, New Delhi: Ministry of Finance, 2007.

Government of India, Ministry of Commerce and Industry, *Medium Term Export Strategy 2002–2007*, New Delhi: Ministry of Commerce and Industry, 2002.

——. *Foreign Trade Policy 2004–2009*, New Delhi: Ministry of Commerce and Industry, 2006.

Government of India, Planning Commission, *Eighth Five Year Plan 1992–1997*, New Delhi: Planning Commission, 1997.

Gowa, Joanne, *Allies, Adversaries, and International Trade*, Princeton: Princeton University Press, 1994.

Guhan, S., "Centre and States in the Reform Process," in Robert Cassen and Vijay Joshi, eds., *India: The Future of Economic Reform*, New Delhi: Oxford University Press, 1995.

Haas, Peter M., "Introduction: Epistemic Communities and International Policy Coordination," *International Organization* 46 (1), 1992.

Hacking, Ian, *The Social Construction of What?* Cambridge: Harvard University Press, 1999.

Haggard, Stephan and Robert R. Kaufman, eds., *The Politics of Economic Adjustment*, Princeton: Princeton University Press, 1992.

Hart, Jeffrey A., *Rival Capitalists: International Competitiveness in the United States, Japan, and Western Europe*, Ithaca: Cornell University Press, 1992.

Herring, Ronald J., "Embedded Particularism: India's Failed Developmental State," in Meredith Woo-Cumings, ed., *The Developmental State*, Ithaca: Cornell University Press, 1999.

Hoffmann, Steven A., *India and the China Crisis*, Berkeley: University of California Press, 1990.

——. "Perception and China Policy in India," in Francine R. Frankel and Harry Harding, eds., *The India-China Relationship: What the United States Needs to Know*, New York: Columbia University Press, 2004.

Hu, Richard Weixing, "India's Nuclear Bomb and Future Sino-Indian Relations," *East Asia: An International Quarterly* 17 (1), 1999.

International Monetary Fund, "IMF Concludes Article IV Consultations with India," IMF Press Information Notice No. 97/11, 16 July 1997.

Jackson, Richard L., *The Non-Aligned, the UN, and the Superpowers*, New York: Praeger, 1983.

Jain, Anil Kumar, *Economic Planning in India*, New Delhi: Ashish Publishing House, 1986.

Jenkins, Rob, *Democratic Politics and Economic Reform in India*, Cambridge: Cambridge University Press, 1999.

Jepperson, Ronald L., Alexander Wendt, and Peter J. Katzenstein, "Norms, Identity, and Culture in National Security," in Peter J. Katzenstein, ed., *The Culture of National Security: Norms and Identity in World Politics*, New York: Columbia University Press, 1996.

Jha, Brajesh and B. B. Mohapatra, "Liberalisation and Agricultural prices: Some Disconcerting Trends," *Indian Journal of Agricultural Economics* 58 (3), 2003.

Jha, Prem Shankar, *The Perilous Road to the Market: The Political Economy of Reform in Russia, India and China*, London: Pluto, 2002.

Joshi, Vijay and I. M. D. Little, *India: Crisis, Adjustment, Growth*, Oxford: Oxford University Press, 1993.

——. *India: Macroeconomics and Political Economy, 1964–1991*, New Delhi: Oxford University Press, 1994.

——. *India's Economic Reforms, 1991–2001*, Oxford: Clarendon, 1996.

Kahler, Miles, "International Financial Institutions and the Politics of Adjustment," in Joan M. Nelson, eds, *Fragile Coalitions: The Politics of Economic Adjustment*, New Brunswick: Transaction Books, 1989.

——. "Orthodoxy and Its Alternatives: Explaining Approaches to Stabilization and Adjustment," in Joan Nelson, ed., *Economic Crisis and Policy Choice: The Politics of Adjustment in the Third World*, Princeton: Princeton University Press, 1990.

——. "External Influence, Conditionality, and the Politics of Adjustment," in Stephan Haggard and Robert R. Kaufman, eds., *The Politics of Economic Adjustment*, Princeton: Princeton University Press, 1992.

Kapur, Devesh, "The Causes and Consequences of India's IT Boom," *India Review*, 1 (2), 2002.

——. "Ideas and Economic Reforms in India: The Role of International Migration and the Indian Diaspora," *India Review* 3 (4), 2004.

Kathuria, Sanjay and Nisha Taneja, *India's Exports: The Challenge from China*, New Delhi: Indian Council for Research in International Economic Relations, 1986.

Katti, Vijaya, "India's Economic Reforms: An Assessment of the Impact on Industry and FDI," *Foreign Trade Review* 28 (1), 1993.

Katzenstein, Peter J., ed., *The Culture of National Security: Norms and Identity in World Politics*, New York: Columbia University Press, 1996.

Kennedy, Paul, *The Rise and Fall of the Great Powers*, New York: Random House, 1987.

Khilnani, Sunil, *The Idea of India*, London: Hamish Hamilton, 1997.

Kindleberger, Charles, *American Business Abroad*, New Haven: Yale University Press, 1969.

Kobrin, Stephen J., "Electronic Cash and the End of National Markets," *Foreign Policy* 107, 1997.

Kohli, Atul, *Democracy and Discontent: India's Growing Crisis of Governability*, Cambridge: Cambridge University Press, 1990.

Krasner, Stephen, *Structural Conflict: The Third World Against Global Liberalism*, Berkeley: University of California Press, 1985.

Krugman, Paul, *The Accidental Theorist*, New York: W. W. Norton, 1998.

Krugman, Paul, ed., *Strategic Trade Policy and the New International Economics*, Cambridge: MIT Press, 1986.

Kumar, Rajiv, *India's Export Processing Zones*, Delhi: Oxford University Press, 1989.

Kumar, Ramani and Pranab K. Banerjee, "Role of States in Export Promotion Efforts: A Case Study of Rajasthan," *Foreign Trade Review* 31 (3), 1996.

LaFeber, Walter, *The New Empire: An Interpretation of American Expansion 1860–1898*, 35th anniversary ed., Ithaca: Cornell University Press, 1998.

Lalvani, Mala, "Sounding the Alarm: Impact of Political Instability on Growth and Fiscal Health of the Indian Economy," *Economics of Governance* 4 (2), 2003.

Lamb, Alastair, *The McMahon Line: A Study in the Relations between India, China and Tibet, 1904 to 1914*, London: Routledge and Kegan Paul, 1966.

Levy, Jack S. and Salvatore Ali, "From Commercial Competition to Strategic Rivalry to War: The Evolution of the Anglo-Dutch Rivalry, 1609–52," in Paul F. Diehl, ed., *The Dynamics of Enduring Rivalries*, Champaign: University of Illinois Press, 1998.

Lewis, John P., "Some Consequences of Giantism: The Case of India," *World Politics* 43 (3), 1991.

——. *India's Political Economy: Governance and Reform*, Delhi: Oxford University Press, 1995.

Little, Ian, Richard Cooper, W. Max Corden, and Sarath Rajapatirana, *Boom, Crisis, and Adjustment: The Macroeconomic Experience of Developing Countries*, New York: Oxford University Press, 1993.

Longer, V., *The Defense and Foreign Policies of India*, New Delhi: Sterling, 1988.

Lyon, Peter, "The Foreign Policy of India," in F. S. Northledge, ed., *The Foreign Policies of the Powers*, New York: Praeger, 1968.

Maddison, Angus, *The World Economy: A Millennial Perspective*, Paris: OECD Development Centre, 2001.

Mahajan, Sneh, *British Foreign Policy, 1874–1914: The Role of India*, London: Routledge, 2002.

Malenbaum, Wilfred, "India and China: Development Contrasts," *The Journal of Political Economy* 64 (1), 1956.

——. "India and China: Contrasts in Development Performance," *American Economic Review* 49 (3), 1959.

——. "A Review of Subramanian Swamy, Economic Growth in China and India 1952–1970," *Journal of Asian Studies*, 34 (1), 1974.

——. "Modern Economic Growth in India and China: The Comparison Revisited, 1950–1980," *Economic Development and Cultural Change* 31 (1), 1982.

Malviya, Gopalji, "The Sino-Indian Security Environment: Inadequate Responses from New Delhi," in Surjit Mansingh, ed., *Indian and Chinese Foreign Policies in Comparative Perspective*, New Delhi: Radiant, 1998.

Manor, James, "The Political Sustainibility of Economic Liberalization in India," in Robert Cassen and Vijay Joshi, eds., *India: The Future of Economic Reform*, Delhi: Oxford University Press, 1995.

——. "India's Reform Strengths," in Edward Friedman and Bruce Gilley, eds., *Asia's Giants: Comparing China and India*, New York: Palgrave Macmillan, 2005.

Mansingh, Surjit, *India's Search for Power: Indira Gandhi's Foreign Policy, 1966–1982*, New Delhi: Sage, 1984.

—— ed., *Indian and Chinese Foreign Policies in Comparative Perspective*, New Delhi: Radiant, 1998.

Marjit, Sugata and Ajitava Raychaudhuri, *India's Exports: An Analytical Study*, Delhi: Oxford University Press, 1997.

Marwah, Onkar, "India's Nuclear and Space Programs: Intent and Policy," *International Security* 2 (2), 1977.

Mastanduno, Michael, "Economics and Security in Statecraft and Scholarship," *International Organization* 52 (4), 1998.

Maxwell, Neville, *India's China War*, New York: Pantheon, 1970.

Mehta, Pratap Bhanu, "Exploding Myths," *The New Republic* 218 (23), 1998.

——. "India: The Nuclear Politics of Self-Esteem," *Current History* 97, 1998.

Mehta, S. S., "Globalisation of the Indian Economy: Nature and Consequences," *Foreign Trade Review* 29 (2–3), 1994.

Mellor, John W. ed., *India: A Rising Middle Power*, Boulder: Westview Press, 1979.

Mittelman, James H., ed., *Globalization: Critical Reflections*. Boulder: Lynne Rienner, 1997.

Miyoshi, Masao, "A Borderless World? From Colonialism to Transnationalism and the Decline of the Nation-State," in Rob Wilson and Wimal Dissanayake, eds., *Global/Local: Cultural Production and the Transnational Imaginary*, Durham: Duke University Press, 1996.

Mosley, Paul, Jane Harrigan, and John Toye, *Aid and Power: The World Bank and Policy-Based Lending*, London: Routledge, 1991.

Murtaza, Naheed, *Parliament and Foreign Policy: Reflections on India-China Relations*, New Delhi: Cadplan, 1998.

Murty, T. S., *India–China Boundary: India's Options*, New Delhi: ABC Publishing, 1987.

Naim, Moises, "Fads and Fashion in Economic Reforms: Washington Consensus or Washington Confusion?" *Third World Quarterly* 21 (3), 2000, pp. 505–528.

Nair, C. N. Purushothaman, ed., *Export Promotion in India*. New Delhi: Discovery Publishing, 1992.

Nayar, Baldev Raj, "A World Role: The Dialectics of Purpose and Power," in John W. Mellor, ed., *India: A Rising Middle Power*, Boulder: Westview Press, 1979.

——. *Globalization and Nationalism: The Changing Balance in India's Economic Policy 1950–2000*, New Delhi: Sage, 2001.

——. *The Geopolitics of Globalization*, New Delhi: Oxford University Press, 2005.

Nayar, Baldev Raj, ed., *Globalization and Politics in India*, New Delhi: Oxford University Press, 2007.

Nayar, Baldev Raj and T. V. Paul, *India in the World Order: Searching for Major-Power Status*, Cambridge: Cambridge University Press, 2003.

Nayyar, Deepak, "The Foreign Trade Sector, Planning and Industrialisation in India," in Terence J. Byres, ed., *The State, Development Planning and Liberalisation in India*, New York: Oxford University Press, 1997.

Nehru, Jawaharlal, *The Discovery of India*, New York: John Day, 1946.

——. *Independence and After: A Collection of Speeches, 1946–1949*, New York: John Day, 1950.

——. *India's Foreign Policy: Selected Speeches, September 1946–April 1961*, New Delhi: Ministry of Information and Broadcasting, Government of India, 1961.

Nelson, Joan, ed., *Economic Crisis and Policy Choice: The Politics of Adjustment in the Third World*, Princeton: Princeton University Press, 1990.

Nye, Jr., Joseph S., *Bound to Lead: The Changing Nature of American Power*, New York: Basic Books, 1990.

O'Brien, Richard, *Global Financial Integration: The End of Geography*, New York: Council on Foreign Relations Press, 1992.

Pai Panandiker, V. A., "The Political Economy of Centre-State Relations in India," in Isher J. Ahluwalia and I. M. D. Little, eds., *India's Economic Reforms and Development: Essays for Manmohan Singh*. New Delhi: Oxford University Press, 1998.

Pal, Mahendra, *World Bank and the Third World Countries of Asia, With Special Reference to India*, New Delhi: National Publishing House, 1985.

Pardesi, Manjeet S., "Understanding the Rise of India," *India Review* 6 (3), 2007.

Parikh, Kirit S., ed., *India Development Report 1997*, Delhi: Oxford University Press, 1997.

Patnaik, Prabhat, *Whatever Happened to Imperialism?* New Delhi: Tulika, 1995.

Patnaik, Prabhat and C. P. Chandrasekhar, "India: Dirigisme, Structural Adjustment, and the Radical Alternative," in Dean Baker, Gerald Epstein, and Robert Pollin, eds., *Globalization and Progressive Economic Policy*, Cambridge: Cambridge University Press, 1998.

Paul, S., *India's Exports: New Imperatives and Newer Vistas*, New Delhi: Commonwealth Publishers, 1992.

Perkovich, George, *India's Nuclear Bomb: The Impact on Global Proliferation*, Berkeley: University of California Press, 1999.

Peterson, Erik R., "Surrendering to Markets," *The Washington Quarterly* 18 (4), 1995.

Pigato, Miria, Caroline Farah, Ken Itakura, and Kwang Jun, *South Asia's Integration into the World Economy*, Washington: World Bank, 1997.

Prasad, Bimla, *The Origins of Indian Foreign Policy: Indian National Congress and World Affairs, 1885–1947*, Calcutta: Bookland, 1962.

Ramu, S. Shiva, *Globalization: The Indian Scenario*, New Delhi: Wheeler Publishing, 1996.

Rao, N. Vasuki, "India: Ripe For Foreign Products As Curbs Lifted," *Journal of Commerce* (New Delhi), 2000.

Rapkin, David P., "The Emergence and Intensification of US–Japan Rivalry in the Early Twentieth Century," in William R. Thompson, ed., *Great Power Rivalries*, Columbia: University of South Carolina Press, 1999.

Rapoport, Anatol, *Fights, Games, and Debates*, Ann Arbor: University of Michigan Press, 1974.

Ray, Hemen, *Sino-Soviet Conflict Over India*, New Delhi: Abhinav Publications, 1986.

Richman, Barry, "Economic Development in China and India: Some Conditioning Factors," *Pacific Affairs*, 45 (1), 1972.

Rodrik, Dani, "The Rush to Free Trade in the Developing World: Why So Late? Why Now? Will It Last?" in Stephan Haggard and Steven B. Webb, eds., *Voting For Reform: Democracy, Political Liberalization, and Economic Adjustment*, New York: Oxford University Press, 1994.

——. *The New Global Economy and Developing Countries: Making Openness Work*, Washington: Overseas Development Council, 1999.

Rogowski, Ronald, *Commerce and Coalitions: How Trade Affects Domestic Political Alignments*, Princeton: Princeton University Press, 1989.

Rosen, George, *Contrasting Styles of Industrial Reform: China and India in the 1980s*, Chicago: University of Chicago Press, 1992.

Rosenau, James N., *Along the Domestic-Foreign Frontier: Exploring Governance in a Turbulent World*, Cambridge: Cambridge University Press, 1997.

Rowland, John, *A History of Sino-Indian Relations: Hostile Co-Existence*, Princeton: D. Van Nostrand, 1967.

Rudolph, Lloyd I. and Susanne Hoeber Rudolph, *In Pursuit of Lakshmi: The Political Economy of the Indian State*, Chicago: University of Chicago Press, 1987.

Sachs, Jeffrey D., Ashutosh Varshney, and Nirupam Bajpai, eds., *India in the Era of Economic Reforms*, New Delhi: Oxford University Press, 1999.

Sandhu, Bhim, *Unresolved Conflict: China and India*, New Delhi: Radiant, 1988.

Sathyamurthy, T. V., ed., *Region, Religion, Caste, Gender and Culture in Contemporary India*, Delhi: Oxford University Press, 1996.

Schelling, Thomas C., *The Strategy of Conflict*, Cambridge: Harvard University Press, 1980.

Scholte, Jan Aart, "Global Capitalism and the State," *International Affairs* 73 (3), 1997.

Segal, Gerald, "Does China Matter?" *Foreign Affairs* 78 (5), 1999.

Selth, Andrew, "Burma And The Strategic Competition Between China And India," *Journal of Strategic Studies* 19 (2), 1996.

Sengupta, Arjun, "Planning for Policies: A Note on the Approach to the Ninth Indian Five Year Plan," paper presented at the National Economic Council, Dhaka, Bangladesh, 15 December 1997.

Shirk, Susan, "One-Sided Rivalry: China's Perceptions and Policies Toward India," in Francine R. Frankel and Harry Harding, eds, *The India–China Relationship: What the United States Needs to Know*, New York: Columbia University Press, 2004.

Shiva, Vandana, *Stolen Harvest: The Hijacking of the Global Food Supply*, Boston: South End Press, 2000.

Shiva, Vandana, Afsar H. Jafri, Ashok Emani, and Manish Pande, *Seeds of Suicide: The*

Ecological and Human Costs of Globalization of Agriculture, Delhi: Research Foundation for Science, Technology and Ecology, 2000.

Sindhwani, T. N., *India's Role in Globalisation*, New Delhi: Capital Foundation Society, 1992.

Singh, Baljit, *Indian Foreign Policy: An Analysis*, New York: Asia Publishing, 1975.

Singh, Jasjit, "India and the CTBT," *Strategic Analysis* 19 (6), 1996.

Singh, Manmohan, *India's Export Trends and the Prospects for Self-Sustained Growth*, Oxford: Clarendon Press, 1964.

Sinha, Aseema, "Political Foundations of Market-Enhancing Federalism: Theoretical Lessons from India and China," *Comparative Politics* 37 (2), 2005.

——. "Understanding the Rise and Transformation of Business Collective Action in India," *Business and Politics* 7 (2), 2005.

Smith, Matthew, and Naing Htoo, "Gas Politics: Shwe Gas Development in Myanmar," *Watershed* 11 (2), 2005–2006.

Solanki, M., "India's Foreign Policy Perspectives in the 1990s," speech given at the India International Centre, New Delhi, 13 August 1991.

Sondhi, Sunil, *Science, Technology and India's Foreign Policy*, Delhi: Anamika Prakashan, 1994.

Spegele, Roger D., "Is Robust Globalism a Mistake?" *Review of International Studies* 23 (2), 1997.

Sridharan, Eswaran, "Coalition Politics in India: Lessons from Theory, Comparisons, and Recent History," Centre for Policy Research, Monograph, New Delhi: CPR, May 1997.

——. "Political Institutions and Economic Reform: Lessons from the Indian Experience 1991–96," Centre for Policy Research, Monograph, New Delhi: CPR, May 1997.

Srinivasan, T. N., "External Sector in Development: China and India, 1950–89," *American Economic Review* 80 (2), 1990.

——. *Agriculture and Trade in China and India: Policies and Performance since 1950*, San Francisco: ICS Press, 1994.

Srivastava, Sadhana, "Competing for Global FDI: Opportunities and Challenges for the Indian Economy," *South Asia Economic Journal* 5 (2), 2004.

Stallings, Barbara, "International Influence on Economic Policy: Debt, Stabilization, and Structural Reform," in Stephan Haggard and Robert R. Kaufman, eds., *The Politics of Economic Adjustment*, Princeton: Princeton University Press, 1992.

Stiglitz, Joseph, *Globalization and Its Discontents*, New York: Norton, 2002.

Strang, David, "Contested Sovereignty: The Social Construction of Colonial Imperialism," in Thomas J. Biersteker and Cynthia Weber, eds., *State Sovereignty as Social Construct*, Cambridge: Cambridge University Press, 1996.

Strange, Susan, "The Defective State," *Daedalus* 124 (2), 1995.

——. *The Retreat of the State: The Diffusion of Power in the World Economy*, Cambridge: Cambridge University Press, 1996.

Subrahmanyam, K., "Indira Gandhi's Quest for Security," in A. K. Damodaran and U. S. Bajpai, eds., *Indian Foreign Policy: The Indira Gandhi Years*, New Delhi: Radiant, 1990.

Subramaniam, Chitra, *India is For Sale*, New Delhi: VBS Publishers, 1997.

Suri, Kamla, *India's Economy and the World*, New Delhi: Vikas, 1992.

Swamy, Subramanian, "Economic Growth in China and India, 1952–1970: A Comparative Appraisal," *Economic Development and Cultural Change* 21 (4), Part 2, 1973.

——. *Economic Growth in China and India: A Comparative Appraisal*, Chicago: University of Chicago Press, 1973.

——. "The Economic Distance between China and India, 1955–73," *The China Quarterly*, No. 70, 1977.

——. "The Response to Economic Challenge: A Comparative Economic History of China and India, 1870–1952," *The Quarterly Journal of Economics* 93 (1), 1979.

Tanham, George, *Indian Strategic Thought*, Santa Monica: Rand, 1992.

Tapscott, Don, *The Digital Economy*, New York: McGraw Hill, 1996.

Tellis, Ashley J., "China and India in Asia," in Francine R. Frankel and Harry Harding, eds., *The India–China Relationship: What the United States Needs to Know*, New York: Columbia University Press, 2004.

Tharoor, Shashi, *Reasons of State: Political Development and India's Foreign Policy Under Indira Gandhi 1966–1977*, Delhi: Vikas, 1982.

——. *The Elephant, the Tiger, and the Cell Phone*, New York: Arcade, 2007.

Thompson, William R. "Why Rivalries Matter and What Great Power Rivalries Can Tell Us About World Politics," in William R. Thompson, ed., *Great Power Rivalries*, Columbia: University of South Carolina Press, 1999.

Vanaik, Achin, *The Painful Transition: Bourgeois Democracy in India*, London: Verso, 1990.

——. "Soldiers of Hindutva: The New Indian Right," *New Left Review* 9, 2001.

Varshney, Ashutosh, *Democracy, Development, and the Countryside: Rural-Urban Struggles in India*, Cambridge: Cambridge University Press, 1995.

——. "Mass Politics or Elite Politics? India's Economic Reforms in Comparative Perspective," *Journal of Economic Policy Reform* 2 (4), 1998.

Verdery, Katherine, "Whither 'Nation' and 'Nationalism'?" *Daedalus* 122 (3), 1993.

Vernon, Raymond, *Sovereignty At Bay*, New York: Basic Books, 1971.

Vertzberger, Yaacov Y. I., *Misperceptions in Foreign Policymaking: The Sino-Indian Conflict, 1959–1962*, Boulder: Westview, 1984.

Visvanathan, S., "A Celebration of Difference: Science and Democracy in India," *Science*, 3 April 1998.

Wade, Robert, "The Market for Public Office: Why the Indian State is Not Better at Development," *World Development* 13 (4), 1985.

Waterbury, John, "The Heart of the Matter? Public Enterprise and the Adjustment Process," in Haggard, Stephan and Robert R. Kaufman, eds., *The Politics of Economic Adjustment*, Princeton: Princeton University Press, 1992.

Waters, Malcolm, *Globalization*, London: Routledge, 1995.

Weiss, Thomas G. and Hans W. Singer, *Multilateral Development Diplomacy in UNCTAD: The Lessons of Group Negotiations 1964–84*, New York: St. Martin's Press, 1986.

Weisskopf, Thomas E., "China and India: Contrasting Experiences in Economic Development," *American Economic Review* 65 (2), 1975.

Wendt, Alexander, *Social Theory of International Politics*, Cambridge: Cambridge University Press, 1999.

Williams, Marc, *Third World Cooperation: The Group of 77 in UNCTAD*, London: Pinter, 1991.

Wolpert, Stanley, *Nehru: A Tryst with Destiny*, New York: Oxford University Press, 1996.

Woodman, Dorothy, *Himalayan Frontiers: A Political Review of British, Chinese, Indian and Russian Rivalries*, London: Barrie and Rockliff, 1969.

World Bank, *India: Recent Economic Developments and Prospects*. Washington: World Bank, 1994.

——. *India, Country Economic Memorandum: Recent Economic Developments, Achievements, and Challenges*, Washington: World Bank, 1995.
——. *India: Five Years of Stabilization and Reform, and the Challenges Ahead*, Washington: World Bank, 1997.
——. *India: Sustaining Rapid Economic Growth*, Washington: World Bank, 1997.
——. *India 1998 Macroeconomic Update: Reforming for Growth and Poverty Reduction*, Washington: World Bank, 1998.
——. *World Development Report 2003*, New York: Oxford University Press, 2003.
Wriston, Walter, *The Twilight of Sovereignty*, New York: Scribners, 1992.
Wyatt, Andrew, "Building the Temples of Postmodern India: Economic Constructions of National Identity," *Contemporary South Asia* 14 (4), 2005.
——. "(Re)imagining the Indian (Inter)national Economy," *New Political Economy* 10 (2), 2005.
Xie, Andy, and Chetan Ahya, "China and India: New Tigers of Asia," *Morgan Stanley Global Economic Forum*, 26 July 2004, http://www.morganstanley.com/GEFdata/digests/20040726-mon.html#anchor6.
Yadav, Lal Babu, *Indo-Bhutan Relations and China Interventions*, New Delhi: Anmol, 1996.
Zakaria, Fareed, *From Wealth to Power: The Unusual Origins of America's World Role*, Princeton: Princeton University Press, 1998.

Newspapers, magazines, and newswires

The following newspapers and magazines were consulted and are cited. Complete citations are given in the chapter notes.

Agence France Presse
Asia Times
Asiaweek
BBC Online
Business India
Business Standard
Business Times
Business Today
Businessweek
Economic and Political Weekly
Financial Express
Frontline
IMF Survey
India Today
Indian Express
Inter Press Service
Los Angeles Times
South China Morning Post
Business Standard
The Christian Science Monitor
Economic Times
The Economist
The Economist Intelligence Unit ViewsWire

Financial Times
Guardian
The Hindu
The Hindu Business Line
The Hindustan Times
Independent (London)
New York Times
The Statesman
Sunday Observer
Telegraph (Calcutta)
The Times (London)
Washington Post
United Press International

Index

www.ingramcontent.com/pod-product-compliance
Ingram Content Group UK Ltd.
Pitfield, Milton Keynes, MK11 3LW, UK
UKHW021247190926
475569UK00002BA/50

9780415776844